Tourists in Historic Towns

Tourists in Historic Towns

Urban Conservation and Heritage Management

Aylin Orbaşlı

London and New York

First published 2000 by E & FN Spon
11 New Fetter Lane, London EC4P 4EE

Simultaneously published in the USA and Canada
by E & FN Spon
29 West 35th Street, New York, NY 10001

E & FN Spon is an imprint of the Taylor & Francis Group

© 2000 Aylin Orbaşlı

Typeset in Times by Keystroke, Jacaranda Lodge, Wolverhampton
Printed and bound in Great Britain by St Edmundsbury Press, Bury St Edmunds, Suffolk

British Library Cataloguing in Publication Data
A catalogue record for this book is available from the British Library

Library of Congress Cataloging in Publication Data
A catalogue record for this book has been requested.

ISBN 0–419–25930–9

To my parents

Contents

Acknowledgements

This book is partly based on work undertaken for a doctorate thesis at the Institute of Advanced Architectural Studies at the University of York, partly on later research and practice experience. I first embarked on the subject in 1990, and in the decade that has passed a much more active debate has evolved in recognition of tourism as an important part of the urban economy and the significance of cultural heritage to urban development. Hardly does a day go past when there isn't a piece of information in the press or a discussion on the subject; and even in the final draft this book was being continuously updated as new information became available.

I am fortunate to reflect in these pages discussions with friends, colleagues and fellow professionals from around the world, many of whom have also provided invaluable friendships and support. Charles Cockburn has guided my work from the beginning and I am grateful for his continuing and dedicated support, and valuable comments on the manuscript; and also to John Warren, for being an inspirational mentor and for supporting and guiding the development of the book. Friends and colleagues contributed to the discussion or took time out from busy schedules to assist with information and comment on various parts of the draft, in particular Jeremy Boissevain, Esra Kurul, Sunil Kumar, Frank Go, Tom Selwyn, Bob Scrase, Reinhard Spilker and Peter Hutchings, to all of whom I extend my sincere thanks. I am especially indebted to Dr Grace Kenny for meticulously reading through the final draft. I would also like to thank many others who have offered more personal support, especially my brother Erol for his encouragement through some difficult early stages, and numerous friends in England, Turkey and across the globe, in India and Japan, who helped keep up the momentum

Others helped with sourcing pictures, including Berin Gür and Filiz Köse. I would like to thank Esra Kurul, Reha Orbaşlı and John Loring who kindly contributed pictures, The Imaginative Traveller for permission to reproduce their brochure material and Joan Burrows for her kind permission to reproduce pictures of York by the late Reg Burrows.

Illustration credits

Figure 2.4 is reproduced by kind permission from The Imaginative Traveller. Figure 6.7a and Figures 1a, 1b and 2 in the Antalya case study are by Esra Kurul; Figures 2.8 and 5.2 by Reha Orbaşlı; Figure 4.5 by John Loring; and Figures 2.11, 6.4, 6.15 and Figures 2 and 4 in the York case study are by the late Reg Burrows. All remaining pictures and illustrations are by the author.

Introduction

Communities live and work in towns and cities; as society changes so does urban form, responding to accommodate change and growth. 'The city is and has always been throughout the ages at the root of our culture, history, arts and traditions. It has been the birth-place of a society in constant evolution' (Cravatte 1977: 13). For its users, residents and visitors alike, the city becomes a cultural interpretation of the physical environment through personal identification and attachment. In the historic environment there are competing demands and underlying tensions between past and present cultures and between the familiarity of the old and the notion of progress attached to the new. 'Progress has come to be identified with improvement in quantitative indicators; these concern mainly economic processes, seldom social, hardly ever cultural' (de Kadt 1990: 9).

Urban heritage is an interpretation of history by a wide range of users; its value, though, is not simply in the historic attributes of the built fabric and spatial aspects of the townscape, but also in the life of its contemporary resident community, differentiating it from other forms of heritage. It is only in the second half of the twentieth century that there has been a growing appreciation and understanding of historic urban settlements, their recognition as 'heritage', and a desire for area-based conservation. Through the contributions of international organisations including UNESCO, ICOMOS (International Council on Monuments and Sites) and the Council of Europe, cultural heritage is becoming recognised as a significant link in urban life and the development process.

The aim of urban conservation must be to enhance the environment and ensure its continuity as a desirable place to live, 'setting the individual person "into place" amid the insecurity of the infinite space and time, and relating him or her to a culture' (Maguire 1982: 23). Conservation is not simply an architectural deliberation, but also an economic and social issue. 'The consideration of the human living environment cannot be divorced from the considerations of the living society itself' (Malik 1993: 82–3). Culture is an essential part of human and urban life, a dynamic and evolving component of community, a continuous link from past to present and through to the future. And as Rogers (1982: 15) points out, 'We must realise that maintaining structures means maintaining the desirability or continuity of a culture – we are in fact conserving cultures not buildings.'

In the urban environment, culture and heritage present a question of ownership. The physical relics of history, including buildings, are 'owned' whereas the historic town as an entity is not, but represents ownership to the local community through attachment and belonging. The designation of an urban place as a World Heritage Site introduces a new international ownership for heritage, also highlighting a growing inside–outside tension of use and decision making, particularly where the future of historic towns is concerned. Society's identification with and ownership of heritage is the primary factor in motivating urban conservation; but it is the securing of financial support that enables implementation.

Parallel to the development of urban conservation, less well recorded and its impact frequently ignored, has been the steady growth of 'cultural' tourism in historic towns. Worldwide, tourism is becoming a growth industry, and in the case of historic towns it is moving from being an 'add-on' economic benefit to playing a significant and sometimes powerful role in conservation and economic regeneration. It is true that urban heritage has been conserved as a result of tourism interest, but a considerable amount has equally been destroyed because of it. The growth of a facadist approach to conservation and the prevalence of 'pastiche' in new developments are becoming a common feature of tourist environments, while medieval towns and nineteenth-century industrial 'heritage' centres are beginning to look very similar with their newly laid cobbled streets, catalogue 'heritage' street furniture, retro architecture and chain retail outlets. The objective of conservation in many places appears to be moving from 'continuity of the lived-in environment' to more aesthetic and external qualities, intended to appeal to the visitor's perceptions in the external realm. There is a complexity of reasons from social to legislative which contribute to the present appearance of many historic towns, and as a major economic component, tourism is one of them.

For the tourist industry, history has become a product that can be marketed, sold and re-created. Historic settlements and urban areas are seen as assets, readily transformed into products that are sold to consumers seeking an 'experience'. A myth is created of a 'clean' replacement industry, jobs and high financial returns, while the burden of economic investment and the drain on environmental, cultural and social resources are frequently ignored. Tourism is a volatile industry, deterred by crisis as it is fashion dependent and a 'spoilt' destination is quickly discarded in favour of the newly discovered. As Murphy (1985: 97) points out, in many Third World situations, '[tourism] involves a lot of noise and activity, but at the end of the day, locals have surprisingly little to show for it'.

Conservation in the interest of tourism is ignoring the depth and dynamism of the urban environment in favour of the re-creation of sterile and 'experienceable' settings. Subsequently heritage is reduced to a chosen interpretation of history and its physical remains as a marketing tool, a specifically selected and packaged product (Larkham 1996). A dichotomy of real and authentic emerges, of a lived-in environment and a 'staged culture'.

> Tourist consciousness is motivated by its desire for authentic experiences, and the tourist may believe that he is moving in this direction, but often it is difficult to know for sure if the experience is in fact authentic.
>
> (MacCannell 1976: 101)

A past time or a 'primitive' existence is being superficially re-enacted in historic settlements simply to satisfy the visitor's desire for an 'authentic' experience. The underlying dichotomy is one of inside and outside, the authenticity of the inside and the facade showcase of the outside, and also of the insider as user and the outsider as decision maker. On a global scale it is also a dichotomy of East and West, the western charters and methods for conservation and the eastern realities of poverty and aspiration; the western tourist (outsider) visiting the imagined exotic (the insider's slum).

Tourism increases the physical pressures on fragile environments and may be seen as a threat to the social unity of culture and community. But tourism is not just a threat that has to be managed, it also has to be viewed as an opportunity to be harnessed.

> Tourism is a twentieth century phenomenon. You cannot put it aside. One must accept it as a phenomenon that exists, good or not so good. Millions of people travel. One cannot stop them. They will come, so let them be used as a source for development.
>
> (Kuban 1978: 84)

Tourism is a unique economic opportunity, but like industrialisation before it, it is also a significant cause of lifestyle change. Tourism potentially brings vitality and economic and cultural dynamism to a place and for heritage, the benefits of appreciation, preservation and conservation. Making tourism work for historic towns and their conservation depends foremost on the objectives of development and the authority to control it. For a high-quality and desirable environment which is competitive and progressive, locally distinct yet globally acceptable, a delicate balance has to be sought in historic towns between the desires of visitors and the interests of residents; between growth and quality of life; between economic development and environmental costs; between the use of space and the interpretation of space; in the decision-making process between public roles and private interests; between the community and the market. Only tourism planning that directly benefits *local* interests and the local economy will serve the realistic continuation of heritage.

Sustainable development is often hindered by the absence of forward planning, reactive rather than proactive urban management and most notably the lack of communication between the two decision-making disciplines, that of planning and conservation and that of marketing and tourism management. It is surprising yet true that at a time when urban conservation and urban tourism are running parallel courses of development, the two fields of expertise directing them rarely communicate, and it is not uncommon for tourism development policy to be contradictory to heritage conservation. In this duality, the community role in decision making is being overlooked and the position of local-level coordination weakened.

Meanwhile, as a new century dawns, the emphasis of urban economy is shifting from production to consumption, while the once strict boundaries between the public and private sectors disappear. Concepts of time and location are rapidly changing as part of a global change taking place since the 1970s and described as 'a process of economic restructuring, spatially dispersed and globally integrated'

(Ghirardo 1996: 176). In the global economy, money and capital are no longer nationally based, but as Tekeli (1998) points out, it is still a globalisation that is working in favour of developed countries, compounding the inequality with the world's poorer nations.

Stimpson and Bhabha (1998) in the UNESCO *World Culture Report* identify three areas of globalisation: in economic and financial systems, in information systems and in entertainment systems. Access to internationally available information is reducing the control of national powers as a global era takes hold, as 'subjective' news bulletins are broadcast worldwide, the music and entertainment industries are valued by global sales only, hotel rooms become identical and restaurant chains offer the same fare on the same chairs in London, Hong Kong, New Delhi or Istanbul. Similarly, culture is losing local or regional identity as global 'cultural industries' start to dominate. Within lies the contradiction, of the familiar being sought by the increasingly mobile punter, who at the same time is seeking the new and the novel among prevailing uniformity. Against a tide of rapid urban growth and change, to users and visitors, historic towns represent a familiarity linked to an 'idealised' past and, in a globalised market of ever-increasing 'sameness', an 'otherness' and a depth not as yet attained in the new. Yet again there is tension, between local culture as it is lived and local culture as it is being marketed and perceived by outsiders.

Visiting historic towns is not about going to a museum or reliving history, and urban conservation is not about preserving the past as an archaeological ruin; it is about enhancing an area which has qualities built upon from the past, as a contemporary living environment. Tourism has to be made to work for historic towns, enhance rather than destroy, support rather than siphon, most of all value the depth, the heart and the spirit of a place. For tourism too, it is the local distinctiveness that is the added value. A valued environment in which people want to live and work is also going to be appreciated by visitors.

The field of urban conservation and the issues relating to tourism in historic environments are as wide ranging as they are complex. This book raises as many questions as it answers. Each town and each case is unique and solutions have to be sought for the specific context, sensitive to the *place* and responsive to the needs of the local *community*. What is proposed represents guidelines only, thoughts and ideas based on past experience. The debate wholeheartedly continues and if past experience is an indicator, there is still much learning to be done.

This book has been written at the end of a millennium and will be published at the dawn of another. It has been written at the end of a century which has seen technological advancement and speed of development like no other before it and one in which the car has changed the way cities are used, and it will be published at the start of another where the achievements of the last century will be overtaken in less than a decade and the successors of the motor industry will revolutionise the way in which cities are used. It has been written at the end of a decade in which a global economy and World Heritage Sites have become common points of reference and it will be published at the start of a decade where many programmes and initiatives are ready to be launched in recognition of the significance of the relationship among culture, historic towns and tourism.

The book

The intention of this book is to examine the relationship of culture, heritage, conservation and tourism development in historic towns and urban centres, by analysing:

- the in-depth characteristics of an historic urban environment, life and local distinctiveness;
- the influences of tourism on urban conservation;
- the pressures of tourism in historic towns;
- how historic places are being packaged by the tourist industry;

so as to develop decision-making and management practices for historic urban environments in the interests of long-term and sustainable development, by identifying:

- ways in which historic towns can benefit from tourism as a developmental industry;
- decision-making practices which are directly responsive to the needs of historic towns;
- the effectiveness and importance of local-level direction and control;
- means for the better representation of community needs;
- a way ahead through innovation, creative vision, forward planning and better management of the heritage environment.

Scope

The book covers historic towns that are established or emerging in the tourist market in both developed and developing countries. The focus is the wealth of historic towns in Western and Eastern Europe and in the Mediterranean region. The common reference to 'historic town' covers the main focus of medium-sized historic towns and historic quarters which are attractive to the tourist market, but it does not differentiate between the legal status of a place as city or as a town. Large cities with historic quarters and smaller rural settlements are not excluded and many of the issues and discussions are equally applicable to these historic environments.

The book is intended for a multi-disciplinary readership including academics and professionals and decision makers in the fields of conservation, heritage management and tourism development. Written from an architectural and urban conservation point of view, the book intends to bridge the gap between conservation and tourism in historic towns.

Structure

The book is divided into six chapters in two broad sections. The first three chapters look at the conservation of historic towns and the role tourism is playing in the urban conservation process. The last three chapters start with an evaluation of existing urban decision-making structures for conservation and tourism, in order then to discuss approaches to tourism planning and the management of visitors in the historic environment.

Chapter 1, 'The historic town', is introductory, and provides an overview of the historic development of towns including urban morphology, industrialisation and change, modernisation and urban conservation. The chapter discusses the recognition of historic towns as heritage and the start of the urban conservation movement in Europe, the approaches and commonly agreed principles of urban conservation today, and its successes and common outcomes in developed and developing countries.

Chapter 2, 'The tourist-historic town', examines the growing appreciation of historic towns as tourist destinations, the role conservation has played in generating tourism and the role tourism has come to play in the recognition, conservation and at times exploitation of historic towns. The pressures of tourism in the historic but contemporary urban environment are discussed, including the tensions arising between residents (hosts) and tourists (guests).

Chapter 3, 'The tourist town', describes historic towns which are being turned into museums, responding to the visitor experience as frozen-in-time set pieces or even theme park-type attractions. Examples are discussed with comparisons drawn with theming and 'Disney experiences'. Town museums, theme parks and heritage parks are evaluated for their implications for the future interpretation of urban heritage.

Chapter 4, 'Decision making for the historic environment', is an examination of the urban decision-making structure in the areas of conservation, economic development and tourism management. The roles played by a wide cast of players from the global tourist industry to the local community are interpreted. The chapter then identifies common areas of conflict and tension between key players, interest groups and development priorities.

Chapter 5, 'Planning for tourism in historic towns', deals with tourism and development planning in historic towns, and discusses approaches which bridge disciplines and the communication gap through partnership, action-based planning and strategic thinking towards achieving sustainable objectives.

The final chapter, 'Heritage management in historic towns', develops ways in which tourism can benefit urban conservation and discusses the use of better management, innovation, good design and added value to reduce pressures and enhance the *quality* of place.

A wide range of historic town examples is discussed throughout the text, and there are hundreds more which could have been cited, but examples have been limited to provide continuity and to enhance points. Alongside the examples given in the text, five case studies are placed between the chapters to illustrate in more detail the issues raised in the previous chapter and to act as an introduction to the following chapter. The case studies represent issues rather than geographical location.

The Albaicín quarter in Granada, Spain, is in urgent need of conservation for even its community spirit to survive. The case study discusses the options for urban conservation in the absence of state grants, and the relationship with tourism, which today is focused only on the Alhambra Palace. The city of York in England is a typical West European historic town, an early and successful example of urban conservation. As other industries have declined, economic dependence on tourism is increasing, but so is the discontent of its residents with the pressures of tourism.

The little over 300 citizens of the walled city Mdina in Malta feel they are a museum exhibit, having become Malta's most popular cultural attraction. Pressures are directly felt and the cost is often borne by locals. Another walled city, Antalya, on Turkey's south coast, was in the process of being sensitively developed through tourism in a clearly defined, well-planned and financially supported development plan. Conflict between professional advice and commercial pressure, however, has resulted in political support of the latter, turning Antalya into another over-developed historic town, devoid of character. And finally, Quedlinburg, a World Heritage Site in the former German Democratic Republic, today faces the task of repairing and restoring a vast stock of rapidly decaying medieval heritage while developing a sustainable tourist market as its main economic resource.

1 The historic town

Introduction

The interaction of human beings with the past and the present, with buildings, spaces and one another produces an urban dynamism and creates a spirit of place. For its user the urban environment is an interpretation through personal identification and attachment to the existing physical fabric, groups of buildings or street network. The (historic) urban environment is a relic of past events, occupation and ownership. Urban heritage on the other hand is the interpretation of history by a variety of users and by decision makers aiming to attract more users. Heritage is finite and the more ancient is rapidly being consumed; yet this loss is increasing the desire to save and to see it, and thus it is also hastening its demise. Lowenthal (1996) thus describes the past as both more accessible and more vulnerable than ever before. Within the heritage environment, as in the city itself, there is an underlying tension between current and previous inhabitants; between local history and world history; between user and visitor; between internal and external space; between depth and superficiality.

The recognition of historic urban fabric as cultural heritage and its identification as a significant link in urban life and development has inspired a desire for area-based conservation. Urban conservation is a long-term political, economic and social commitment to an area with the intention of providing a better quality of life for its users. Conservation encompasses not only the physical urban fabric, but also an understanding of the spatial morphology and a social dimension which makes urban heritage so distinct from the more 'object' qualities of the singular built heritage. Both the conservation and the effective management of the historic townscape are dependent on a sound understanding of its historical and spatial structures (Conzen 1981; Larkham 1990), an understanding of social and community structure, and an appreciation of the private and religious uses of urban space. 'Civilisation resides in communities, not in things' (Youngson 1990: 85), and the conservation of the object is not enough when communities are changing and developing.

This chapter is an introduction to historic towns, quarters or areas and urban conservation, and considers the following questions:

- What is urban heritage?
- Who does heritage belong to?
- What does urban conservation seek to achieve?

Urban form

Morphology

The city is an ecosystem, in form a compilation of past and present layers providing a framework for the contemporary mechanisms of urban economy and life. No living environment is the product of a single historic period and even the most puritanically planned cities have experienced change within several years of completion. Descriptions such as 'Georgian Bath' refer to the significance of a certain period and predominant architectural style. Nor can a place be associated purely with a single culture, religion or nationality. Throughout history, cities have been established and planned, they have grown and expanded, they have been invaded or sacked, and ultimately they have been rebuilt, developed and replanned. In the process they have acquired a collective identity of urban theory, architectural style, defence, culture and human life. In Caniggia's description of urban morphology, in each period a leading style 'type' is created. Initially appearing on the periphery, the new type gradually features more centrally as its details are adapted in alterations to existing buildings. Growth and development continue in this fashion as new leading types are continuously introduced (Larkham 1990). What is referred to as 'historic town' is this synthesis and overlap of style, which is becoming ring-fenced or frozen as 'heritage' in the present.

The heritage interpretation or re-creation of an 'historic town' is not so much urban history, as a modification and romantic vision of what the viewer or the decision maker, on behalf of the potential viewer, would like it to be. Although an underlying spatial morphology and a certain amount of the physical fabric are of a past era, the experience is of a contemporary 'heritage-town', in which layers of history in the urban fabric, use of space and contemporary human life interact, both in harmony and in tension. Conservation may be a form of interpretation, but it has to respond to the spatial pattern and morphology of a city.

History and form

The underlying street pattern and urban morphology of many European and Mediterranean towns and cities can be traced back to a Roman grid plan. Cities as far apart as York and Antioch or Trier and Istanbul share a Roman past. The Roman grid was seen to dissolve gradually as feudalism took over and walled cities provided protection in the new political climate where the church had gained power. The walled medieval city was typically located on a hilltop or a riverside, built around a church or a cathedral in the centre, often with a market square and a narrow and winding street pattern. As power shifted from the church to the bourgeoisie, trade revived, urban form adapted and new buildings such as town halls gained importance.

In the East, Byzantine rule gave way to Islamic dynasties, spreading in the Middle East, North Africa and into Spain. The Islamic rulers were building on an existing and often sophisticated urban tradition established around the

Mediterranean. The new urban population often came from a nomadic back-ground,[1] contributing new traditions to urban life. The fifteenth-century city was typically located around a citadel with an inner bailey housing administrative buildings, and artisans and upper-class residents within the outer fortifications, while peasants lived outside the walls. Urban form and location responded to the environment, with cities built on hillsides to allow sunlight into the houses or huddled together against desert winds. Markets and caravanserai evolved as international trade became more important in urban livelihood.

Meanwhile, the Renaissance started to change the face and form of the more important towns of Europe, as grand avenues were created to connect palaces and public squares. By the seventeenth and eighteenth centuries, new quarters were being built outside some medieval towns,[2] and others, including Paris, were being completely redesigned with new avenues and facades in the 'Grand Manner'.[3] Diagonal axes followed, framing distant vistas of palaces, monuments, triumphal arches, commemorative columns and statues. Medieval towns that had lost their importance were saved from 'classical' intervention and have become some of the best-known 'historic' towns of today.

During this period of stylistic and morphological change for European towns and cities, the traditional form was retained in eastern ones; their spatial organisation reflects an underlying ideology that each part of the city is a whole within itself, locking into a street and spatial pattern and becoming part of the overall whole. The religious, administrative and commercial public centre was separated from the private residential neighbourhoods, connecting through a succession of transitionary open, semi-open and closed spaces; a social hierarchy of public, semi-public, semi-private and private place within the urban structure was created. Although there are examples of planned towns, organic formation and growth are the main characteristic of Islamic towns, resulting in a network of winding streets and cul-de-sacs. It is of course impossible to make stylistic generalisations on Islamic architecture or urban form as a single entity; and for many Islamic countries urban form is a result of belief combined with national identity and local tradition.

Although the traditional urban pattern may date back over several centuries, individual buildings within the old towns are not that old, a result of the 'Moslem respect only for the permanence of God, which had inbred habits of building afresh instead of maintenance' (Goodwin 1992: 450), with the residential fabric being frequently renewed.[4] Unlike European historic towns, with buildings spanning several centuries from as early as the thirteenth, Islamic towns often present stylistic homogeneity.

Urban growth in the post-industrial era

Industrialisation has been one of the most significant turning points of urban development and urban living. From the nineteenth century on, many western cities were revolutionised, with the introduction of heavy industry, mass transportation, associated developments and new pollutants. Urban boundaries rapidly expanded, with rural immigrants moving in as the new urban 'industrial' workforce. Transport networks made suburban life possible for the middle classes, who were abandoning the old central areas to incoming migrant populations and to frequent deterioration into overcrowded slums. In the post-industrial period, entire neighbourhoods and the many historic buildings within them were demolished in slum clearance programmes and development initiatives. Central districts, which had become isolated from residential use because of planning zones, developed into prime business and retail real estate. Consequently, increasing property values accelerated the pressure for demolition and redevelopment. Heavy-handed renewal schemes paid very little respect to the original scale, layout and cityscape, and many of the developments were real estate driven.

In this period Britain, as a leading industrial nation, was also following the practices of modernism – building 'big' and 'new' buildings, town centres and roads, often regardless of the historic urban fabric. 'Improvement Areas', specified by local authorities in the 1950s and 1960s, often resulted in large-scale developments (Balchin and Bull 1987). The general attitude of post-war Britain was to demolish slums and rehouse residents in new multi-storey tenements. For Newcastle the 1961 grand plan included a proposal for demolition, with the exception of a few buildings identified as 'masterpieces', and the building of new motorways and shopping malls. The politicians' vision for Newcastle was of a 'New Brasilia', an international city of the future with efficient road networks and high-rise buildings (*Architects' Journal* 1980). Following demolition, the clearance site was built up with shopping centres closed to the outside and fourteen-storey blocks decorated with sculptures. 'It was this sort of unquestioning belief in the benefits of redevelopment that kept the 1961 grand plan alive so long' (*Architects' Journal* 1980: 59). The New Brasilia plan was only abandoned after 1975, when growing public and environmental concern combined to curtail finances.

Similar developments were also under way in many other European city centres including Brussels, where an ambitiously named Manhattan Project was launched to replace the central Northern Quarter, which was regarded as a slum. This historic part of town housed low-income groups, including the elderly and relief-dependent foreigners; many of them were attached to the area for their livelihood, social benefits, and the safety of their tight community. The grand project, which was to provide jobs, entertainment, shopping facilities and upmarket housing, was never completed due to a recession (Appleyard 1979).

In the late twentieth century, industrialisation for many developing countries is a bid to catch up with developed industrialised nations. The consequences of this accelerated and large-scale industrial activity for the urban environment has been dramatic and often beyond the control of local managing powers. Inner-city conservation projects not only have to tackle economic deprivation, but are also faced with a complexity of rapidly evolving formal and informal traditions and often a desire for renewal. In Lahore for example, the nineteenth-century walled city is home to as many as 500,000 people, many of them unskilled or semi-skilled labourers. A pre-industrial economy and social organisation still dominate urban life in the quarter, which faces serious problems of decay, overcrowding and sanitation. At the same time the population is moving towards a post-industrial consumerism which has been generated through technology (Mumtaz 1978). Responding to technological developments, a new mobility of capital, and the rapid urbanisation of the world population, the urban environment is in a continuous process of spatial and social restructuring. The centre of Ankara, Turkey, for example has been rebuilt twice since its original conception in the 1930s; the centre of Mexico City has been replaced at an even faster rate.

Today an information revolution is bringing more change to work, living and leisure in the urban environment. On the one hand heritage and identity are fighting for survival amidst rapid growth, and on the other hand leisure, culture and tourism industries are recognising the historic urban environment as a commercial asset. At a time when commercial value is being attached to the 'historic' element of the urban environment, mass tourism according to Page (1995: xv) may be the next big change to urban life after the car. The post-industrial urban labour market is also moving from the industrial to the service sector, creating new spatial and social relationships, which according to D. Harvey (1989) are subsequently accelerated through tourism and growing urban consumption.

Urban heritage

History and heritage

Heritage, as derived from inheritance, is defined in the *Oxford English Dictionary* as 'that which has been or may be inherited', and involves both previous and future generations. In the urban context, it is the power of continuity from one generation to the next, it 'is not only something we want to hand down to future generations, it is also something we want to appreciate and experience to the fullest extent' (Masser *et al.* 1994: 31). According to Millar (1995: 120), 'heritage is about a special sense of belonging and of continuity that is different for each person', whereas Ashworth (1997) prefers to refer to heritage as 'the contemporary uses of the past', and Lowenthal (1996: 1) considers heritage to be a new cult, 'whose shrines and icons daily multiply'.

History is itself a written interpretation, intended for a certain audience, a tribute to the person who commissioned it, glorifying the deeds of a ruler for example. Not unlike the written word, buildings provide historic evidence in stone and mortar from which social history is interpreted. 'Historians operate as agents of society and produce histories to service that society' (Kavanagh 1996: 4). National history becomes a form of intellectual colonialism, written by and for the ruling classes. But as nationalism loses its once protected boundaries to institutional globalisation, and cross-national culture is exemplified by communications and media technology, there is a noticeable move towards the reinterpretation of history, to an interpretation that is inclusive rather than exclusive, and one which will possibly be more honest and fact derived (Boniface and Fowler 1993; Tekeli 1998). While African significance is being incorporated into a previously 'white' American history, a previously white South African history is being reversed to a predominantly black one (Ashworth 1997).

Urban heritage as a link to history is a combination of physical parts, historic association and mythical story telling. 'Contemporary life, divorced from the roots of our history, can be an extremely superficial and meaningless experience' (Worksett 1978: 3). As hopes of progress fade, heritage consoles us with tradition (Lowenthal 1996). Heritage has been regarded as accumulated experience, an educational encounter and a contact with previous generations, and, according to Conzen, an 'objectivation of the spirit of society' (Whitehand 1990: 371). 'History explores and explains pasts grown ever more opaque over time; heritage clarifies pasts so as to infuse them with present purposes' (Lowenthal 1996: xi). Ashworth and Voogd (1990: 67), on the other hand, argue that heritage is an urban product, an assemblage of selected resources bound together by interpretation.

Urban heritage cannot be narrowed down to individual buildings or monuments of historic interest, nor can it be interpreted simply as a totality of built parts. Urban heritage exists in the physical attributes of buildings, public spaces and urban morphology; it is experienced by users (inheritors) in the present and it is concurrently in the making of the next generation of heritage. The fall of the Berlin Wall in 1990, for example, revolutionised urban life, form and interpretation of the city. Some unlikely and previously intimidating aspects such as Checkpoint Charlie have been transformed into the new urban heritage. More heritage is being created in Potsdammer Platz for example, where the new signature architecture is both an historical symbol of a unified Germany and a prime tourist attraction.

Whose heritage? Identification and conservation

The identification with heritage and a communal claim of ownership (possession) bring about the (communal) desire for the protection of the physical relics of urban history. Although this identification with cultural heritage is a primary prerequisite, conservation depends fundamentally on the availability of funds. Tourism may become an important contributor to the economic realisation of a project, but there is the delicate balance between tourism being a support to conservation and tourism becoming the reason for conservation. Like history, who does urban history relate to, whose heritage is it and who is it being conserved for? Such identifications and distinctions are not easy to make, but remain essential to the understanding of a situation and a well-balanced outcome. Identification with a cultural object often evokes feelings of ownership and of belonging. In an example from Sardinia given by Oddermatt (1996), villagers identify prehistoric monuments near their village as 'theirs', because they are in a place where they gather for celebrations and which they frequent for communal activities. Frictions occur when the Sardinian authorities identify the ruins as an important part of the national heritage and safeguard them with a fence, denying the villagers access. Both the government and the villagers have a stake in the 'ownership', but resentment is intensified when the authorities' claim is seen to be for touristic and commercial reasons.

Warren (1998: 12) points out that 'society owns the historic town', because unlike the individual, community has a continuous life, and with it an ownership of the environment. Cultural heritage undoubtedly has communal value and the links between cultural objects and national identity have long been understood. The severe damage to many central European cities from heavy bombing in the Second World War led to a post-war effort of re-establishing historic buildings, reflecting the importance of rebuilding severely damaged national monuments for the dignity of nations and the citizens' desire for a memorial (Jokilehto 1998). Many buildings and facades facing public squares across Europe were rebuilt as replicas, often on the mere evidence of pre-war photographs and drawings. Although 90 per cent of Nuremberg's buildings were destroyed during the war, the 1950 guide for reconstruction required the use of steep roofs and the reddish and yellow tones of rendering typical of the nineteenth-century city (UNESCO 1980).

Fig. 1.1 Architectural heritage is strongly linked to identity: in returning to their homeland in the early 1990s, after fifty years in exile, the Crimean Tatars immediately set about the restoration of the Palace of Bahcesaray, formerly the seat of the Crimean Khanate.

Careful reconstruction of buildings of historic significance following war damage is an expression of national and collective identity, an important step in post-war recovery. Ivo Andric, in his historical novel *Bridge over the River Drina*, describes the restoration and strengthening of the sixteenth-century bridge that had become the symbol and probably the most familiar structure of the town of Višegrad, following each conflict including the First World War. The bridge was subsequently bombed in the Second World War, repaired and once again heavily damaged during more recent conflicts in the region. Post-modern warfare, against international convention,[5] is often seen to specifically target major monuments and historic urban centres. Armed conflicts in the former Yugoslavia have severely damaged the popular tourist-historic towns of Split, Dubrovnik, Sarajevo, Mostar and many others. The bombing of Dubrovnik by Serb forces in 1992 purposely targeted the historic fabric, as the world watched a black cloud of smoke rising from the walled city. Ironically, many residents had taken refuge within the medieval walls, assuming the old town would be spared for its historic significance.[6] The rebuilding process, in a conservation-conscious Europe, clearly recognises the potential of 'heritage' tourism as a major source of income. In a more macabre twist, 'post-modern' tourists in search of alternative experiences are visiting bombed-out cities, like Beirut, to view the aftermath.

It is, however, misleading to associate cities simply with a collective national identity. The world population just within the past fifty years, through war, revolution and economic forces, has experienced migration and unprecedented human mobility. While a politically divided Berlin has been reunified, Sarajevo has been restructured to accommodate two conflicting ethnic communities. The former occupants of East Berlin in turn were surprised to find West Berlin inhabited by immigrant guest workers. People are moving as refugees or migrant workers

Fig. 1.2 The old walled town of Dubrovnik in Croatia was specifically targeted and shelled by Serb forces in 1992.

and making new places their home; a rural to urban migration continues the world over, boosting urban populations and introducing new inhabitants to the urban cauldron. There is a general mobility with new border arrangements between European Union countries: these include a new European job market and the freer movement of European residents such as northern Europeans moving to southern France or Spain in retirement. This mobility is changing not only urban form, but also its nature and human identification with it, while migration is sharpening nostalgia for a lost heritage. Travel brings another transient group into the urban arena, with different demands, priorities and interpretations.

Not only war, but a community's concern for heritage at risk, increases the pressure for conservation. A rapid pace of change is adding value to the familiar and heightening nostalgia for the past. Urban heritage holds within it both collective identity and diversity, and possesses a different meaning for each individual identifying with it. Often incorporating within its borders conflicting cultural claims, the state ultimately has a responsibility to develop and nurture cultural heritage. 'The modern states achieved certain success in unifying different ethnic groups and regions in a national heritage they more or less shared' (Canclini 1998: 157). Alongside static archaeological or museum displays, the state is recognising the significance of supporting urban rehabilitation to keep a desired history alive. The approach, however, varies from a mixture of national identity and local association for inhabitants old and new, to simply supplying a picture-postcard image to the transient visitor. Not all identification is of appreciation, and heritage valued by some may have negative connotations for another social group.

Heritage provokes in the individual a sense of being part of and belonging to place and community. The ownership of heritage is in the public realm; there is a dichotomy of individual association and collective claim, a growing tension between what constitutes the boundaries of the public realm and the physical remit of 'collective'. Not only ancient sites and monuments, but entire cities are being inscribed in the World Heritage List, described in the World Heritage Convention as

> groups of separate or connected buildings which, because of their archi-
> tecture, their homogeneity or their place in the landscape, are of outstanding
> universal value from the point of view of history, art or science.
>
> (UNESCO 1972)

Lowenthal (1996: 5) points out that 'global popularity homogenises heritage' in the ways in which it is defined, addressed and treated, ultimately in a language created by the western world. International recognition may also highlight a conflict between local association with a place and global ownership of it; it may create new pressures for the environment and residents living in a World Heritage Site.

Increasingly, the identification of culture is that of a major economic sector, as the economic potential of cultural industries is being recognised (UNESCO 1998). Developing an historic area specifically for tourism can range from an appreciation of its urban qualities to a re-presentation of a past era and a creative interpretation of history. The limits for creative intervention can only be judged for each situation individually, but above all they must remain honest. The 'doing-up' of facades to create a glossy pattern-book streetscape is regarded as pastiche, whereas the regeneration of industrial heritage reusing a redundant building as a vehicle for economic revival in the often depressed post-industrial environment is acceptably removed from the grim historic reality. More and more, what has come to be known as 'heritage' is becoming consumer driven, and so is the authenticity that is attached to it (Ashworth and Larkham 1994), as historic towns become products which are being modelled to be acceptable to the market. A conserved and beautified assembly of buildings is what is seen as desirable and what the market is perceived to demand of an historic environment. Once again the point is one of conflicting arguments, between the need to provide a deeper understanding and the superficiality of contemporary life.

The Old Market Square of Warsaw is inscribed on the World Heritage List for what must be its cultural value and not its authentic one, since the square was rebuilt after the Second World War. But this can only further encourage an assemblage of parts formula for urban beautification, moulding urban heritage into sought-after images – the tried and tested formula of cobbled squares and outdoor cafes. Historic towns are in danger of becoming the same global product and, as such, an increasingly superficial experience.

Urban conservation

Conservation in the urban environment

'The old city exemplifies the human scale, individuality, care and craftsmanship, richness and diversity that are lacking in the modern plastic, machine-made city with its repetitive components and large scale projects' (Appleyard 1979: 19). Historic areas remain familiar in a changing environment and provide a sense of place, which Conzen refers to as *genius loci*. This is one reason for urban conservation, together with the aesthetic, cultural and historical values identified as heritage, and the educational, spatial and townscape values (Larkham 1996), combined with environmental concerns and economic viability (Lichfield 1988). Conservation is a reflection and accumulation of values placed upon our traditions and culture. Without it 'we would all be much poorer, deprived of roots, more uncertain about who we are and who we were' (Fethi 1993: 160). Even lived-in surroundings are not identified as heritage; 'people attach considerable value to aspects of their immediate environment . . . which give them a sense of identity and pride of place' (Butt 1988: 1). Urban conservation is a political, economic and social concern; and tourism-, image- or fashion-led conservation will only be superficial.

Fig. 1.3 Urban conservation is a long-term commitment to an area; well-conserved buildings that are being used encourage more projects to be realised (Erfurt, Germany).

Many definitions have been provided for conservation. According to Fethi (1993):

> Conservation is the careful planning and management of limited and selected resources. It is a conscious process to control and manipulate change to a minimum – to a rate that ensures the survival of cultural heritage over a long time.
>
> (Fethi 1993: 161)

Lichfield (1988), on the other hand, describes conservation as action to cope with actual or potential obsolescence. Historical environments serve a social purpose and their loss as irreparable cultural loss has been demonstrated in post-war rebuilding. Conservation is necessary for society both practically and in the academic sense of the historic knowledge (Whitehand 1981).

Fig. 1.4 In-between spaces, squares, formal and informal, are as important a part of the urban fabric as the buildings by which they are defined (Seville, Spain).

Urban conservation differs significantly from building conservation. First, it is multi-dimensional, and it involves, as well as the building fabric, the urban pattern, streets, open spaces, green areas and urban vistas. Second, it involves the services of a much wider range of disciplines and persons, and it is influenced by political decision making at local and national levels. Third, and probably most importantly, it involves a social aspect. The users, the residents, the property owners, business interests, and other citizens who use the area, and those who depend on it for their livelihoods, are all part of the conservation process. Urban conservation policies are often area based, through the designation of conservation or protection areas. City walls that once protected towns from invasion have also protected them from destruction, and nowadays they provide the boundaries for conservation areas. However, even within set boundaries, conservation has to be proactive and to permit growth and change in the urban structure, responding to the functionality of historic quarters and their spatial organisation in relation to contemporary urban problems.

Urban conservation has three dimensions: physical, spatial and social. All three interrelate and overlap, in context and in the responsibilities of key players. All are encompassed within the fourth dimension of *time*. The conservation of an historic urban environment is not an isolated project, but a multitude of projects, not all of them physical, which are interlinked to take place over an extended period of time, embodying public desires and private vested interests. Urban life continues during the conservation process and it is wrong to expect a finished product, for a city as a living organism is never complete and the urban environment grows and develops with and through its users.

The *physical* dimension is closely linked to building conservation, in that the emphasis is on appearance, and it covers projects involving old buildings, groups of buildings, new structures and many other aspects such as street furniture. The physical conservation of the urban fabric involves historians, archaeologists and

Fig. 1.5 Local use of a place, such as this early evening gathering in the Mathilden Brunnen in Quedlinburg, is part of urban life.

specialist architects, and it is controlled by city planning authorities and conservation departments. Others, including amenity societies, non-governmental organisations, grant-awarding bodies or community groups, may also take an active interest. The physical attributes of a 'finished' product, on the other hand, are of interest to the tourism marketer, but the direct beneficiary will be the owner, an individual, a group of individuals, an organisation or a private sector developer.

The *spatial* dimension is the urban planner's view of the city as a whole, including relationships between spaces and their use, circulation and traffic, and the internal and external space relationship. The spatial aspect of urban conservation is predominantly the role of the city planning department, overlapping with a city manager and closely linked to economic planning. Main considerations include traffic and circulation, and, in large cities, the historic area may play a small part in a much larger plan. Urban designers play an important role in design interpretation and in the organisation of external spaces, while tourism promoters and managers are likely to make demands on the urban planner for the provision of better access or parking facilities. The private sector wishing to invest in an area will also have demands for access and even on space use.

The third and *social* dimension concerns the user, the local community and the urban population. Compared to the physical and spatial dimensions, the social dimension of urban conservation is the most difficult to define, but arguably the most important, as continuity in conservation can only be achieved through the continuation of urban life. None of the professional groups identified above has a direct link to residents unless lines of communication are specifically established. The relationship is through the city authority answerable to the local community, and, in the case of an elected city council, the political decision makers also have a role as community representatives.

Historic towns were not built to accommodate many modern-day inventions including electricity, centralised services and the motor car. Inhabitants' demands for better amenities, from indoor bathrooms and running water to cable television and accessibility and car parking facilities, have had an impact on historic areas. Narrow streets are not ideal for cars and they are even less so for lorries or tourist buses, which are prone to cause damage to the historic fabric, particularly at tight junctions. Demographic and social changes are resulting in smaller nuclear families, and incomes are no longer able to pay for servants or the escalating maintenance and heating costs of large and draughty houses; there will also be a growing concern for personal and property security. To continue to be attractive to residents, old houses and towns need to provide for contemporary living standards.

Not all benefits of rehabilitating existing property can be measured against direct costs. The conservation and rehabilitation of old neighbourhoods are also a form of recycling – reusing buildings and in some cases maintaining an informal industry dependent on this process. When restoration costs are compared to new-build costs, energy and environmental costs for the production of new materials are not being calculated, and the need for maintenance of new buildings is frequently overlooked (Lichfield 1988). Furthermore, the immeasurable cultural value of these places is ignored.

An urban conservation movement

It is only in the second half of the twentieth century that there has been international recognition of historic urban areas as part of the built heritage, an appreciation of the everyday vernacular as 'heritage'. Historic town conservation has become a populist trend and Lowenthal (1996) questions whether too much is being kept and whether too much of our lives recorded for future heritage. The realisation that urban tissue could be as important as the monuments that it surrounded, and from which it had previously been methodically removed, led to a conscious urban conservation movement in Western Europe. The Charter of Venice, signed in 1964, stated:

> The concept of an historic monument embraces not only the single architectural work but also the urban and rural setting in which is found the evidence of a particular civilisation, a significant development or an historic event.
>
> (ICOMOS 1971)

An interest in history is not new in Europe. The Romantic movement in architecture of the eighteenth and nineteenth centuries, evoking an interest in the picturesque, was initiated in England and led by some of the most prominent architects of the time – Nicholas Hawksmoor, John Nash and Sir George Gilbert Scott.[7] This interest in historic buildings also initiated an interest in building restoration, later known as preservation,[8] in the late nineteenth century.[9] Even though both the definitions and the approaches to preservation and restoration have changed, the interest in, and love of, history continue in England. The history of building conservation and early legislation is well documented elsewhere (Erder 1986; Larkham 1996; and most recently Jokilehto 1999). In many instances local interest promoted awareness for the conservation of historic townscapes. In England a love for history, landscape and the picturesque had evolved, and with it came a feeling of responsibility for the environment and the appearance of amenity societies. The first national amenity society was formed in 1846 and by the turn of the century many more were established, most notably the National Trust[10] and the Town and Country Planning Association.[11]

International commitment to the historic value of urban areas started to be realised in the mid 1960s. In 1966, the Bath Symposium concluded with a statement on 'principles and practice of active preservation and rehabilitation of groups and areas of buildings of historical or artistic interest' (Council of Europe 1977: 33). The Symposium raised architectural and town planning issues, including communication and accessibility, with a precise brief to prevent historic areas being transformed into lifeless museums. The outcome of a 1967 symposium in The Hague particularly stressed that town planning schemes should include conservation links and awareness.

The European Architectural Heritage Year, 1975, not only increased awareness of the built heritage but also encouraged city authorities to tackle the problems of their historic centres, and a number of pioneering projects were launched. The declaration by the Council of Europe on the occasion stated the aim of the year:

> To awaken the interest of the European peoples in their common heritage;
> to protect and enhance buildings and areas of historic interest; to conserve
> the character of old towns and villages, and to assure for ancient buildings
> a living role in contemporary society.
>
> (Wood 1975: 1)

In contrast with the ongoing modernist schemes, in the early 1970s conservationist attitudes were growing and reports were being commissioned by many European governments on their historic towns. This new consciousness for urban conservation started to change the approach to 'development' in inner-city areas.

Worldwide, interests were also awakened and the United Nations, under UNESCO, and other international bodies, started publishing recommendations on historic conservation,[12] enhancing the conservation of culture and community within the urban context. The 1976 *Recommendations Concerning the Safeguarding and Contemporary Role of Historic Areas*, published in both Warsaw and Nairobi, stated that:

> The conservation of historic towns and urban areas is understood to mean
> those steps necessary for the protection, conservation and restoration of such
> town areas, as well as their development and harmonious adaptation to
> contemporary life.
>
> (ICOMOS 1987)

The restoration of buildings in the late twentieth century is very different from the practice started in the nineteenth century and it has become a well established and recognised field of expertise today. Institutions have been set up to provide specialised training at all levels from architects to craftspeople. The use of original materials and techniques is widely promoted, as is the supervision of projects by suitably qualified experts. The diverse elements of urban conservation, including the human element, are also being recognised in multi-disciplinary teams.

Urban conservation in Europe

Appleyard (1979: 8) refers to the theory that the conservation movement in Britain only gained momentum when the middle classes began to realise that the older neighbourhoods were perfectly habitable and possessed qualities above those in the suburbs and new towns. Probably for much the same reasons, by the late 1970s and early 1980s a surge of conservation activity could be detected in Europe's run-down historic quarters. Projects were set up and initiatives supported to improve urban areas and settlements across Europe. In each case the precedent and the outcome were different. Sometimes it was urban revival in a recognised and well-known historic city, in other cases the rehabilitation of an industrial slum.

The medieval town of Bruges in Belgium had been an important trading city in history, hardly touched by the industrial Revolution or by bombing during the war. However, by the early 1970s the historic centre, no longer responding to the demands of a twentieth-century industrialised society, had became poverty stricken with one in eight houses lying vacant. But demolitions by the city council provoked heavy protest and a plan was launched in 1972 for a multi-functional city centre, conserving cultural and aesthetic values and responding to present-day needs. The plan aimed to make the centre attractive to a greater proportion of the population and to achieve this through private initiatives. The city council was able to pay up to 50 per cent of repair costs on visible parts of listed buildings and 30 per cent for other parts, also promoting the insertion of high-quality modern architecture into vacant plots (UNESCO 1980: 44). The scheme achieved most of its targets of making the centre of Bruges attractive again, as the population of the inner city increased along with the art galleries and smarter boutiques which started to boost the local economy. Today Bruges is another smart European town, a successful example of conservation and modern development. While economic targets have been met and exceeded through tourism, the town centre has become overcrowded by visitors to the extent that overcrowding is ruling daily life (Jansen-Verbeke 1995) and it is becoming less attractive to residents.

For the residents of Venice, however, there has been little choice. A World Heritage Site, Venice has continuously received funding for the conservation of its grand monuments, particularly following numerous and devastating floods, but rarely for improvements to the housing, which suffers from rising damp and associated decay (Sammuels 1990). Lack of policies for public housing and almost non-existent grants led to many houses becoming dilapidated and eventually abandoned, as residents moved out to the suburbs when living conditions in their old properties became unbearable. Properties bought up by affluent Europeans and Americans as second or third homes now often lie empty for much of the year. But property is no longer affordable for Venetians who want to live in the old city in spite of the tourists, in the belief that it is only they, the Venetians, who are the true caretakers of Venice (Cessarelli 1979).

In the market economy there is a social price to be paid as new ownership patterns emerge. 'Western cities are creations of the capitalist order, where investment fuels an economy and becomes part of the cycle of wealth creation' (Larkham 1996: 3). Many areas in their rehabilitated and modernised forms have once again become popular among the middle classes, often at the expense of their poorer latter-day inhabitants. Low rents do not pay for repairs and once properties

Fig. 1.6 Bruges in Belgium is a successful example of urban conservation. Most of the historic architecture has been restored and modern buildings successfully incorporated into the historic fabric.

have been repaired, the new rents are no longer affordable to the old tenants. Large houses are now divided into small flats and studios for a growing demand from urban professionals choosing to live close to city centres. Soane (1994: 173), for example, describes the re-establishment of the old town of Dresden on the Elbe as 'a comprehensive reintroduction of the wide variety of high-quality cultural, retail and tourist facilities that existed in this area before 1945'. On the one hand it is a natural cycle of urban environments; on the other hand a less desirable layer of urban history is being conveniently dismissed in this latter-day 'clean-up'. While interest, support and campaigning from the public were the main guiding elements in the western conservation movement, implementation has often been at the residents' expense.

Jordaan, traditionally a working-class area of Amsterdam, had become dilapidated once small and dirty industries had taken over much of the housing. When the city council took action to remove industry, pedestrianise certain streets, concentrate commercial activity and subsequently gentrify the area, it was a group of professionals and students who campaigned for Jordaan to be returned to its working-class community, 'where people knew their neighbours and a community spirit existed'. However, in order to make their point many of them moved into the area, which resulted in the neighbourhood gaining a new image, that of an intellectual community, which 'did not use curtains and never spent time talking on street corners' (Appleyard 1979: 235); the working-class inhabitants had still been alienated.

Kreuzberg, a run-down area with poor and foreign tenants and high unemployment in the former West Berlin, came to the attention of the authorities when social unrest and protests in the 1980s resulted in a student-led movement. Consequently rehabilitation plans were tied in with the then ongoing IBA[13] project and attracted private and public investment. Living standards of 'those who were able to stay' improved, as houses were rehabilitated, new parks and gardens were created and traffic in the area was reduced. As Duwe (1989: 62) points out, the original tenants no longer live in Kreuzberg and 'the former students use splendid white tablecloths and silverware for their exquisite dinners'. Both IBA and social rebuilding appear to be forgotten as the fall of the Berlin Wall has relocated Kreuzberg from an undesirable border region to prime real estate in the city centre.

While for the well-known historic quarters of Western Europe the architectural environment has been improved, as have housing conditions and amenities, the objective of protecting the resident community has very rarely been achieved. Throughout Europe only a small number of urban renewal schemes attempting community participation have been successful in achieving community objectives. Community participation appeared on the agenda of major conferences organised by the Council of Europe for the year of European Architectural Heritage (1975). At the Edinburgh conference the importance of amenity groups in the process, and the publicity of successful projects were discussed, while in Bologna it was demonstrated that it was only through public participation that local development could occur, involving all the citizens, not just the home owners, but also the not so privileged tenants, so as to enable them to remain in the area after rehabilitation.

Bologna has probably been a rare successful example when it comes to community benefit. The attitude of the local 'communist' leadership was that the city was the property of its inhabitants. Prior to the decision to revitalise the historic centre, eighteen neighbourhood councils were established of about 30,000 people each. A conservation programme was developed with these local councils, and detailed surveys undertaken on building types and the families living in them. The City bought up a considerable amount of property, to rehabilitate and use as public housing for the people of the area. Private owners were given repair grants, on the condition that rent levels were maintained, and the city council held the right to buy renovated property before it became available on the market. Although this was an immense task, the long-term result has been that many of the original communities have remained in the revitalised neighbourhoods. Heralded as a success story, it has nevertheless failed to become an example for capitalist and market-based developments in other Italian or West European towns. Appleyard (1979) has pointed out that similar results can only be achieved in neighbourhoods 'which are not yet the object of large-scale tourism'. In the twenty years that have passed, tourism and not the Bologna example has been the winner.

Today, many of Western Europe's old towns are strict conservation areas, with laws and regulations protecting the historic fabric and permitting little and only rigorously controlled modern intervention. Although conservation work may be more modest than that of a major monument, resources required for the urban environment are much greater and unlikely to be available as a single lump sum, nor would this be desirable. Improvement budgets are provided as a tool for

Fig. 1.7 Like many other Western European historic town centres, the well-conserved historic core of Strasbourg caters for tourist activity.

economic regeneration and rely on the knock-on effects of the early initiatives. In England Town Schemes have injected money into areas and grants have been made available to owners to repair their properties.[14] More recently larger regeneration funds have been made available, including European Union-backed schemes, covering a wider remit of industry and job creation based on public–private partnerships. Nevertheless, there is considerable competition for such funds and city authorities are at times investing precious time and resources into unsuccessful bids.

Local governments controlling conservation programmes in the 1970s and 1980s were often in a fortunate position to award supporting grant funding to projects. However, even though they are able to control and regulate the quality and standards of conservation work, councils have often been unable to resist the commercial powers of the market, and gentrification has become the inevitable outcome in most cases. As western society has turned to leisure and recreation, many historic centres have evolved into providers of leisure services, supplying a 'picturesque' and 'authentic' setting for pleasant cafes and restaurants, small hotels and good shopping facilities. Conservation can become an exaggerated concern to keep everything as it is; this is neither possible nor realistic. Nor is flawless conservation where the results appear more like a themed heritage park than a town. The conservation process, policy and planning decisions have to consider long-term future growth and development. Furthermore, problems perceived by the expert outsider may not be the problems that are experienced by the inhabitants or a priority to them.

Urban realities and conservation in developing economies
Rehabilitation in many European towns may have ended up with gentrification of areas, but at the same time considerable progress has been made and lessons learnt. A conservation culture has developed, supported by established legislation, policy and control mechanisms. It is not, however, always possible to apply all these

principles to cities of the developing world which are facing rapid and uncontrolled urban growth, with related consequences for urban services and debt-ridden national economies. For less stable economies where pressures for development are much greater and where the funds available are negligible, urban conservation as has been developed in Western Europe is near impossible, and where progress is being made there is still much to be accomplished and a greater complexity of issues to be tackled.

Conservation charters, although international in name, are predominantly generated in Europe and by Europeans, and do not fully respond to cultural differences and social realities, nor can they be supported by the economies of many developing countries. For many places it is simply not economically possible to retain an entire stock of urban heritage. Planners in both Riga, Latvia, and Tallinn, Estonia, are trying to protect neighbourhoods of grand buildings in the Art Nouveau style as well as the medieval quarters. There is no funding for the repair of these tumbling mansions and in many cases ownership disputes continue. Planners are unwillingly faced with some harsh and critical decisions for their future. However, it must also be recognised that being old does not necessarily qualify architecture as heritage.

Major issues facing conservation in general and urban conservation in particular in developing countries are that:

- urban growth can be phenomenal and is taking place at a much greater pace than has ever been experienced in the West;
- urban resources are limited and under greater demand;
- national or local budgets rarely stretch to urban conservation;
- aesthetic and cultural appreciation of the historic environment can be different than in the West;
- there is a desire to modernise and pressure for related development.

Today developing countries account for over 70 per cent of world population, but benefit from only 30 per cent of the world income (Antoniou 1981: 33). In the twentieth century many developing countries have experienced accelerated industrialisation and are currently coming to terms with technical innovation, and in many countries rapid and uncontrolled urbanisation prevails. In bids to catch up with western development, consequences for the traditional urban fabric are much greater, with a growing gulf between the urban rich and the urban poor. High rates of rural to urban migration are leading to the rapid urbanisation of many previously rural cultures and the unprecedented expansion of cities. Urban change and growth are further accelerated as populations double in as little as thirty years, with conditions being made more difficult by the fact that there are increasingly fewer resources and greater demands on services.

Recognition of historic quarters with a view to preserving some of their qualities, or rehabilitating them, is a very new concept for many cash-starved governments and local authorities. 'The issues involved in monumental and historic conservation are not strictly speaking those of preserving inner-city neighbourhoods for their residents' (Habitat 1984: 37). Priorities have often been politically driven and architectural and historic concern achieved through eviction, demolition and

*Fig. 1.8 An entire
quarter of Art Nouveau
buildings
are rapidly decaying in
Tallinn, Estonia, while
ownership disputes and
severely limited
finances curtail the
work of architecture
and planning
departments.*

disruption to the existing patterns of life and informal economy. There is increasing awareness, and projects with socio-cultural development objectives are being promoted. However, while most conferences and publications to date have tended to examine issues or voice the problems, action is still variable.

Funding for conservation can become a low priority when there are pressing demands on budgets for better sanitation, healthcare and schools. Further problems arise from the insufficient funding for the training and education of professionals or specialist craftsmen to undertake and organise conservation work. There is at times insufficient legislation to protect individual buildings; and where conservation legislation does exist, there is inadequate control or lack of financial assistance. Inevitably, urban conservation only becomes recognised as a product of tourism development.

While the blight of modern cities and the dilemma between old and new are a problem the world over, in the East, historic continuity is frequently being disregarded in favour of the status of the modern (Kuban 1980). For many developing countries there is an aspiration towards western styles of living, while the traditional is rejected for being backward.

> The great bulk of buildings constituted by vernacular architecture are being wantonly destroyed, because their cultural and symbolic, even economic, values are not subordinated to the exigencies of new life patterns, to the status of new forms and materials and speculative profits of staggering dimensions.
>
> (Kuban 1980: 10)

Fig. 1.9 In Istanbul the traditional timber architecture is in a fight for survival against urban growth, increasing land value and the desire for 'modern' dwellings.

Western architectural styles are replicated in the name of modernisation, often with little respect for local cultural, climatic or building needs. While many have been blamed for creating inappropriate or 'irrelevant and inefficient' environments (Khan 1980: 32), the replication of traditional models is perceived as a western wish to see a lower culture, a reflection of an ongoing East–West tension in development and control.

Western-derived charters, methods and conservation philosophy are not necessarily appropriate to non-western cultures or to the realities of developing economies. Aestheticism, historical continuity and materialistic wealth, for example, are predominantly European values. In some societies, symbolic, religious and naturalistic values may constitute a greater reason for conservation (Oliver 1982: 3). In Japan for example, there was no post-war policy for rebuilding heritage as in Europe, and it was not until the 1960s, through international stimuli, that a material-based cultural heritage policy was formulated. It is vital to understand people's values and standards, which differ according to their cultural and economic backgrounds. It could be argued for example that conservation denies the Muslim philosophy that housing is but a temporary earthly shelter which is renewed in response to the changing size and needs of the extended family. Proposed conservation programmes also have to recognise the realities of a situation. Providing design guidelines publications to residents who are unable to read them, or, more significantly, unable to afford to realise repairs in accordance with them, is counterproductive. Situations have to be approached in response to local needs and in keeping with local culture.

Many large cities are faced with a growing poor population, often crammed into the old city centres, where overcrowding and poor sanitary conditions are rife. In Fez the old town grew from 100,000 inhabitants to 220,000 between 1920 and 1970 (Bianca 1978). Residents depend on the central areas not only for accommodation but also for access to their daily economic activity. Projects simply directed towards the salvation of historic fabric have often involved the removal of the poor population in order to create restoration images that satisfy Ministries of Heritage and Tourism. However, providing alternative housing on the urban periphery as happened in Cairo, Egypt, potentially cuts off the vital connection to the centre for jobs and socio-cultural ties. Like many examples of European housing upgrading programmes, rehabilitated or renewed housing demands higher rents. Even though new trade patterns are being introduced, in many sprawling metropolises and towns alike there continues a thriving informal sector and moving people out of a central 'historic' area has implications for the inner-city economy.

Invariably in the smaller towns, where many residents have been born in an area, there continues to be a stable population and social collaboration. Research carried out for a regeneration project in the old town of Fez, for example, revealed that spontaneous building in the squatter settlements still followed traditional patterns (Bianca 1978). Despite pressures for growth and economic constraints, and an outwardly portrayed modernisation of developing countries, the following urban qualities should also be recognised in favour of conservation:

- a continuing link to a traditional way of life, which has been lost in developed western cultures;
- the existence of informal trade and small-scale but thriving informal economic activity in town centres;
- the continuing significance of religion and belief, in urban life.

Conservation programmes in developing countries, with pressing demands and low budgets, must be able to consider a more pragmatic approach responding to a careful assessment of priorities. It is more important to provide adequate bathrooms, if this is the required standard, than perfected facades which inhabitants are unable to maintain or afford to live behind. Religion, too, continues to play a role in urban life and has a presence in urban morphology and spatial use. The continuation of a certain lifestyle makes conservation closer to continuity than the step-back-in-time images being created in the West. Although a lack of funding, expertise and control predominates, the benefits of a continuing craft tradition and low labour costs cannot be overlooked.

Summary and conclusions

Urban heritage represents to the user and visitor an appreciation of the past which may be more tangible than that illustrated in grander monuments, possibly a social insight into the life of a previous or foreign era, and more often a sense of identity and of belonging within physical surroundings responding to the human scale. It is not just through international heritage bodies, but also through the, often passive, appreciation of users and visitors that urban conservation is gathering momentum. For conservation to be a reality, a place has to present a meaning to its users and occupants and there need to be finances available to initiate and realise urban conservation programmes.

As the world population increasingly becomes an urban one, the importance of the city as a place to live in, work in and relax in increases. There is an ever-present dichotomy, however, of past and present, of resident values and marketplace values; of developed and developing. Contradictions are apparent between re-habilitation for the provision of better living environments for residents and preservation and the retention of the urban environment through restoration projects often aimed at beautification. It is also a dichotomy of inside and outside: the resident seeking the modern facility and a damp-free environment while the visitor values the external appearance, at times the romantic ruin, ignorant of the living conditions of the occupant.

In urban conservation there is also an East–West dichotomy, involving urban morphology, economic realities and future aspirations. Whereas the rehabilitated western city is a mere historic reference or even a prop for modern-day living, in the East the historic environment is still likely to be lived in and a contemporary extension of tradition. Although the difference plays an important role in the visitor's interpretation and the use of these towns by tourism, many of the pressures and demands brought on the historic environment by tourists are similar.

The following case study of Granada highlights some of the difficulties facing urban conservation in the absence of major funding or high-profile commercial activity. The next chapter discusses the influence of tourism on conservation and the safeguarding of historic urban areas in the face of the new demands tourism places on the historic environment and on urban life.

Notes

1 Including the Berbers, Bedouins and Turkomans.

2 For example the New Town of Edinburgh or the Neustadt of Strasbourg.

3 These new 'straight' streets not only promoted public order and better communications, but also added ceremonial aspects and an axis to the city, reflecting the current social ideology and political climate.

4 Houses were often built out of perishable or low-quality material (Küçükerman 1985), and even in Istanbul few houses date further back than the eighteenth century (Goodwin 1992), and those that have survived for over a century are likely to have been intended for a mere fifty-year lifespan.

5 The Convention for the Protection of Cultural Property in the Event of Armed Conflict, or the Hague Convention, 1954.

6 First hand accounts from Dubrovnik residents, 1993 and 1994.

7 The eighteenth-century architect Nicholas Hawksmoor respected the old architectural styles of London and designed buildings to harmonise with the existing townscape. The romantic and picturesque movement followed, led by John Nash, in which buildings of every period were highly valued and admired. During the nineteenth century, in the reign of Queen Victoria, Sir George Gilbert Scott became a central figure for his numerous church restorations, but not all were successful as he was criticised for being too 'authentic' in his approach (Erder 1986).

8 John Ruskin in his book *Seven Lamps of Architecture* (1849) criticised the popular 'restoration' process of demolition and rebuilding on a stylistic basis. William Morris, in support of Ruskin's views, introduced the 'preservation' movement by establishing the Society for the Protection of Ancient Buildings (SPAB).

9 In England the first Bill for the Protection of Historic Monuments was passed in 1882, enabling government protection of sixty-eight selected monuments. Mainly in London, historic buildings were classified. In 1921 a list of classified buildings, some of which were residential properties, was published and the buildings came under government protection for alterations or restoration.

From 1910 government grants were made available for repair work and the Town and Country Planning Act of 1947 introduced early initiatives for environmental conservation (Erder 1986).

10 The National Trust of England was established in 1895 'to act as a Corporation for the holding of lands of natural beauty and sites and houses of historic interest to be preserved for the nation's use and enjoyment'. The Trust owns houses and opens them to the public, as well as protecting chapels, wind and water mills, medieval barns, farms and even villages (National Trust).

11 The Town and Country Planning Association (TCPA), founded in 1899, is Britain's oldest independent voluntary organisation concerned with planning and the environment.

12 These include the Venice Charter, the UNESCO Recommendation on the Conservation of Urban and Rural Historic Centres, the Bruges Resolution on the Rehabilitation of Historic Centres, the Amsterdam Declaration and the Charter on the Architectural Heritage adopted by the Committee of Ministers of the Council of Europe.

13 Internazionalle Bauausstellung, a building exhibition completed in Berlin in 1988. Organised prior to the unification of the city, the exhibition's purpose was to utilise public and private funding with some of the most prominent architects in the world to realise a city-wide building and rehabilitation programme (Ghirardo 1996).

14 In England there were several sources of grants and financial aid for the repair and maintenance of historic buildings. Local Authorities were receiving grants from English Heritage ranging up to 40 per cent of eligible costs from Town Scheme Grants and 25 per cent of eligible Conservation Area Grants. Furthermore, individuals in possession of a listed building could apply to the Secretary of State at the Department of the Environment for a grant to cover a maximum of 50 per cent of all the cost (1953 Historic Buildings and Ancient Buildings Act) and Local Authorities could make grants available to owners of non-listed properties in Conservation Areas (1962 Historic Buildings Act).

Case study
The Albaicín quarter
of Granada, Spain

Europe has been at the forefront of area-based conservation, and even though most historic quarters are today protected through designation as conservation areas, not all of them have had access to the necessary financial support to back rehabilitation and conservation programmes. Consequently, poor resident populations continue living in dilapidated buildings in a fight against ongoing decay, as in the Albaicín quarter of Granada in Spain.

The place
In Spain the high mountains of the Andalusian coast separate the long sandy beaches, well known to the holiday industry, from the hinterland of what were once prosperous Moorish cities and villages. The only part of Western Europe to have been ruled by Asia for over six hundred years, up until the fifteenth century, to this

Fig. 1 The Albaicín quarter, located on the opposite side of the Darro Gorge to the Alhambra Palace, is a cluster of whitewashed houses, contrasting with the modern-day city which has grown around it.

Fig. 2 The sophisticated interconnecting courts and gardens, the magical succession of spaces, and the courtyards with water features are barely visible as tourists overcrowd the Alhambra Palace, an 'Oriental gem' in Western Europe.

day it has remained a mixture of East and West, with features unique to both Europe and the Islamic world. Two very different architectures live harmoniously together: the light and ornamental Islamic alongside the massive latter-day Christian. Granada became the centre of Moorish Spain, best remembered for the presence of the stunning Alhambra Palace, but the modern-day city continues to be an important regional centre.

The Albaicín quarter had been a Muslim neighbourhood serving the Alhambra Palace. Although much of the craft industry died down in the eighteenth century, the quarter continued to thrive and to this day retains close to 200,000 inhabitants. Like many of the old Muslim quarters of the region, it contains a mixture of small white-washed houses clustered together in narrow, winding streets, today an island in the modern city that surrounds it. The underlying Islamic morphology and pattern are visible in the irregular public squares and busy streets leading to narrower and calmer alleys, which in turn give onto internal patios behind high walls to provide cool seclusion and much-valued privacy. Most houses in the quarter are of brick, adobe or timber-frame construction, lime-washed on the outside. The large timber patio doors with heavy metal knockers are similar to those of North Africa. Arab-style decoration can still be seen in many forms, inside and outside (Gallego 1985), while 'later' windows or balconies open onto the street, adding colour with the flowers that fill them. Due to the steepness and narrowness of many streets, cars are at times unable to penetrate into the heart of the quarter and horses are still used for transport.

The modern city has developed around the old quarters. The commercial centre of the Islamic town remains separated from the neighbourhoods and is embedded in the modern city centre of Granada, but the old silk market, even though more recently rebuilt, is still a warren of small shops lining narrow passages with a colourful array of goods. A major slum clearance project towards the end of the nineteenth century resulted in demolitions in the Albaicín quarter to make way for

Fig. 3 The narrow streets are part of the Albaicín's character, but difficult to negotiate with modern-day transport.

a fashionable avenue, the Gran Via. Today the classical-style 'new' buildings are an important part of the conservation area.

Prospects of urban conservation

The Albaicín today is mainly occupied by a lower-income group and labourers, nevertheless a tight-knit community for whom the area represents a meaning apparent in the neighbourly gatherings on summer evenings or the lively fiestas that take over the area (see Figure 4.5). Although many of the inhabitants are the owners of the properties, in the absence of external financial support the houses are too expensive to maintain, and those who could afford to, have moved out to better conditions in the newer suburbs.

In Spain the Directorate General of Fine Arts and Archives Technical Office, a Department of the Ministry of Culture, is responsible for the protection and conservation of sites and monuments.[1] In 1990 the Instituto del Patrimonio Histórico was formed in Seville, providing heritage funding previously unavailable to the region. In collaboration with the Architecture Departments of the universities, the Institute has embarked upon the laborious task of recording the historic buildings in the two hundred settlements of the region. The emphasis is on monuments rather than urban areas, however, and much of the resources have been taken up in recording rather than rehabilitation. There is growing concern among conservationists that the building traditions of the region will be lost due to ignorance and inaction. The Spanish Government has been promoting 'culture for

Fig. 4 Dereliction and decay are a reality in the Albaicín, but the doorway secluding the 'private' courtyard also appeals to the 'romantic' vision of the Western eye.

all' with the intention of encouraging community interest in local culture and as a means of boosting domestic tourism. The Ministry of Transport, Tourism and Communications, responsible for the promotion of cultural tourism, has directed some funds towards the conservation of the nation's heritage, though again to monuments.

Decentralisation policies since 1985 have shifted responsibility for protection and policy enhancement to local authorities. In Granada, with more local-level decision making there is a growing interest in the historic town. But only limited local council grants are available for repair, and owners of historic property are expected to finance improvements themselves, although some tax exemption schemes do exist. Home owners are strictly obliged to keep to the old styles when making alterations to properties within a conservation area.

The Albaicín is one of the poorer areas of Granada, and although emigration may have saved the old quarter from overcrowding, depopulation, in its turn, is leading to an increasing number of houses being abandoned to dilapidation. Much of the conservation initiative and planning work to date has fallen on the Department of Architecture at the University of Granada. Although a Granada Conservation Area Plan was drawn up in 1989, it was unable to attract financial assistance, while heritage interests have focused not so much on the residents, but on tourism potential, for example a project to preserve the city walls. Nevertheless, the benefits of tourism for the future survival of the quarter have to be seriously considered.

Prospects for tourism

The ravages of mass tourism have completely changed the small coastal towns of the Andalusian coast, but they have hardly penetrated into the hinterland. In Jaen, an inland town, many of the buildings in the old Muslim quarter are still intact, whereas in Almería on the coast, historic buildings have been replaced by large-scale tourist developments. But the investment of tourism development money in coastal areas has curbed inland development. While sun, sea, cheap beer and competitively priced flights from Northern Europe have made the Spanish coast a popular holiday destination, it is partly through tourism that the Spanish economy has come to play in the same league as Northern Europe. But despite campaigns to attract more cultural tourism, Spanish tourism remains predominantly coastal.

Tourists rarely stay in the inland towns, and the three historic cities of Granada, Seville and Córdoba are invaded daily by tour buses from the coastal mass tourism destinations. As in many inland attractions of the Mediterranean region, the visitor numbers are considerable but the duration of visits is very short. In Córdoba, streets of the older quarter around the Great Mosque have been taken over by restaurants and souvenir shops, providing for the day tours and coach parties. While the street scale makes an ideal shopping environment, architectural quality is often lost behind the shop fronts and displays, a stark contrast to the streets further away from the central attraction and not under tourist occupation. Here houses are lived in and a strong neighbourhood atmosphere is apparent in the small and intimate squares. Nevertheless, the properties are generally in poor condition, another stark contrast to the 'shiny' facades of the tourist streets.

In Granada, having visited the Alhambra Palace, visitors are frequently taken straight back to their resorts. There is pressure on services and roads, but very little distribution of gain to the local economy. Córdoba benefits, albeit slightly, over Granada in that first, the attraction that is the Great Mosque is smaller than the Alhambra, and therefore 'faster' to visit, and second, as it is situated in the heart of the old quarter, tourism activity spills into the surrounding streets.

Issues and options

Conservation and community

The Albaicín is in need of urgent maintenance and rehabilitation to survive. With only very limited access to grants for the repair of historic properties, the authorities are facing the problem of maintaining a fast-disappearing urban heritage. The resident community value the area but are unable to contribute to the repair of properties. Much of the spirit and character of the area comes from the community; valuing their needs and working with them is essential in ensuring a safe future for the quarter.

Tourism could destroy the whole character of the quarter and diminish its spirit

Whether tourism would be beneficial to 'save' the Albaicín is questionable, but in the absence of other sources of funding it may become a serious consideration. The authorities' choice in repairing the city walls could be considered a step in that direction.

Tourism may be an active way of supporting the conservation of the quarter

Diversifying tourism in Granada could become a means of reducing pressure on one single spot and extending visitors' stay. If planned and managed adequately by the city authorities, this would be a means of increasing tourist gain and decreasing environmental pressure, as well as enabling the initial steps for conservation in the Albaicín. Alongside the architectural attraction of the Alhambra, the Albaicín residential quarter in its unique setting could potentially offer the visitor the feeling of a 'character' and 'lifestyle' still maintained by its residents.

The future

Will any intervention in the quarter simply result in eventual gentrification, new, richer residents and an inevitable loss of identity?

Notes

1 The first law governing the protection of national monuments in Spain was passed in 1926, although a list of National Monuments had appeared back in 1860. A second law was passed in 1933, which with the exception of several amendments in 1936 and 1955 remained in force until 1984, when the new legislation was introduced (Council of Europe 1985).

2 The tourist-historic town

Introduction

As historic towns gain tourist potential, historic quality gains market value. A new urban society is emerging, seeking leisure, culture and a high-quality environment, and cities are moving from being industrial centres of production to becoming centres of consumption (Page 1995). For historic towns faced with limited financial opportunities, cultural tourism is seen as a significant economic alternative and the attached commercial value is turning the past into a product of the present. Today historic towns and quarters are competing to attract tourism, and previously unknown locations are appearing on the heritage market; Eastern Europe has become accessible again, and former industrial cities look to discover historic areas with 'potential' within their urban fabric.

The urban language of a past era and the townscape value inherent in a hierarchy of street patterns, open spaces and intersections combine to create a physical attraction. A walkable and pleasant environment and a familiarity not as yet gained from modern developments of our own time increase appreciation for leisure purposes. Unlike historic monuments or archaeological sites, however, the city continues to be lived in, and it is the 'life' within that is as much the attraction as the physical qualities of the setting; but it also presents a dichotomy of the lived-in inside and the experienced outside, the streets and spaces framed by the built fabric of the townscape.

This chapter discusses the market potential of historic towns and quarters and the portrayal of the sought-after 'historic' and sometimes 'exotic' image in response to the perceived expectations of the visitor. More than historic quality, however, it is the location, size and accessibility of a place that play an important role in both its success as a tourist destination and the consequent impact of tourism on the built, cultural and social environment. The interpretation of heritage and the haste to attract more visitors have significant implications for the urban environment, including impacts and pressures caused by crowds. The chapter considers the following questions:

- What makes an historic town a tourist destination?
- How can tourism contribute to urban conservation?
- What impacts does tourism have on historic towns?

Historic town as 'product'

The international tourism marketplace

> [Tourism] is a major source of income and employment for individuals in many places deficient in natural resources other than climate or scenery. It makes use of resources, which may not be used otherwise, in particular of unemployed labour in developing countries and regions with few or no alternative sources of employment.
>
> (Burkart and Medlik 1974: v)

In 1990 the annual turnover from world tourism had reached 5.9 per cent of world GNP, and over 6.7 per cent of world capital investment was in the tourist sector (WTTERC 1992: 2). The industry worldwide employed 118 million people in 1990 and was predicted to create a further 38–55 million jobs by the end of the 1990s (WTTERC 1992: 2). Further jobs are created indirectly, such as within the construction or aviation industries. However, it should be noted that it is common for the better-qualified and managerial jobs to be taken up by the facilitators of tourism, mainly the western developed nations, while destination locations are often the last to benefit, with the local labour force filling the ill-paid and seasonal service sector jobs.

In the developing world, tourism diversifies the economy and is seen as a relatively clean way of earning substantial 'hard' foreign cash. The benefit of tourist spending, however, is not a direct gain as there will be a cost to pay for infrastructure and facilities that are provided, including an increase in foreign imports. Providing 'home comforts' for visitors frequently involves the provision of western facilities and products at a time when local product bases are being lost. In Hawaii for example, so much agricultural land has been given over to tourist developments that the islands now import pineapples, previously a major product.

Tourism earnings are often calculated from the gross figures of foreign exchange earned, not discounting the costs for imported goods and services or payment towards royalties and shares held by multinationals. Money leaves the country on expenditure involving imported goods and services, interest on foreign capital, overseas advertising, overseas training of tourism personnel and foreign management salaries (Erlet 1991). There is also the capital expenditure on the building and maintenance of airports, hotels, infrastructure, roads, water supplies, communication systems, etc., all likely to be borne by the host country. Tourism is a volatile industry and there is very little guarantee of its continuation at stable levels, for a variety of reasons including changing fashions. Moreover, over-investment leads to over-capacity, which in turn leads to fiercer competition and price wars. When the prices go down, so does the quality of clientele, and the destination is eventually branded as being overbuilt and 'spoilt'.

Tourism and tourist developments are greedy consumers of the natural environment and of culture. Once it has become a tourist attraction, a small or fragile monument is often surrounded and overwhelmed by sign boards, parking facilities, souvenir shops, restaurants or cafes. Although a monument may be safeguarded, the surrounding environment is often not. Green areas and natural beauty spots on the other hand are used up for large hotels and resorts, leisure centres, car parks and airports, adding to traffic and noise pollution. Crowds become a threat to the fragile balance of nature and to the fabric of historic buildings and settlements.

Tourism has the potential to yield economic development, at both regional and national levels; however, the gain that penetrates to the community is usually not known, and is often immeasurable. The trickle-down effect attributed to top-down development can only be assumed and is rarely an adequate substitute for its consequences. The profits of tourism are calculated through the profits of major tourist facilities but the costs are not as easy to calculate. In an example from England, 'costs are much more difficult to pin down. They include the social penalties borne by those who live or work in central London or in other big tourist towns like Oxford, Bath, Stratford or Edinburgh' (*Economist* 1977: 90). The benefits of tourism are distributed differently among residents, and improved facilities are likely to be appreciated more by those living outside the centre, not affected by the immediate disruptions (Laws 1995). Furthermore, the benefits of an improved environment and better services and facilities can only be valued if they are within the purchasing power of the inhabitants.

The urban form and fabric of an historic town are the primary attraction to visitors, and are a free commodity. Hospitality services and commercial outlets within the town are secondary attractions, but they constitute the greatest opportunity for financial gain. The investment in infrastructure and the conservation of urban fabric and environment consequently do not benefit from a direct financial return. For the local population, most of the financial gain is through knock-on effects and jobs created in the sector. However, locally run or owned small businesses do benefit directly.

Although new employment opportunities may reduce the amount of migration from an area, an established local economy may still be threatened through tourism activity. It has often been the case that the comfort of temporarily higher wages and the glamour of tourism lead to the abandonment of local agricultural jobs. Thus the loss of subsistence agriculture accelerates emigration and leads to increased imports and rising prices. Increasing prices can make tourist-based areas and land, including beaches previously used by fishermen, inaccessible to local inhabitants. In city centre locations too, high land prices result in rents and prices that are no longer affordable to local residents and businesses. Consequently town centres are given over to tourism-based seasonal use and create related environmental impacts, including the need for housing on the periphery, added transportation costs into the centre, as well as the social and financial burden of a seasonally underused centre with associated vandalism and security problems.

Tourism: a new urban economy?

As the dirty industries created in the nineteenth century close down or are moved out of cities, authorities look towards new and cleaner industries to replace them, tourism being a favoured option. The knowledge that history and heritage are a popular tourist product has made many town authorities reconsider or reinterpret urban heritage as a marketable attraction; and even places previously perceived as centres of industry and business have started to develop new 'heritage' images. Newcastle and Brussels for example, both recipients of 'modern' new developments in the 1970s, have turned to tourism to boost economic activity. In Newcastle the riverside has been redeveloped with a focus on its entertainment and shopping potential. In Brussels the historic image of the Grand Place and the wealth of Art Nouveau-style architecture of the 1920s are being promoted. Good rail links and growing leisure interests have been increasing the tourism potential of both cities.

Bradford, in the North of England, is another post-industrial city seeking new economic opportunities. A busy trade and manufacturing centre in the eighteenth and nineteenth centuries, it was also, according to a sanitary conditions inspector of 1846, 'the filthiest town he had visited with little paving and sewerage conveyed by open channels discharging into the beck of the canal basin' (Bradford Council 1991: 2). The streets may be cleaner today, but the industrial era has left Bradford with a stock of derelict warehouse buildings, soaring unemployment and a high Asian immigrant population, once enticed by the industry. The authorities have turned to tourism and are keen to market Bradford as an historic town with Asian attractions; they hold an annual festival on a European theme, to revive the now empty merchants' quarter in the city centre known as Little Germany.[1]

Sydney, more likely to conjure up the image of a major Pacific Rim city, has also paid tribute to its older settlements in developing the harbour area. The former residential quarter known as the Rocks at the foot of the Sydney Harbour Bridge, dating back to the early settlement, has been restored in part and developed and pedestrianised to become a significant part of the city centre activity. The area is publicised for tourism and could be considered a predominantly tourist district with light entertainment, cafes, restaurants and an abundance of souvenir shops.

In Dubai a perfect climate for beach tourism in the winter and the availability of existing business hotels and related services have facilitated the development of leisure tourism to a wider market. Better known as a business centre and for its lavish shopping facilities in the Gulf region, Dubai's vernacular heritage is being rejuvenated as the tourism base is expanded. A marketing campaign under the name of 'Arabian Adventures' offers cultural excursions to traditional wind tower houses, local souks, and spice and gold markets (Laws 1995). Much of the traditional urban heritage previously removed to make way for the grand hotels and offices is now being revalued and reinstated as tourist attractions.

A role for tourism in urban conservation

History can become exclusive, dictated by the ruling classes who identify with selected periods of history, post-independence perhaps or a class distinction, identifying exclusively with an upper-class past. There is naturally more demand for conserving buildings relating to a period of particular national or local significance, at times loosely linked to political messages and propaganda. Tourism, on the other hand, can become a valuable means for widening cultural understanding to include less valued monuments and overlooked traditional urban environments. In many instances tourist interests have activated conservation programmes for archaeological sites, monuments or vernacular buildings, and, more recently, entire urban areas.

Tourism has been instrumental in conservation programmes of the classical 'Greek' heritage in Turkey and in the preservation of historic towns associated with being Ottoman in Greece.

> In Turkey, the arrival of increasing numbers of westerners who had come to tour the Greco-Roman cities, especially Pergamon, Ephesus and Priene on the west coast, must have made the inhabitants aware that the ruins were highly valued by others (even for reasons they could not understand). The most popular sites soon acquired an economic value and it became more profitable to act as guides, sell souvenirs or to work for archaeological expeditions, than to demolish piecemeal.
>
> (Turner and Ash 1975: 133)

Tourism can also increase cross-cultural understanding, and regional marketing enhances both the 'product' and the links between neighbouring regions or countries. However, at the same time, an earning power is being attached to history and archaeology, as Breeze (1994) questions the value of archaeological sites that do not 'earn', and their perceived diminished cultural importance.

Tourism is potentially an important catalyst for the safeguarding of historic fabric and the initiation of conservation on an urban scale. Appreciation of the historic environment by visitors not only becomes a reason for conservation but can increase local interest in the environment. Although tourism is not a direct financial resource for conservation, indirectly it opens up previously unavailable investment finances. The restoration and reuse of redundant buildings encourages other environmental improvements, adds life and activity to a place, provides an example of conservation, and may boost the economy to a level which will enable other small-scale improvements to happen.

For the nineteenth-century old town of Tunis, tourism was specifically seen as a catalyst for development when a project was launched with the specific aim of maintaining a balance between tourism development and public interest. The old town had many buildings worthy of restoration, but had been in decline when the Association pour la Sauvegarde de la Medina (ASM) took over. The ASM's work has involved recording existing buildings and making proposals for new ones in the vacant plots, one suggestion being a luxury hotel aimed at catalysing development and renewal. The objectives were set for renewal that would maintain existing residential use and retain trade patterns. The programme included a pilot project to renovate municipal buildings for tourist use, and new residential units for sale to reduce overcrowding in the centre. Other proposals were for the restoration of municipally owned buildings to be let at low rents, and to make loans available to encourage private and public participation (Serageldin 1982). Fadel and Serageldin (1997) report on the success of the scheme in achieving targets for affordable housing.

Appreciation by visitors can lead to better local understanding and insight into some of the values of the immediate environment. Understanding and response to local heritage are different and to local inhabitants the *community* value of a neighbourhood may be more important than the historic value of the physical environment appreciated by the visitor. For many developing countries for example, 'old' continues to be associated with 'backwardness'. Tourism, nevertheless, has to be a two-way process and appreciation of local community values by the visitor is also important in developing cross-cultural relations.

The attraction of visiting historic towns and quarters lies in the qualities offered to the visitor, including a lifestyle that is essentially not exploited by tourist commercialism. While visitors appreciating and frequenting towns encourage conservation, restoration of more buildings and 'in-character' facilities increases time (and therefore money) spent by visitors. Through slow and conscious activity there is the opportunity for resulting tourism to become a growth industry that is not simply measured by bed spaces; tourism becomes a balance between sustainability of the product and emphasis on local-level income generation and associated human growth and involvement. Sir Angus Stirling (1995: 16) calls for 'a constant re-iteration of the long term benefits of conservation', pointing out that 'no well-run industry would dissipate the assets on which its wealth is based, but rather seek to plough profits to augment those assets; only tourism at its worst, does the opposite'.

In summary, tourism can play an important role for the future of historic towns because:

- tourist interests generate a greater heritage awareness and the conservation of less obvious historic buildings;
- well-conserved buildings that are being used encourage more projects to be realised;
- community awareness of the benefits of conservation increases local involvement and demand for conservation, and the forming of local associations;
- uses are provided for otherwise redundant buildings as tourist accommodation;
- the promotion of architectural and historic values (locally and nationally) motivates cross-cultural communication.

Redundancy and reuse

Through life-cycles and use-cycles buildings become redundant, no longer able to serve the function for which they were originally built. Some are adapted to new functions, others lie vacant; they may be valued for their historical quality, association or contribution to the townscape, but urgently require a living role for this relationship to prosper. Tourism not only encourages new economic activity, but also introduces new uses and often more flexible demands on space. It is an opportunity for otherwise redundant buildings to be rehabilitated and reused, providing continuity through active use. The reuse of existing resources reduces new construction and related environmental pressures, while increasing use in central locations. Financial viability illustrated in the restoration and revitalisation of one building can encourage others to follow the example, while continuing local ownership and small-scale activity enable local economic involvement, reducing the export of benefits.

Within historic town centres there will be a wide range of building types of different periods and varying artistic merit. The potential for reuse is different for each building and is closely linked to ownership, private, public or institutional.

Where buildings are no longer suitable for present-day requirements or the purpose for which they were built, and where adaptation would detract considerably from their unique character, tourism may provide the right reuse with minimal change to their historic character. The biggest space requirement for the tourist industry is in overnight accommodation followed by related services, commerce and cultural activities. Palaces, castles, mansions and religious buildings such as monasteries provide an alternative form of visitor accommodation in unique and authentic settings, with a living function closely linked to the original. Large public buildings and halls are being converted to museums or exhibition spaces, while industrial buildings are finding a new lease of life in riverside regeneration and associated cultural, leisure and residential developments.

Major historic buildings have frequently come into state ownership and there are successful examples of nationally supported reuse projects. In 1911 the Spanish State initiated a programme in which outstanding but redundant buildings were restored as hotels or guest houses. Known as *paradores*, these converted buildings can be found all over the country, creating authentic and high-quality leisure environments for guests. Inevitably the project has encountered some minor problems where buildings have not been easy to convert; castles for example often lack sufficient ventilation and daylight (European Heritage 1975). But the conversion of many underused buildings into hotels has had many advantages. The impacts on landscape and environment are negligible, particularly in comparison with a new development on these sites of natural beauty, and the appropriate scale and existing relationship of the building to the place have brought direct economic benefits to many small towns.

In India changes to state governance following independence have led to a number of former maharajas' palaces being successfully converted into high-class and atmospheric hotels, and in Europe priories and monasteries are being converted to host new 'cultural' pilgrims. In Turkey the Touring and Automobile Association has successfully converted Ottoman mansions in Istanbul and Safranbolu into atmospheric and popular hotels. In a flagship project by the Association in the Kariye district of Istanbul, it was possible for a mansion to be converted into a hotel and smaller units to be restored and rented back to the original tenants. As a non-profit organisation, the Touring Club was able to divert the income from a tourist development towards housing, using tourism as a means for regeneration.

A balance, however, has to be sought between the demands of the market, such as air conditioning, and the limitations of the building fabric and maintaining the character and authenticity of the surrounding environment. The attraction for the visitor is the setting and a sense of nostalgia; this must not be compromised when simpler solutions, such as better use of natural ventilation and the level of facilities made clear on publicity material, can be applied.

In retail too, it is often the smaller units that continue to be occupied and that are easy to maintain, whereas larger complexes, once fallen into disrepair, are more likely to be left to decay. The once profit-making *han* of Islamic towns are frequently abandoned or only partly used in the face of ongoing decay, as the cost of repair is no longer feasible for the commercial community and rental income continues to fall. Tourist-based activity potentially rejuvenates traditional buildings, but it can also take over from existing commerce. In İzmir, Turkey, an eighteenth-

Fig. 2.1 In the Kariye project in Istanbul, this row of houses, restored with proceeds from hotel and tourism-related projects, was leased back to tenants.

century *han* was not only 'liberated' of fully functioning workplaces, but also completely demolished for an imaginative rebuild in order to serve the tourist industry, compromising livelihood, tradition and cultural heritage (Keleş 1992).

Planning and development are a long-term process and the reuse of redundant buildings for tourism and cultural activities involves a sympathetic approach to historic unity and a creative use of space. Reuse for tourism-based activity should not be permitted to take over from reuse for local needs. For example, the reorganisation of a ground floor for retail or restaurant use may be at the expense of much-needed housing above. Appropriate choices for initial or pilot projects for reuse, focusing on promoting local architecture that is otherwise redundant for an activity which will provide a good return, will help establish a visitor pattern and encourage other rehabilitation projects.

Historic town as an 'attraction'

Historic buildings, their associated relics, the morphological pattern of streets and spaces, and historical associations have all become tourist resources of the historic town. Alongside a host of well-known and even world-famous historic towns are a growing number that are being specifically developed for the historic town market. A combination of architectural style and social significance creates for each town a distinctive 'character'. Historic towns are valued most for their special character, a physical link with the past and the continuing tradition of a lived-in environment, most notably for:

- the physical attractiveness of buildings, streetscape, townscape, views and vistas;
- the light craft-type industries which ensure that they are clean and comfortable places to visit;
- the human scale and feeling of intimacy;
- their walkable and explorable characteristics;
- the life within;
- the occasion for communication, lost in the larger 'modern' metropolis;
- the opportunity to become temporarily a *part* of urban life.

Historic towns may also become tourist destinations for their association with a famous event or personage. Sarajevo, previously associated with an assassination triggering off the First World War, is now better known for the atrocities of a more recent civil war. Dublin or Stratford-upon-Avon on the other hand are famous for their literary associations. More recently a European Union treaty signed in Maastricht made this small Dutch town a better-recognised location. The use of a place for a film location may also make it an attraction, to the extent even that a film location may become more authentic than an actual (historic) location. The town of Stamford in England has now been inaugurated as the mythical Middlemarch in George Eliot's novel as a result of its use as the film-set for the dramatisation of the novel. Common associations such as 'Paris is romantic' also boost tourist potential. Third, the attraction may be linked to the quality of services provided, including good shopping facilities, good restaurants or cultural attractions. Vienna is associated with music and opera and the centre of Brussels is promoted for its restaurants as much as its historic attractions. Dublin's good entertainment facilities add to the city's cultural and historic attractions. Boniface and Fowler (1993) point out that most important is for the destination to be able to appear more attractive than the visitors' home town, thereby making it worth the visit.

Some historic town destinations such as York, Bruges or Heidelberg could be described as *naturals*; they contain all the right ingredients to attract visitors and are visited simply for their historic and townscape values. Other places have become *must-see* destinations from which tourists cannot be deterred, Paris and Venice among them, where seeing these destinations has become a ritual. Sometimes it is a fashion or interest set off by a film, for others it is a never-ending popularity. MacCannell (1976) describes a trip to Europe as a pilgrimage, in which one must see Paris, in Paris the Louvre and in the Louvre, the Mona Lisa. This does not mean that there are no other good paintings in the Louvre, good museums in Paris or interesting cities in France.

In a larger metropolis the historic attraction is often restricted to a quarter, forming one of many other attractions. The Barrio Gótico, the medieval heart of Barcelona, for example, has become a focus for much of the tourist activity, but it is by no means the exclusive attraction of Barcelona or the reason to visit. Other towns are better known for being part of a region or landscape setting, those in Tuscany in Italy for example. Often it is a combination of factors that influences a visit: a known historic town, some familiar associations and the knowledge of good 'culture', services or shopping facilities. Moreover, the underlying attraction is the 'life' within – the added value of a place where people live, work, shop and entertain (Jansen-Verbeke 1995).

Interpreting the historic image

Hilltop views or the quality of a riverside, coupled with the 'charm' of a major cathedral set in the midst of streets and squares lined with 'historic' facades, are nowadays recognised as tourist attractions. 'Picturesque' is the sought after, typified in the narrow and winding medieval street pattern. The vision is perhaps epitomised in the tourist posters showing aerial views of Italian towns, with the main square and texture of the roofscape, ironically a view visitors only seldom experience.

Fig. 2.2 The love affair of travel literature with a romantic image (compiled from travel literature by the author, 1991).

The attraction and facilities offered by large cities, small towns or rural hamlets are very different. Large cities, by their nature, are expected to be cosmopolitan centres, where historic quarters contribute to a mixture of attractions. The visitor expects there to be a cultural component, museums and art galleries and a diversity of entertainment facilities, but probably little contact with the 'locals'. Smaller towns on the other hand are attractive for their 'heritage value', which may be coupled with other cultural activity. Visitor expectations of a rural settlement are more likely to be of a primitive existence or lifestyle and a vernacular culture, yet also an opportunity for communication (Table 2.1).

Medieval towns such as Winchester, Trier, Granada, Bruges or Perugia, having escaped industrialisation, have become favoured tourist towns marketed for their visual qualities, modern boutiques and smart cafes.

Table 2.1

HERITAGE	VILLAGES	SMALL TOWNS	LARGE CITIES
Monuments	None	Some May be attraction Varying degrees of maintenance	Many Prime attraction Well maintained
Urban heritage	Rural vernacular	Lived-in neighbourhoods	Often lost to new development
Cultural continuity	Yes	Partial	Very little modernisation, transition and urban movement
TOURISM			
Numbers	Large impact	Noticeable, saturation point easily reached	Absorbed
	High interaction	Partial interaction	Minimal interaction
Facilities	None or very few (imported)	A selective range	Plentiful, serving all requirements and all price ranges
Interest	PEOPLE Rural life	Human scale, lifestyle	BUILDINGS Monumentality, urban complexity including nightlife
Experience	Primitive	Past urban life	Exotic

And yet how many fascinating and often tragic destinies are hidden behind. . . . Many of them, once great centres of influence and power, have become mere tourist sites, providing a journey six, seven or eight centuries back into the past, but deprived of their former might and glory.

(Bairoch 1988: 156)

Whereas other qualities of a medieval past are best forgotten:

Waterborne sewerage and sewerage disposal was virtually non-existent, refuse collecting spasmodic and refuse disposal concentrated in a few 'muck hills'. Horses, pigs and chickens roamed the streets. Squalor, dirt, discomfort and disease were the accepted lot of medieval man.

(Burke 1971: 62)

Needless to say, the stench and unsanitary conditions which accompanied medieval towns are not part of the idealised picturesque image of a bygone era.

There is clearly no expectation of reliving the past or experiencing any lifestyle associated with it, yet romanticised images continue to be attached to places. In a

Fig. 2.3 The narrow winding streets of medieval towns, such as York, are an immediate attraction to tourists.

simple yet typical example the small Turkish coastal town of Kalkan is described in a UK travel advertisement as follows:

> If you want to stay in a village of whitewashed houses, shuttered windows, draped in brilliantly covered Bougainvillaea, winding cobbled streets lined with colourful local shops, cafes and restaurants, leading down to the pretty harbour and town beach, then Kalkan is for you. A delightfully unspoilt and romantic fishing village, nestling in the foothills of the rugged Toros Mountains on Turkey's Turquoise Coast.

The image is picture perfect, yet the description is factually conflicting. First, a fishing village the size of Kalkan is traditionally unlikely to have been awash with cafes, restaurants and shops, more likely a traditional (male only) coffee house and a local shop – the 'colourful local shops' actually means 'tourist souvenir shops'. Second, a 'romantic' image is being built up of what has been well documented[2] as a difficult existence dependent entirely on the sea, as farming and even transportation across the 'rugged' Toros landscape have been near impossible. The setting as it is today is romantic to the western visitor and the fact that it is a fishing village appears to add to this romanticism, though it must be assumed that the tourist cafes will be safely distanced from any 'fishy' smells.

As in the above example, in the West a distinctively more romantic image of travelling to the East or the 'orient' is created, which can on occasion be translated into a backward lifestyle. An element of exoticism or oriental mystique is added to the anticipated experience of eastern travel, and therefore a hidden demand for staged culture. For the Middle East or North Africa for example, a typical image is of half-veiled women, and exotic items on open stalls in spice markets, with men wearing the fez, or riding across deserts on camels, in many ways a 'flying carpet' image created by the film and advertising industries. Urban conservation is in danger of responding to the expected imagery and the status of the 'picturesque' or even 'exotic', and therefore not to an understanding of present-day urban life.

Nevertheless, expectations of past periods or simplistic surroundings are strictly limited to the marketplaces, and the hotels are expected to provide all the modern comforts and possibly swimming pools, at times in deliberate ignorance of Third World realities and poverty. Comfort and hospitality demands tend to remain a constant whatever the travel destination. A trip to Kathmandu is sufficient to see western youth flock to western-style coffee bars for cappuccinos rather than frequent simpler local establishments.

Guidebooks and the literary traditions of a society are a cultural framework within which foreign places are interpreted. Travellers choose guidebooks that are culturally familiar to them and this too has implications for heritage and cultural observation (Boniface and Fowler, 1993). A common complaint of local guides is

Fig. 2.4 Travel literature uses images of exotic markets or similar settings to entice travellers.

'Not Lonely Planet again'. The guest's image of culture and society is the image that has been marketed. Trying to fulfil an unrealistic expectation results in a cheap product attempting to satisfy a sought-after image. Moreover, the expected image may well be in stark contrast to the desires and self-image of local residents.

What may seem very attractive and 'picturesque' to the visitor, may simply be old and dilapidated to the resident. Interpretation and priorities in the lived-in environment are different for each culture. For example, the western eye will be quite taken by the image of a weatherworn timber doorway on a narrow cobbled street set against the texture of flaking plaster, in part revealing the mud brick or timber-frame structure, overhung with the greenery from an inner courtyard or garden. For the residents it is simply an old house on an inaccessible road. 'The taste for decaying mud walls is a Western one, deriving from our passion for the romantic and the picturesque' (Lewcock 1978: 73). Civic pride, too, is a western value and may be less of a priority in other cultures more concerned with personal and spiritual wellbeing than the cleanliness of streets, often uncontrollable by overstretched municipal services.

Fig. 2.5 The realities of developing countries may not live up to some of the romantic images imagined by the traveller. Old Delhi survives not because it is immaculately restored, but because it is a thriving economic centre.

Historic town as destination

Location

Global position and global holiday patterns play an important role in the way a place is perceived and used in the cultural tourism marketplace. Location plays an important part in the potential for tourism development, the type of tourism that is attracted and the type of attraction a place becomes. Most tourism is generated and monitored by the developed world, with the US, Germany, Japan and the UK leading the market, contributing to half the world's total tourist expenditure (Erlet 1991: 10). The European Travel Commission figures also show that 59 per cent of world tourist arrivals are to Europe (Leu 1998).

As a destination, Europe represents the 'old world' and offers a well-preserved résumé of history combined with good cultural facilities. Northern European historic towns attract a high number of overseas visitors as well as benefiting from internal and regional tourism, predominantly for cultural purposes. Culture has become a reason for travel, and historic towns combine pleasant surroundings with culture, heritage and entertainment. European cities, including those on the Mediterranean coast, are being visited year-round as short-break holiday destinations within the European market. Visits within Europe are often off season and less likely to be in large groups, and the amenities provided are also attractive to the resident community because their cultures are similar. New historic town destinations have appeared as the former communist countries have opened up their culture and doors to tourism. The 'undiscovered' nature of these towns, and particularly their cheap prices, are proving attractive to the market. Europe's historic towns also find themselves on the busy itineraries of long-haul visitors, 'doing' Europe on intensive tours concentrated over the summer season. Simpson (1990) notes concern that tourism in Edinburgh is subject to a short summer tourist season and a fickle American market 'doing Europe in three weeks'. Nevertheless, overseas visitors continue to spend more than European domestic tourists do (Leu 1998). A growing mobility in Eastern Europe, on the other hand, has added to the pressure on many of Western Europe's must-see destinations. A common scenario for historic towns, particularly at high season, is increasingly of day visitors, and an increase in seasonal and mid-day pressure but a downward trend in tourism income.

Around the Mediterranean, including parts of North Africa, tourism is closely linked to European tourist patterns. The attraction is unquestionably a favourable climate – sun, sea and associated leisure activities. The rich culture of the region is a secondary attraction and is frequently consumed in day-trip breaks from nearby beach destinations. One of the first Mediterranean countries to develop mass tourism, Spain, has paid a cultural price for rapid tourist development and there is a general feeling that tourism 'robs Spaniards of their heritage in terms of natural beauty of the country' (Debelius 1972: v); a priest complains that the tourists 'come for our alcohol rather than our art' (*Economist* 1974: 38). Historic towns off the beaten track are unlikely to attract visitors and those in resort areas are frequently overwhelmed by tourism as shops, bars and restaurants move into historic buildings considered 'quaint' or 'romantic' settings for such activity. Side, on Turkey's Mediterranean coast, for example, once a small settlement among the ruins of an important archaeological site, has become 'in two decades, the most blatant example of the destructive nature of uncontrolled tourism' (Kuban 1985: 54). Already in 1975, 'a barrack like hotel and a number of makeshift shacks had appeared on one of its beaches. The Turkish village, built picturesquely in among the ruins, is now full of signs advertising pensions and discothèques' (Turner and

Ash 1975: 134). Since 1975 the coast has been heavily built up with high-rise hotel buildings and the 'village' transformed into a tourist ghetto of souvenir shops, pensions, bars, discos and restaurants. Ironically in such situations, in attempts to make the visitor 'feel at home', the Spanish vernacular is more likely to be transformed into a 'traditional' Dutch bar and the Turkish house converted into an English-style 'pub'.

Inland towns and villages become recipients of day-trip tourists from coastal resorts. On the Spanish sunshine coast, the Costa del Sol, for example, the historic towns of Granada and Córdoba are relinquished to day tourism. Picturesque villages are in danger of being turned over to the quintessential 'see local village life' day trips. The small and picturesque mountain village of Şirince, in close proximity to the Turkish resort town of Kuşadası, is overwhelmed by tourist buses in the high season. Even the small-scale economic activity generated by the village women selling handicrafts has turned into a highly competitive business giving rise to village rivalry and commissions to tour operators. The increasing popularity of the 'all-inclusive' holiday, spreading from Caribbean resorts to the Mediterranean, where the cost of food and drink is covered by the holiday price, means visitors are less willing to spend money on facilities when on trips out of the resorts.

More recent campaigns have aimed at emphasising the cultural product. Spain for example dropped its 'Everything under the sun' campaign of sun-drenched beaches in 1992 in favour of more historic and cultural imagery while Turkey adopted the 'and the rest is history' slogan; both campaigns are a reaction to low-spending package tourism, but meanwhile historic towns are becoming itineraries on cultural package tours.

Locations outside this hive of tourism activity – the Middle East, the Indian sub-continent, South-East Asia, South America or sub-Saharan Africa – are long-haul destinations from the tourist-generating countries. Consequently a longer distance

Fig. 2.6 The village of Şirince in Turkey has become a day trip option from nearby coastal resorts, and the small-scale village enterprise is known to be manipulated by tourist guides.

travelled at greater expense means that these travels are more likely to be seen as either a luxury holiday or one with exotic overtones and some 'mystery' attached to the destination. Holiday objectives vary, but are likely to include travel to see history and culture, the experience of a living and exotic culture, landscape, activity sports or simply leisure. Trips to see a distant country and experience a foreign culture are combining past and present as the attraction. Although major centres, like Bangkok, conjure up images of an exotic night life and even prostitution, the smaller historic towns have a much less familiar image than European towns do. There is generally less knowledge of the culture and the way of life; but there is a vision fed by the exotic cliché images of spice markets and souks appearing in travel literature.

In a recent debate with post-graduate students at Tribhuvan University in Nepal we compared tourist attitudes and knowledge on arrival in Nepal and in Turkey. Turkey, despite its cultural riches and natural diversity, is predominantly a coastal holiday destination to which reservations can be made as little as 24 hours in advance as one of many options for a beach holiday. The visitor's knowledge or expectation of the destination, the culture or the language is likely to be minimal and will remain so for the duration of the stay. Nepal, on the other hand, benefits from being at a greater distance and a more expensive airfare away, and has the advantage of predominantly catering for a specialist market. Visitors are more likely to have planned their trip, saved up, purchased guidebooks in advance and probably acquired some background knowledge on the country. Travellers on

Fig. 2.7 The central Durbar Square of Kathmandu, Nepal, combines local life with tourist interests.

activity holidays, such as trekking or mountaineering for example, frequently allow time for cultural visits in the Kathmandu valley area. Needless to say, twenty years previously Turkey also represented an 'exotic' destination.

Much is determined by the international tour agenda, referred to in Scotland as the 'milk run' of popular sites visited by most tours. Lesser known historic towns in Europe need not apply to be on the two-week tour, which is unlikely to go much beyond the London, Paris, Heidelberg, Venice and Vienna circuit. A 1993 survey of travel literature in six European countries identified only eighteen cities out of 144 destinations which were described as 'classic' and extensively marketed in all six countries (van der Borg 1994). In India, too, much of international tour-based tourism is strictly concentrated on the Delhi, Agra, Jaipur golden triangle.

Closely linked to location is the accessibility of a town from a major transport interchange, air, rail or road network, or its proximity to other established destinations. Connections to major transport networks also play an important role in the success of tourism development. York, conveniently located on a high-speed rail link between London and Edinburgh, attracts many day visitors for its easy accessibility and distance from two major attractions, while the opening of the Eurostar rail services has increased the tourist potential of a number of historic towns. Efficient access, however, also means an efficient departure, as York has also experienced a fall in the number of overnight visitors.

Urban spatial use

The movement of a visitor in the urban environment is one of discovery and appreciation; tourists will wander and linger, taking in the surroundings rather than seeking the shortest route. In spatial terms urban tourism is a predominantly external activity. In historic towns the primary attraction is the narrow, winding 'cobbled' streets, captured vistas, glimpses through urban fabric, texture created by the architectural facades, open squares, a piazza or river front. The visitor arrives

Fig. 2.8 Most tourist activity in historic towns takes place in the external realm (Prague, Czech Republic).

and moves through the external space, and it is possible for a day visitor to spend an entire visit in the external domain. This interpretation or use of urban space means that the emphasis of finance is shifting to improvements to the external environment and facades. Gradual movement from open and semi-open to closed space is significant to the extent of penetration into the urban fabric and therefore into cultural attractions such as a cathedral or museum, and service providers such as cafes, restaurants or shops. However, it is equally important that secondary attractions are reached as it is at this point that income from tourism begins to be generated.

A conflict arises between host and guest in the different cultural uses of urban space. In the East for example, in the privacy of neighbourhoods the street is considered a natural extension of the residential unit, a place for neighbourly interaction claimed private in the hierarchy of the street network, while in the public commercial districts the street becomes a natural continuation of commercial activity mingling with social and at times religious life. The transformation of streets around a Friday mosque from a hive of commercial activity to rows of prayer mats for the Friday noon prayers is a typical example.

Religious space is also under pressure from tourism, as commercial operation and religion confront one another in cathedral cloisters or mosque courtyards, and tourists climb over temples or wander into Buddhist prayer in monasteries (Orbaşlı 1998). For users and worshippers this space is sacred, and a lack of respect for a community's culture undermines tourism. In addition to 'sacred' space clearly

Fig. 2.9 A cul-de-sac is considered a private space by residents (Córdoba, Spain).

determined by the boundaries of a place of worship, there is also an associated sacred space within the urban realm, and spaces that are deemed sacred by the users; these are more difficult to define physically and manage with unwritten codes of respect, noise or the consumption of alcohol for example. For some religions nature is sacred, such as a holy mountain, lake or river. A less obvious presence in an urban surrounding may lead to misunderstandings and cultural conflict. For example, what appears to be a pleasant riverside esplanade to the western eye could in reality be an important bathing ghat for pilgrims to a sacred river.

In any urban environment there are spaces considered 'private' by the users. For some it may be the safety of an inner courtyard as a children's play space, for others it is a tight residential community on a small cul-de-sac, for the students of Oxford and Cambridge colleges it is quadrangles not shared with hundreds of camera-sporting visitors. Privacy, often part of an historically defined spatial hierarchy, can easily be disrupted through insensitive planning and new patterns of public use. The growth of tourism, especially of foreign visitors, may bring with it a loss of privacy for residents in a neighbourhood community. It is not uncommon for residents of a popular tourist spot to experience people peering through their windows, and once this becomes a common occurrence frustrations start to be felt. Residents in the small walled town of Mdina in Malta have even found curious tourists in their front rooms. Parts of a local urban culture such as leaving patio doors open, customary in southern Spain for example, or the privacy attached to a cul-de-sac are unlikely to be known to the curious visitor seeking authentic culture.

Interaction and confrontation in urban space

'Tourism was and continues to be a major contributor to, as well as a manifestation of, a process of cultural invasion' (Helu-Thaman 1992: 8). Tourism, heralded as a means for cross-cultural understanding, is also the cause of cultural confrontation and misunderstanding as international tourism more often confronts than integrates (Bodlender and Lickorish 1991). The impacts of tourism are largely dependent on the physical and cultural capacity of a place to cater for and absorb tourists without them becoming an obstruction to daily life. The successful meeting of tourist (visitor) and resident (host) is determined by their cultural differences and the size of the place. While the centre of a large metropolis, such as Istanbul or Cairo, can absorb the impacts of tourism, pressures are much greater on the smaller towns, including cultural pressures where a more traditional way of life continues, and in rural settlements where impacts are immediately felt (see Table 2.1).

In smaller towns and particularly in rural locations the opportunity for interaction is much greater but is likely to lead to resentment if a local community is being inconvenienced, but not benefiting from tourism. While several bus loads of tourists are easily absorbed into a metropolitan location, a single bus may upset a delicate balance in a small rural settlement, be it a famous film location in the Yorkshire Dales or a small African village. Individual travellers in rural areas are more likely to communicate with locals and be less of a burden on scarce resources or hospitality. Interaction between resident and visitor at the rural level is direct as the rural population is also often part of the object of a visit. While communication and dialogue are beneficial for both host and guest, there is a significant difference between being a 'guest' and viewing, including looking down upon a primitive existence, especially in developing countries where rural poverty is endemic.

Historic towns under tourist pressure

Overcrowding: people pressure

World-famous monuments are being eroded and historic towns choked by mass tourism, many of them intended for use by far fewer people. The Acropolis of Athens is being visited by more people in a week now than had ever set foot in it in a hundred years in antiquity (*Art* 1990: 64). York Minster alone was visited by over 17,000 people a day in 1978 (Lowenthal and Binney 1981), totalling around two million visitors a year. Congestion is caused in many other cathedrals, including Coventry, Canterbury, Durham or St Paul's in England, Chartres or Notre Dame in France, the last of which is visited by over ten million people each year. In the Palace of Minos at Knossos, the restoration work shows signs of tourist erosion. In tourist towns, overcrowding not only congests streets, but creates pressure on services and can disrupt local lifestyles. Even world cities such as Venice, intended to welcome visitors, are ultimately vulnerable to overcrowding. The problem is greater in small but hugely popular historic towns such as Bruges, York or Stratford-upon-Avon, and tourists have even listed 'overcrowding' as their single biggest complaint about London (*Economist* 1977). Due to time constraints, popularly recognised 'highlights' of must-see destinations are intensively visited and other surrounding attractions commonly ignored. As travel becomes intensified through mass tourism, some world-famous cities are becoming unbearable at peak visitor times. Tourists, however, do not like admitting to being part of an archetypal group and even though they usually all want to see the same things, they tend to be annoyed by other tourists 'polluting' a site.

While tourism is a major source of income and may contribute to the costly process of preservation and conservation, large numbers of tourists are damaging

Fig. 2.10 One of the things tourists dislike most is 'other' tourists 'polluting' a site (Kensington Palace, London).

heritage sites and the historic fabric of towns. It is inevitable that tourism development causes erosion (Newby 1994), depreciating the finite heritage resource. Mass tourism is potentially destructive of attractions, both physically through the erosion of surfaces, traffic fumes, etc. and also because attractions lose their popularity once they are perceived as being 'overcrowded' or 'spoilt', for 'nothing annoys some tourists more than the presence of other tourists' (Turner and Ash 1975: 134). As Israel has become an increasingly popular holiday destination, the overcrowding in Jerusalem has become acute. While authorities would like to diversify tourism, it is inevitable that most visitors to Israel wish to see the 'holy city' and within it the holy sights. Back in 1970 'tourist pollution' in London, Venice and Florence was reported to have reached dangerous levels. On extremely crowded summer days, Venice police are known to close the causeway to stop people entering the historic town. In the 1990s the affluent visitors to Venice were being replaced by East European visitors keen to see the major sights of Europe, but with very little money to spend (Boniface 1995). The day trippers are not benefiting Venice, and overcrowding is deterring the richer, longer-staying visitors. In Prague, a more recent addition to popular historic towns following the Velvet Revolution, high popularity is prompting authorities to consider means for limiting visitor numbers.

For Bruges, which attracts high numbers of visitors throughout the year, tourism is now considered to be of secondary importance in the planning programme. Tourist promotion is being limited, yet the city, with its waterways, well-kept medieval buildings, streets and smart shops, continues to be a magnet. The townspeople expressed concern that they had

> no wish to be considered a kind of urban museum, a cultured 'Disneyland', whose inhabitants act as museum attendants or small stall keepers for visitors who come to steep themselves for a few hours in the somewhat folkloric and decadent atmosphere of an 'art city'.
>
> (van den Abeele 1975: 26)

Although tourism is appreciated for bringing an international and cosmopolitan atmosphere to the town, and is valued for economic and employment benefits and the continuation of crafts such as lacework, tourist pressures on Bruges, including overcrowding, often unconscious vandalism, traffic and parking problems, have become a serious concern for both the authorities and the residents. Urban spatial use and functions change as residents are deterred from using central areas at times when they are expected to be overcrowded, but the major social cost is frustration and irritation on the part of the relatively small number of people directly exposed to tourists. In Bruges organised resident activity against tourism actually took place in 1990 (Jansen-Verbeke 1995). Similarly, 'in high summer, disaffected residents of York can be spotted wearing anti-tourist badges' (Stancliffe and Tyler 1990: 3).

The urban fabric may not be as valuable as a monument and the wear and tear on a medieval street not comparable to the erosion of the threshold of the Parthenon, but constant overcrowding of a narrow street detracts from its appearance and streetscape value. When the anticipated image of a narrow pedestrian street for example can no longer be appreciated, then it also loses value. 'Tourism development carries with it the seeds of its own destruction' (Murphy 1985: 39). For each locality or region there is a saturation level; 'if that level is exceeded, the costs of tourism begin to outweigh the benefits' (Young 1973: 111). The threat of tourism is that it eventually destroys its very resource. The real loss is to the ordinary people, who not only lose a source of income, but also experience irreversible damage to their environment.

For each place there is a threshold beyond which the urban environment no longer continues to be attractive. Carrying capacity is a combination of physical capacity and social tolerance, 'the capacity of any local population for the painless integration of tourism development into their lives' (Korça 1993). Jansen-Verbeke (1995: 26) lists indicators for when a critical point has been reached:

- a decline in the number of overnight visitors;
- a growing absence of the original target groups;
- an over-capacity in the hotels, which leads to 'price-dumping' campaigns;
- a loss of quality of products and services;
- a decreasing interest in the city from project developers, investors and sponsors of events;
- an indifferent or even an antagonistic attitude of the locals towards tourism and tourists.

Traffic and parking pressures

Motor traffic can become a serious threat to historic buildings, urban fabric and environmental quality. An increase in the number of tour buses, cars and service vehicles leads to traffic jams, as well as disruption and destruction to the historic environment. Fumes not only blacken surfaces, but can cause irreversible damage to surfaces. Narrow streets, tight corners and low overhangs within the traditional urban environment are easily damaged, particularly when speed limits are ignored or oversized vehicles attempt tight corners. Large delivery vehicles supplying retail outlets, backing into narrow streets and tourist buses trying to park in close vicinity to an attraction all increase the liability of damage. While popular tourist towns are able to impose restrictions on vehicle sizes and parking, towns trying to increase their tourism potential readily bow to operator demands.

Closely linked to traffic are the provision and location of parking space. Seasonal or peak-time demand on parking has to be resolved in designated areas as there is little space in historic towns for on-street parking. Large parking garages are out of scale and character with the historic towns, while ground-level parking requires a large site, which may cause the loss of otherwise green spaces and be disruptive to the spatial and visual qualities of an historic town. Frequently, available open spaces including town squares are given over to parking.

> The streets and piazzas the tourists love to photograph are crammed with Renaults, Fiats, Volkswagens, and Fords, let alone motor scooters, mopeds, vans of all sizes and shapes, and other forms of motorised transport. All these have contributed dramatically to the sense of congestion that pervades European cities today.
>
> (Appleyard 1979: 13)

Fig. 2.11 Heavy delivery lorries are out of scale, obtrusive and damaging to the historic fabric of old towns (Monk Bar, York).

Fig. 2.12 Used as a car park, the market square in Bruges has little appeal to visitors.

The pleasure of walkable spaces and the link to the human scale are spoilt by vehicular traffic and in many town centres pedestrianisation schemes are being introduced to rekindle pedestrian activity. Removal of traffic in historic quarters, while creating a pleasant environment for visitors, has at times deterred residential use of the area due to strict parking and access regulations. In York it was found that restaurants were locating outside the historic core, because once shops closed in the evenings, the area did not attract tourists and resident customers preferred locations with fewer car parking restrictions. Similarly, one of the reasons residents have been moving out of the central but historic parts of Madrid is parking and access restrictions.

Services and infrastructure

An increasing number of visitors imposes pressures on the local administration for the provision of adequate infrastructure, superstructure and other municipal services. The carrying capacity of existing services in historic towns is likely to be very limited, and sufficient provision for a peak season may become a very costly capital investment with little direct return to the investor. The insertion of infrastructure into an historic environment is tricky and there are many associated implications to the historic fabric, both above and below ground. Most dramatically, for Venice there is also the threat of sinking.

Seasonal fluctuations in the number of users create a dilemma for the service provider. The size and capacity of a transportation network adjusted to a high season for example incurs additional maintenance and staff costs in the low season. Similarly, services such as garbage collection have implications for resources and jobs. Often the least obvious but the most vital element of urban redevelopment is infrastructure works, modernising obsolete networks or upgrading transportation networks (roads etc.). A recent World Bank-assisted development project for the old town of Tbilisi, the capital of Georgia, started out by addressing the serious underground water and waste problem (World Bank 1998).

Sudden increases in user numbers bring extra pressures on services and higher maintenance costs. With no direct payment made by visitors to a place, these costs must be borne by the local municipality and will inevitably be passed on to residents as taxes and rates. In efforts to attract private sector developers for tourism projects, municipal governments are also likely to be under pressure to provide the necessary infrastructure for a development to take place.

Changes to ownership patterns

The previous chapter discussed the change of ownership in historic quarters as many rehabilitation and conservation projects have resulted in gentrification. The loss of urban space to tourism brings new demands and space use patterns to historic towns, including an increase in retail, leisure and entertainment uses. For city centres isolated in the 1950s and 1960s through zoning, a revival of multi-purpose use, combining residential with retail and services, is welcomed. However, if a city centre no longer caters for residents' needs then this will also affect the residents and residential uses in the area. If a centre is only being used seasonally then the 'real life' perceived by the visitor is only a seasonal 'real'.

One of the characteristics and attractions of living in old towns is the mixed use. A balance has to be met, between retail rents that are not alienating and a centre that is still a pleasant environment for living in; increased commercialism and the presence of the entertainment industry are unlikely to be welcomed by residents. The Plaka district of Athens, for example, became a favoured tourist spot because of its wealth of nineteenth-century vernacular architecture and its proximity to both the Acropolis and the city centre. In the 1970s many properties were taken over by the commercial and 'aggressive' entertainment industry, including tavernas advertising their presence using amplifiers (UNESCO 1980: 161). The district became renowned as a red light area and a centre for drug trafficking. Not only were the residents moving out, but even the tourists were appalled by the noise and atmosphere of depravity. By 1979 there was serious concern that the area was losing both its attractiveness and its residents (Zivas 1979). Strong campaigning from residents forced measures to reverse the trend.

In several Bulgarian towns the old nineteenth-century quarters, associated with the period of national independence, have been carefully restored for cultural promotion purposes and to attract tourism. The restored old cities were envisaged as scenes for festivals, traditional music and crafts and a means of promoting national culture (UNESCO 1980). In Plovdiv, although the scheme was discussed with the local inhabitants, in reality it involved moving them out to new suburbs. The immaculate restoration carried out by the then communist regime, with most of the nineteenth-century mansions regaining their elegance, did not prove sufficient to attract tourists.[3] Within a year it was realised that the area was underused; there were too many art galleries, reception rooms and government guest houses reserved for important visitors, and the buildings which had previously been housing up to three families were now being used for only one-third of the year or less. Visited in mid-July by the author, the historic quarter lay quiet, apart from a few tourists on one of the main streets and a few affluent locals in the cafes, which were too expensive for most.

The historic town of Salt in Jordan is a traditional trading and market town with stone buildings which today presents a unique settlement in Jordan. In 1981 a masterplan was prepared, specifically targeting a tourist strategy for historic conservation by establishing hotels and a tourist village (Fakhoury 1987: 45) with little reference even to the traditional street character. A typical top-down view on

Fig. 2.13 In Plovdiv in Bulgaria, although the buildings were immaculately restored in the old quarter, the 'life' was lost once inhabitants were moved out of the area.

tourism and conservation, the project was not realised, but a later study again identified tourism as an important factor in reviving the economy of Salt, described as 'a mixture of heritage, charm and tourism potential' (Alzoabi 1992: 1), and pointed out that 'there is a potential for Salt to become the vibrant fashionable cultural heritage city' (RSS 1991: 3). The local market is identified as an amenity which is an

> attractive old market street where tourists will spend time and money, and [which will] create new workspaces and shops for craftsmen, often trained in the local institutes, who will offer goods of interest for tourists to buy.
>
> (RSS 1991: 4.5)

In this example too, tourist interests are being considered rather than the needs of the community.

Fig. 2.14 Hammam Street in Salt, Jordan, an 'attractive old market street where tourists will spend time and money', according to a development report.

Changing commerce

In the market economy, consumerism has become a leisure activity, and shopping firmly linked to travel. Historic attractions are supplemented or even engulfed by commercial outlets which can range from quality crafts to tacky souvenirs. Even once 'alternative' and new age festivals are today accompanied by hundreds of stalls selling a range of souvenirs and Third World memorabilia; while Kathmandu has become a shoppers' paradise catering for all budgets. As shopping has become a leisure activity of the consumer society, historic environments have come to provide an ideal setting for leisure shopping. The success of Covent Garden in London as a pleasant pedestrianised shopping district with atmosphere is undeniable, yet the fight for the conservation of this redundant market hall in the 1970s was another triumph for local residents and businesses, many of them since driven out of the area by high rates. The city of Bath is described as a 'retail gold mine' (Pettifer 1990: 4) and, as in York and Chester, shopping has become the main activity of the city centre. Retail is one of the biggest opportunities for financial gain in historic towns, and everyday shopping facilities are first taken over by tourist and luxury outlets and then in turn by chain stores.

Trade patterns in historic towns are changing notably. Small workshops and crafts move out because they can no longer compete with mass production or they are seen as too noisy and dirty to be in central areas of a city. Simpson (1990) notes

Fig. 2.15 London's Covent Garden is an example of a successful transformation from abandoned market hall into a prime retail attraction.

Fig. 2.16 Chain stores, with standard shop frontages, rather than small local shops have come to dominate the historic townscape. This example is from Maastricht in The Netherlands, but it could be anywhere.

how city centre industry such as carpentry and other craft trades have been forced out of Edinburgh for a 'sanitised tourist city'. Escalating tourist demand suggests that many staple food outlets such as grocers and butchers are also being replaced with souvenir shops, smart cafes, fast food outlets or specialist retail outlets, of little use to the local residents, especially when they cater for a more affluent visitor. Accordingly, the shops serving local demand are no longer able to afford the inflated rents. In Eastern Europe, for example, the attractively low prices in cafes and restaurants are too high for locals, who feel they are gradually being alienated from their city centres. Even in towns like Bath, York or Bruges, many shops reflect the buying power of rich visitors or represent novelty values for weekend shoppers. When increased economic activity is allowed to exceed its capacity, then 'the character of the town will be altered – at best compromised and at worst ruined' (Worksett 1989: 2).

In the East, commercial areas are traditionally composed of small-scale labour-intensive and often family-run organisations which are easily accessible, ensuring production to sale takes place in the same area with little need for transport. Street sellers provide many supplementary services while the more valuable items are sold closer to the centre. For developing economies an informal sector requires little capital or infrastructure yet provides much-needed employment and economic activity. Many of these commercial centres continue to be vibrant economically, with the smaller establishments depending on the inner-city network for their business connections; but the informal sector operating in historic centres having to compete with the tourist trade is not able to generate sufficient resources to maintain shop units once tourist trades take over. The dirty, unsightly but locally needed commercial activity is being replaced by an attractive souvenir market comprising sought-after exotic ingredients.

Successful commerce in tourist-historic towns is a delicate balance between creating attractive retail facilities to encourage visitors and continuing to provide a retail service for local needs. The reuse of buildings for tourism-based retail may provide new life for otherwise redundant buildings, but must be carefully planned to consider existing use, location and access. Increasing retail potential allows for growth as a regional centre, and for attracting visitors from a closer catchment area. In York or Lincoln for example, their popularity as retail centres for the region attracts regional visitors around Christmas, when other visitor numbers are low. In many western countries today, the 'attractive' high street shopping facilities are also in competition with out-of-town retail centres, as small historic towns compete with the growing popularity of the shopping mall import from the United States. The advantages of malls for modern-day living and lifestyles are undeniable: adequate car parking, protection from the weather and entertainment facilities for children. The consequence for historic towns is a growing pressure to provide similar benefits in order to remain competitive.

Summary and conclusions

So long as leisure, culture and travel remain a lifestyle of affluent Western society, historic towns will compete to attract tourists. As production in the city loses its importance, tourism as a clean alternative and an easy option for economic gain and employment creation becomes a favoured development option for local authorities. Nevertheless, the realities of tourism as an industry must be recognised, especially concerns for the environment, type of employment and the global volatility of the industry. But tourism can also make a contribution to cultural heritage through raising awareness, strengthening cross-cultural relationships, for releasing finances and investment previously unavailable for the conservation of historic buildings and by occupying redundant buildings. These opportunities cannot be overlooked, and well managed they will all contribute to the future of the place.

For local inhabitants, however, tourism may be the cause of depreciation in *quality of life*. Page (1995: 142) describes residents' response to tourism as initially embracing, then tolerating and adjusting and finally withdrawing. Constant rises in land and property values, spoiled landscapes, pollution, traffic and overcrowding are among typically unwelcome changes. Small industries are forced out, along with the residents, who can no longer afford the increased rents and property values as tourist services take over old towns. Even the new middle-class residents of gentrified areas are deterred by the absence of amenities and increasing noise levels. The movement of residents out of a tourist area, however, gradually turns a stable town centre into a transient one of seasonal occupation by service sector employees; while flawless, at times 'colourful' and stage-set external restoration and tourist-based approaches to conservation hasten devaluation. The following case study of York illustrates both the feat of conservation on an urban scale and the pressures this small city is facing from tourism. Chapter 3 considers the outcomes of a tourist-oriented response to conservation in historic towns.

History has a price, with a market value attached to the location and the attraction offered. The historic towns' assets of historic buildings, charm and character are finite resources and face the imminent danger of being consumed and discarded by tourism. Lichfield (1988), in defining conservation as an action to cope with actual and potential obsolescence, highlights the fact that the current market builds obsolescence into its products to ensure future sales. The overworked tourist historic town is rapidly reaching its 'sell by' date. A 1998 travel article on Dubrovnik finishes with: 'Visit it before it becomes once again too popular for comfort' (Thorncroft 1998).

Notes

1 The area is known as Little Germany because of the East European immigrants who traded in the area from around the 1860s.
2 The famous Turkish writer Cevat Şakir Kabaağaçlı (1890–1973) wrote extensively on the difficulties of life in these coastal fishing villages.
3 Bulgaria attracts most of its tourists to the Varna and Bourgas coastal areas. Western visitor numbers have always been low and this has been accentuated by troubles in the former Yugoslavia. Eighty per cent of tourists to Bulgaria utilise package tours and the 'culture' element is very low in the image created with cheap sun, sea and charter flights. Plovdiv, among other places, is only offered as an additional attraction (Anastassova 1993).

Case study
The city of York, England

Supported by grant schemes, conservation has been ongoing in the city of York since the late 1960s and today the medieval city centre is a celebrated example of urban conservation. The issues concerning the authorities are no longer 'saving' heritage and conservation but the management of thousands of visitors, and maintaining a high-quality environment for visitors and residents alike.

The place

The city of York, in the North of England, has played an important role in Britain's history, as a Roman legionary fortress and later as a Viking town known as Jorvik. Particularly popular today for its medieval character, by the eleventh century York was established as an important ecclesiastical centre in the North of England. York Minster, completed in the fifteenth century, is the largest Gothic cathedral in Europe, and has been a famous visitor attraction ever since it was built. Today so are the narrow, winding medieval streets and a wealth of architecture spanning several centuries snugly held together by the city walls. In the nineteenth century the introduction of the mainline railway helped maintain the city's importance as an important railway centre, and the railways became a major employer. Although the railway industry has declined, the National Railway Museum has become another important tourist attraction.

A conservation example

Early efforts at conservation in York were largely due to the interest and commitment of York residents. Planning attitudes in the 1960s were different from today's, conservation areas had not been introduced and only a few examples of buildings of any particular period were being protected or conserved. In York too, modernist infills were readily given planning permission with little thought to the context in which they were being built. Eventually, a proposal for a new ring road backed by the authorities resulted in public protests. A Feasibility Report published by the City Engineer in 1967 claimed that an inner ring road was the key factor to the future of the road network of York. However, building this road would involve the demolition of a number of Georgian properties. No public reaction had been

Fig. 1 The medieval street pattern, a wealth of architectural style and good shopping facilities make York attractive to visitors.

anticipated but by 1971 petitions were being signed, informal gatherings were being held and a citizens' group was being formed under the name of 'York 2000', raising funds to fight a legal battle against the ring road (Cummin 1972: 1).

Parallel to these developments, in 1966 the Minister of Housing and Local Government and City Councils commissioned a report on the historic towns of Bath, Chester, Chichester and York. The York study, carried out by the architect/planner Lord Esher, not only identified the assets of the historic town but also made suggestions for the reuse of empty properties. The Esher Report, as it was known, proposed alternatives to the ring road, including considered suggestions on new traffic patterns, car parking and pedestrianisation, supported by a detailed cost analysis. The report, criticised and dismissed by the City authorities of the time, was, however, welcomed by York inhabitants and it is largely because of the pressure exerted by the people of York that the inner ring road was never built and that York continues to be so well preserved today.

The Esher Report and the Civic Amenities Act of 1967 prompted the local planning authority to designate much of the historic town a conservation area. From a nationwide urban renewal initiative known as 'The Town Scheme', starting in 1966, York was able to benefit from over £2 million in public grants for the restoration work, supported by a further £10 million contributed by the private sector. This funding crucially enabled comprehensive and high-quality restoration to be undertaken within the city walls and 'demonstrated the value of a sustained partnership between Central Government and Local Authorities' (York City Council 1993: 1).

Today, the work of the city council is supported by a number of groups including the York Conservation Trust. The city council has a key role in the promotion of conservation policies for the city. Since the 1970s more than 1,500 historic buildings have been restored and the area within the city walls has become a well-managed conservation area.[1] The council, now at the forefront of conservation, provides assistance and advice on the restoration and repair procedures for York's many historic buildings, as well as assuming a management role for the conservation area including streets, squares, pavements, street furniture and trees. York citizens are informed of new projects through the local media, council displays and public meetings.

Picture perfect?

In 1971, John Shannon, the long-standing chairman of the York Civic Trust, said on the future of the city:

> We believe that a city like York ought to be conserved for itself, but if commercial reasons are wanted, I would only add that it has the biggest tourist potential of any city in England and properly handled so that it doesn't become a 'pretty pretty' self-conscious city, the money that will flow from this will more than pay for its conservation.
>
> (Wallis 1971: 1515)

A certain 'pretty pretty'ness has, however, become the case as the York street-scapes are turned into images of what the Americans think the 'old country' should look like and shops have so-called authentic names bearing 'Ye olde . . .'. Shopping streets are dominated by souvenir shops, specialist outlets and smart boutiques, not grocers or butchers, as York has become a model town, initially as an example of good urban conservation but more recently as a purpose-built 'model'.

> York's fate as a collective monument of historic and architectural interest is a matter of primary national concern: it is the English Toledo or even Venice. Hence the interest in conservation, often carried out to a point which born Yorkers regard as exaggerated and intrusive; but which they must come to accept as natural and inevitable.
>
> (J. Harvey 1975: 21)

The conservation of the old city is almost complete but such immaculate conservation is at times suffocating the city.

New buildings in the historic centre may no longer be insensitive to their surroundings, but they are increasingly turning to stylistic imitations of the past, devoid of an 'individual' character. Most of the new buildings have been retail centres. The largest, the Coppergate Centre, built in the 1980s and incorporating department stores and a multi-storey car park, is a sensitive modern design responding to the scale of York through smaller shop units and a central square (Figure 2). Later schemes completed in the 1990s, Stonegate Walk and Swinegate,

Fig. 2 The Coppergate shopping centre is a modern development incorporating department stores and a multi-storey car park, while successfully responding to the scale of York in a contemporary idiom.

Fig. 3 The later Swinegate development, having opted for an 'instant heritage' approach, 'colourfully' replicates Victorian shop frontages.

have instead created a series of Victorian-style shop fronts, the pastiche accentuated by the alternating colours of the fascia (Figure 3). The 'classical' style of the public conveniences has also attracted attention (see Figure 6.15).

Retail facilities in the centre are increasingly a major attraction for shoppers from the region, particularly at weekends and in the pre-Christmas period. Retail is big business for York and alongside a 'specialist' niche, growing competition from large-scale shopping centres in the region has triggered debates concerning a new retail centre which is able to accommodate the demand for the larger department stores and car parking.

On the other hand, few York inhabitants live in the city centre. Properties located above shops have often not been made available for development; parking restrictions and a lack of domestic shopping outlets further discourage potential residents. Most shops are closed by 6.00pm, leaving a quiet and underused town centre, a further deterrent for residential use. The two-hour parking restriction in the pedestrianised historic core is also seen as limiting for evening uses.

Tourism and tourists

York consequently is a tourist haven attracting large numbers of foreign and British tourists. Even though visitors to York are often the sought-after wealthy tourists, including Americans, and British people taking second holidays, many stay for less than a day. This is partly due to the convenience of the high-speed rail link connecting York to London or Edinburgh, and proximity to an area of natural beauty where longer holidays are taken. Day visitors increase traffic pressure and at times contribute little to the local economy.

Museums and tourist facilities are constantly being increased and improved. Even back in the early 1970s it was reported that York spent more money per head of population on its museums than any other British city (Wallis 1971: 1518). A

Fig. 4 Similarly, the use of 'heritage' furniture and lamp posts on the Parliament Square redevelopment bear little truth to the historic precedent for the square, which previously has also been used as a marketplace.

major attraction is the Jorvik Viking Centre, where part of the Viking town excavated in the 1970s has been turned into a museum-attraction. In what has become a prototype copied across Britain, the Viking town was rebuilt as an underground museum on its original site based on archaeological evidence. This town, with 'original' smells and models, is toured on a small electronic cart system with a running commentary. The Viking identity of York is further enhanced through an annual Viking Festival in February, a low season.

With a decline in the coal and textile industries in the region, and confectionery and railways in York, the service and tourism sectors have become the major employer. Many of the jobs created, however, are not permanent or skills based and are likely to be poorly paid. Two reports commissioned by the Council in 1984 estimated that 85 per cent of jobs in York were tourism related (York Chamber of Trade and Commerce 1984: 23). But tourism is not seen as the only development target; on the contrary, in a bid to diversify the economy the City authorities are committed to attract more companies and government organisations to York in an effort to increase local employment opportunities for better-trained staff on a permanent basis. The aim of the Tourism Services Section, established in 1985 under the York City Council Marketing Division, is stated as: 'to mobilise and co-ordinate the management and promotion of the development of tourism in the city, in a form that will be acceptable to visitors and benefit York residents' (York Chamber of Trade and Commerce 1984: 12). The decision-making influence of local establishments and the private sector is evident in planning for tourism.

A study by the English Tourist Board in 1972 reported that York citizens felt tourism was good for business and that it made public services and the preservation of old buildings possible, but listed disadvantages as increased traffic congestion, overcrowding in the streets and parking problems. Since then, numbers have continuously increased; in the summer months or holiday weekends the central area is often so congested with pedestrians that it is almost impossible to walk. Today, while traffic and congestion continue to rank high as residents' concerns, there is also the acceptance that the number of facilities available in this relatively small city are due to tourism.

Issues and options

The image: town or museum?

Even though effective conservation has made York the envy of many towns and the focus of international interests, there is a noticeable movement towards a somewhat 'Disney' interpretation of heritage. In an admirable attempt to keep the old street patterns, new commercial buildings are being designed as a pastiche of past styles, thus perhaps 'freezing' the city centre more and more in its past, almost as a museum, resulting in reduced residential and community life in the city centre. Attractions added to increase the potential can also be short lived. Even the Jorvik Viking Centre, which opened to international acclaim and long queues of visitors, has failed to maintain the early interest as the concept was rapidly and often poorly copied across the country, reducing its value to York.

Management

While continuing to attract visitors, one of the biggest issues for the authorities is the efficient management of high visitor numbers within the city walls. There are many aspects involved, from the effectiveness and extent of a pedestrian area to the provision of car parking. But most important is for the urban management to work with the promotional concerns for the city.

The competition

There have been many attempts to attract longer-staying and higher-spending visitors to York, including the promotion of York as a base from which to visit the attractions in the surrounding area, including the Moors, Dales or the coast. Like other historic cities, York also intends to attract more conferences and conventions, as delegates not only stay longer, but are also known to spend more money than the day visitor. Competition is high, as many other cities in England and the region, including Leeds and Bradford, are also promoting themselves as tourist centres offering good accommodation, dining and shopping facilities and promoting the arts, and the chance to visit York on a day trip. To avoid other places taking over the tourist market York has to keep up its standards, advertise effectively and market sufficiently.

The future

The city council is faced with the task of managing visitors, encouraging longer-staying, better-spending tourism, possibly increasing the attraction base to do so and promoting retail against regional competition. At the same time it is obliged to diversify the economic base of the city, to ensure it is a desirable place to live and to market it as such.

Notes

1 The Town Scheme was discontinued in 1993, reducing financial support available to individual projects.

3 The tourist town

Introduction

Newby (1994: 208) describes the relationship between culture, community and the visitor as three stages of a continuum; first coexistence then exploitation and finally the staging of culture as imaginative reconstruction. Where tourism and culture coexist, tourism does not dominate the economy and an ongoing pattern continues within the urban environment; in the case of exploitation, culture is used to generate cash flow and commerce and consequently presentation is predominantly for the external market; eventually culture is re-created, shaped and packaged to a recognised formula, for the benefit of the market and immediate financial gain.

Over the course of four decades, traditional urban fabric has been officially recognised as an important part of the cultural inheritance, programmes have been launched and methods have been developed for the conservation of historic towns, and their survival has been fought for. In what could be considered a reversal of fortunes, historic towns are now in danger of being valued for their tourist commercial worth only, as they are turned into theatrical backdrops devoid of urban quality and historic reality, and as townscapes are simplified into products of heritage tourism. An expanding cultural tourism market and the cultural and heritage tourism industry seeking a wider market appeal are leading to the re-creation of heritage and recreational heritage, as historic experiences are invented where they never existed before, and new attractions and entertainment with 'experience' value are appended to historic towns.

The boundaries between urban environment and museum are becoming increasingly and at times dangerously blurred. Some recent developments point to signs of an identity crisis in historic towns and a loss of 'spirit' as a chosen image is perfected, attractions are added and *places* are transformed into lifeless theme parks. Tourism is becoming an important tool for economic regeneration and development in historic towns, but at times tourism development is taking over from the urban and community development needs. Remodelling urban heritage into a stage-set, a themed attraction or an 'experience' for the benefit of the visitor is no different from building a new 'heritage' theme park on the urban fringe, and furthermore it is destroying history, culture and community life. This chapter considers the following questions:

• What is authenticity in the urban environment?
• Can a town be a museum?
• Can a museum or park be a substitute for an urban experience?

The historic town perfected

The period architecture stands proud, it is neat and well maintained, and unsightly modern buildings have not crept into the streetscape. The cobbled streets are quaint yet wide enough to avoid congestion, and the nearby car park is successfully out of sight. There is no poverty and the streets are safe; this is not an oppressive regime but part of the free world and everyone is happy to be here. Not only do the building owners benefit directly from tourist spending, but they are not burdened with heavy maintenance costs either, because the building elevations are fibreglass. Welcome to Disneyland!

The stage-set townscape

Tourist interface with the external has resulted in an over-emphasis on the physical, external aspects of heritage and conservation, invariably at the expense of an in-depth understanding of urban culture. A preservationist attitude is prevailing where historic towns are becoming frozen predominantly in their external appearance as a fear-laden response to spoiling a desired 'image'. 'The activists who want a policy of preservation at any price are the enemies of urban conservation. A city must continue to renew itself. What matters most is the quality of the renewal' (Feilden 1990: 17). The outcome of an image-based approach results in either facadism or the replication of historic style and pastiche.

A facadist approach is not unlike the 'Disney' glorification of urban heritage. The previous chapter referred to tourism in the urban realm being a predominantly external activity, and the emphasis of conservation moving to the external aspects, streets and public spaces, and the facades of buildings. Facadism in conservation has become a long-debated subject, seen as the loss of a totality (Britain), the cutting of losses and a chance to modernise in 'character' (France, Germany) or simply a means of keeping the authorities happy and a loophole in listed building legislation (Turkey).

Germany pioneered facade re-creation on modern concrete buildings in the post-war period. Today, rows of 'authentic' vernacular facades in Frankfurt's Römerberg front the large department stores behind them. The practice of keeping the front and renewing the back has remained popular in Germany and a similar approach was observed in Erfurt in 1994, where conservation work in the old quarter was under way following German unification. On the other hand, an 'ideal solution' for the dilemma faced in Ulm in the 1980s, between an appreciation of vernacularism and a demand for modern and technological advancement, involved the building of facsimile buildings, not only with modern internal design, but with new dimensions (Soane 1994). Authenticity and preservation factors appear to be quite loose in this somewhat extreme, yet misguiding example, relating only to external appearance and not to urban scale or morphology. As Simpson (1990: 23)

Fig. 3.1 (left) Facadism: the front of an old building is propped up before a modern addition is built behind it in Brisbane, Australia.

Fig. 3.2 (right) The retention of this facade in a developer's scheme in İzmir, Turkey, is a token gesture to conservation legislation.

stresses, 'buildings may be complex, but are defined by plans and sections, structures and finishes, not just by principal façades'.

There is a danger that an initial emphasis on the external will gradually move to a stage-set approach which is no longer linked to the reality of the urban environment. MacCannell (1976) in discussing 'authenticity' refers to front and back regions as in a stage show for tourists. In the six levels of interaction described, the front is the facade, the region on display, and the sixth level is the back, which is strictly private and therefore the 'true authentic'. Boissevain (1996), however, expresses concern for the back as the privacy of the authentic is breached as cultural tourism is marketed to the masses. The facadist approach is two-dimensional and theatrical, awaiting animation yet denying life. Facadism has become first, a conservation solution for maintaining image, character and streetscape while providing for modern space demands, and second, a means for 'keeping up appearances' to the outside visitor. The facade has become a lie for the building behind it. Millar (1995) points out that theatrical re-creation is a short-term response to boom-time tourism; it is a two-dimensional image, the antithesis of the texture created in the roofscape.

The tourist stage-set takes on many guises. In Istanbul the Soğukçeşme Street project involved the recording and demolition of a street of houses backing onto the Topkapı Palace before they were replaced with new buildings with imitation facades which are used as a guest house, a restaurant and a library. With only conceptual links to the original, the street is needless to say 'quaint', with heritage street lamps and a modern cobbled street. The ultimate betrayal comes from Rome, as Appleyard (1979) reflects on the irony of the peeling original facades staging the desired effect while being just a romanticised front for the modernised interiors, the culturally authentic private back described by MacCannell (1976). Never-theless, it is often the professional mind which is concerned, while the public welcome the familiar (historic) exterior, particularly for visiting, and demand the modern facilities of the interior for living in.

Fig. 3.3 Soğukçeşme Street in Istanbul, with its new clean-cut image, is a compromise 'tourist' solution to safeguarding a rapidly disappearing heritage.

Fig. 3.4 The decaying facades of Rome satisfy the visitor 'image', but front the modernised interiors desired by the inhabitants.

The continuation of an 'historic' imagery is also spreading as a design trend to the facades of new buildings in the name of contextualism. In Canterbury for example, where the policy is described as conservation, continuity and context, the new building approach described by the chief planning officer is:

> a philosophy of repair for the damaged fabric of the city, which is not just repairing and restoring historic buildings, but it extends to repairing the historic townscape – for example filling gaps in streets caused by wartime bombing or post-war clearance, or where there is an opportunity to replace

poor quality modern buildings with traditionally designed buildings that fit
the historic street and plot boundaries.

(Jagger 1998: 76)

New buildings should not look out of place in the townscape, where external
appearance is important; but replication is resulting in the contextual becoming
historicist (Warren 1998) or the use of a local vernacular tradition in a revivalist
style which Larkham (1996) refers to as 'pseudo-vernacular'. Revivalist and
pastiche approaches have become a common approach across Britain, often
supported by local planning authorities and compounded by the availability of
mass-produced 'traditional' materials (Larkham 1996).

The visitor 'experience' of culture

The *Oxford English Dictionary* defines experience as 'personal observation of or
involvement with fact, event, etc.', an everyday occurrence in human life. Visiting
a foreign town is in itself an experience, the experience of a way of life in a unique
environment. Increasingly, in the tourism and entertainment sector, there is a
growing notion that experience has to be provided, and therefore managed and
controlled. Theme parks are built for the purpose of selling a pre-determined
experience where human interaction with the environment is carefully stage-
managed.

An increasing use of interactive tools taking over from the traditional descriptive
and didactic content is regulating the museum experience. It is said to be because
of the popularisation of culture as an activity that leisure attractions, including the
media and museums, are catering for increasingly short attention spans. But as a
result, human activity is becoming managed and tightly regulated with little room
for self discovery. This is either because previously 'elite' attractions are being
made more widely available or because gross generalisations are being made about
contemporary society. Recent research in England has identified a territory between
museums and heritage theme parks which has popular appeal, including the
experience of history with gunfire and noise simulations, which is seen as exciting
(Moore 1997). 'Lifetimes', an interactive attraction based on local history and
interest in Croydon, England, is located in a shopping complex and deliberately
not named a 'museum', so as to attract a wider audience than the (traditional)
museum-going middle classes.

A new generation of 'intelligent' museums is appearing, encompassing
technology in full while virtual reality is being used to reconstruct the past. Wallace
(1995), however, points out that multi-media, or the expensive investment that it
entails, is not a guarantee for a high-quality product. 'Many times a simple, low-
cost solution, well executed and which responds well to the interpretative plan can
be much more successful' (R. Harrison 1994a: 314). Material culture which is
central to human life and society, clearly demonstrated in conflict and when it
is threatened (see also Lowenthal 1996), is being lost as museums are increasingly
moving away from the material or object, relegating them to mere props of the
interactive display environment (Moore 1997).

Discussing mining museums in Wales, Davies (1996) compares two different
approaches to visitor interpretation. The near-real preservation at the Big Pit Mining

Museum in Blaenafon has left the pit as far as possible in its 1980 condition when it was closed, simply sanitising and providing access in accordance with public Health and Safety regulations. The intention is to give visitors a realistic impression of the coal industry and the conditions and life of miners. On the other hand, the Rhondda Heritage Park offers visitors an 'experience' named 'A Shift in Time', where reality has been remodelled or ignored in favour of creating an 'experience' which includes the opportunity for visitors to set off an explosion, trivialising a complex and dangerous process. The mine has been repackaged for the heritage consumer by succumbing to mass 'tourist' appeal, described by Davies (1996: 109) as a 're-created workplace which fails to interpret working conditions'.

As the leisure industry expands, so does 'experience' culture; the Millennium Dome in London's Greenwich for example is marketed as the New Millennium Experience. Furthermore, a news article in February 1999 reported that a proposal for a school and health centre in the new Greenwich Millennium Village, submitted for planning approval at the time, could be used as an interpretation centre for visitors to the dome (*Building Design* 1999: 2); not only is the 'experience' provided, but so is the 'interpretation' of the experience. In the shadow of these millennial 'experiences', the historic town of Greenwich, it is feared, will become a 'theme park façade' for passing visitors, displacing historic, cultural and social integrity (V. Hall 1998: 13).

Museum interpretations of town histories, often an addition to information centres, provide an introduction to the history of the locality, increasingly through multi-media presentation, such as Dublinia in Dublin. Fleming (1996) points to two restrictions in museum representation of cities: first, that museum collections are only representative of the city in the narrowest areas and second, that it is impossible to capture through collections modern urban society, which is too changeable, dynamic and complex. 'No museum in any city in the world can encapsulate the city's experience completely' (Fleming 1996: 136), but interpretation centres can play an important role by acting as signposts for the activity within the city and a background to the history of a place. A multi-media type of interpretation may be useful and capture the attention, but it may also over-simplify history and urban experience. More significant is retaining the boundaries between experience fake and urban real. At the entrance of the tiny walled town of Mdina in Malta a signpost reads 'The Mdina Experience'; immediately a confusion arises, for unless one knows about the associated multi-media and film show, does the unsuspecting visitor not assume that the walled town itself is the experience? (Figure 3.5).

Experience in the urban environment is closely related to a pre-determined image, the expectations of visitors influenced by the portrayal of a destination through marketing and popular media. The depth of the city is no longer fully understood as the product, and the visitor experience becomes superficial and devoid of content. As D. Harvey (1989) points out, the experienced outer faces of cities are becoming the same, as a growing uniformity appears, obliterating distinctiveness. The use of 'tried and tested' formulas and the architectural application of the same heritage products create a bland and uninteresting attraction, and an 'experience' experienced elsewhere loses attractiveness for the visitor. The Dublinia multi-media presentation and the Delhi sound and light show for example

Fig. 3.5 The sign post to the 'Mdina Experience': is it pointing to the multimedia show or the small town itself? One person's town can become another person's experience.

are not that dissimilar, with the theme based on a narrative by their respective 'female' rivers, differing in historic fact rather than style.

Despite the individual value of heritage, the heritage product industry is in the business of mass production, which consequently leads to uniformity. Even the 'craft' heritage for sale in the West is likely to be mass produced in South East Asia. But more important is the larger-scale uniformity as historic towns become increasingly similar in appearance, as the same chain retail outlets take over from the specialist shops, and as attractions are the copies of the same product found elsewhere. Once historic towns become global products rather than distinctive places, the reasons to visit them will be vastly reduced.

In fast-growing and developing environments, old quarters are rapidly swallowed up into the progressive modern developments determined by competitive market forces. Historic quarters become an afterthought, a hint maybe of nostalgia but more likely a lost tourist opportunity, Dubai and Singapore being no exception. The loss nevertheless is being compensated for, as traditional quarters or marketplaces are re-created, at times in new out-of-town locations. Architect designed, they are sanitised and managed and provide ample room for coach and car parking. In Dubai not only are traditional buildings, most of them lost to affluent building programmes, being revived for tourist purposes, but a new tourist village is being constructed in the desert to simulate the old Dubai, originally a small fishing settlement, so as to provide an opportunity for visitors to 'participate in traditional pastimes' (Laws 1995). In Amman in Jordan, more discreetly, an old stable complex has been converted into a one-stop history and culture experience: a smart night out at the restaurant with waiters in themed attire and an opportunity for leisurely shopping at the 'traditional' marketplace souvenir shops. Ironic and superficial as they may be, they appear to be catering for a demand, and furthermore it could be argued than the 'real' traditional quarters are kept safe from tourist invasion, pressures of overcrowding and resulting social conflict.

Attractions in the urban environment

The leisure market is forecast to grow and cultural industries will continue competing for their market share. Even museums, traditionally educational establishments, are today in competition with leisure and entertainment activities. Information technology is changing not only working patterns, but also leisure activity, the way people travel and the way in which places are being perceived. Museums, once established institutions of an urban place, are now less location based as their exhibits can be accessed and toured virtually from anywhere in the world. 'Is virtual access going to reduce visitor numbers?' is a common question being asked as business plans are being updated. In an age where information can be stored and communicated electronically, more paper is being used and more books are being purchased; so it is probable that virtual reality and compact disc technologies will inspire travel rather than be a substitute for it, enticing visitors by providing more in-depth knowledge than the standard brochure pictures. Similarly, open-access systems like the World Wide Web are becoming an opportunity for locally initiated marketing to reach a wide recipient audience at low cost.

Human mobility is increasing and is forecast to continue to do so. People still want to see the 'real' thing, as crowds to recent mega-exhibitions of the works of Cézanne or Monet have shown. Authenticity and being real are an historic town's most valuable assets, made attractive through the power of interpretation. McKean (1993), in referring to New Lanark in Scotland, an industrial heritage village, makes the observation that interpretation can potentially make the ordinary seem extraordinary. The addition of any interactive experience is capital intensive and may well be short lived; as children become bored with buttons to push in museums, and the cultural tourist wearies of riding in carts and smelling authentic smells in darkened chambers. Attractions require substantial investment and often high running costs for what may become a short life span. Browne (1994: 20) suggests good-practice guidelines for the development of future attractions in Ireland, which could be summarised as general suggestions for historic towns:

- attraction development must be sustainable and relevant to the local community and it must not trivialise it;
- attractions should be authentic (in the true sense);
- attractions should be used to enhance heritage, not be copies of already successful attractions;
- major attractions should be of significant scale in order to make an impact on a holiday experience;
- the attraction must be clearly defined, concentrated and focused in its interpretation to ensure a high-quality product;
- the attraction plan must be an integral part of a city-wide visitor management plan;
- the attraction must provide all the facilities expected of it.

The development of attractions has to be based on sound market research and should consider the following questions:

- What will the benefits be and who will benefit?
- Will the attraction pose a danger to the asset?
- Can a high-quality product be produced and maintained?

Adding a tacky, inappropriate and ill-researched attraction to the historic environment will only degrade and lessen value. Whatever the choice of development it must remain appropriate to the place.

The slow success of EuroDisney, for example, could be attributed to the 'historic' images attractive in the USA or in Japan, appearing 'unimaginative' in the heart of Europe (Boniface 1994). On the other hand, a tourism development proposal for Salt in Jordan, which aimed at turning this traditional town into the 'cultural centre for Jordan' (RSS 1991), as it has become the last surviving example of architectural heritage on an urban scale, paid little respect to the local reality. Salt is neither on a main tourist route nor is it wealthy, but it is lived-in with a resident community keeping the older quarters alive and the commercial centres bustling. Heritage is being lost, mainly through decay and lack of maintenance, but the imported values of a cultural centre and the implanted tourism based heritage ideals will do little to serve or 'save' Salt.

Theme park reality

The Disney Corporation might be acknowledged as having devised the so-called potted history. The first Disneyland in California re-created the American Main Street of the nineteenth century, ensuring it was clean, tidy and colourful. The Main Street is used as a base from which to explore foreign countries and cultures of the world in the safety of the park, where human 'senses are titillated in safety and comfort, secure in the knowledge that home and the hamburger are never more than five minutes away' (Evans 1994: 53). It represents an historic interpretation, but functionally it is consumer driven: the 'Disney vision of systematic commercialised reality' (Ghirardo 1996: 42). Not only are political and economic problems eliminated, but so are the difficulties of maintenance as building materials are faked in prefabricated glass fibre. Nevertheless, the theme park industry continues to grow as the Disney Corporation expands worldwide and others follow the example. Alongside Egyptian pyramids, imaginary historic towns appear to be an enticing backdrop or setting for theme parks. What is provided is a sanitised and choice image, Egypt without the dirt or the unbearable heat for example, a desirable mixture of pyramid and souk and only a short distance from the oriental pagoda and the hamburger booth. Boniface and Fowler (1993), discussing the choice of imagery in theme parks, point to the common occurrence of locations thought to be exotic, and cliché images such as dragons or belly dancers – images which may even be degrading to the community cultures concerned, but which are equally becoming the symbols to be adapted in national promotional propaganda because of their familiarity. Theme parks are, nonetheless, responding directly to the visitor expectation of a provided experience, and are of course able to accommodate all the desired facilities.

Heritage is being distorted and culture cheapened, while association and meaning are lost. In Singapore the Haw Par Villa and Tiger Balm Gardens were a public pleasure garden with a collection of Buddhist scriptures and sculptures depicting Chinese folklore, legend and history. In the 1980s the Singapore Tourist Board, seeking to re-establish a 'lost oriental mystique' for visitors, converted the gardens into a theme park with action rides. As forced iconography was mixed with technology the 'real' heritage of the park and associated authenticity were irreplaceably lost. More significantly, the park proved neither a sustainable tourist attraction nor an attraction for the locals, who were deterred by the high entrance cost (Teo and Yeoh 1997).

Las Vegas is probably the ultimate example of theatrical commercialisation of historic iconography, with the re-creation of Egyptian pyramids and Greek temples to house gambling establishments. A casino in Atlantic City, supposedly a life-size replica of the Taj Mahal, a tomb, either is in poor taste or there is a relation between the two; whatever the case, the relationship to history is a kitsch stylistic gesture. The theatre continues with an Aladdinesque oriental image with veiled blonde maidens and doormen in pointed slippers.

Ironically, while 'authentic' is what is being advertised, authenticity is the very thing that is absent in these park environments. 'Authentic' is defined in the *Oxford English Dictionary* as 'genuine, of legitimate or undisputed origin'; for a British conservationist it is the original thirteenth-century stonework in a cathedral or an original oak frame in a timber-framed building, while MacCannell (1976) refers to 'authentic' as the back region, the real private life in the urban environment. In Disney-speak, however, 'authentic' appears to mean anything vaguely resembling, in appearance only, the real thing, be it an historic town or a distant culture.

The themed environment employs culture and heritage images as a backdrop to a controlled event within defined boundaries, where the actual attraction is often the rides and adventure that are provided. A growing popularity and availability of theme parks the world over have repercussions for historic towns competing

Fig. 3.6 This example in Sydney's Rocks area could be used to demonstrate authenticity: the house that is left as it is, albeit as a museum, against the carefully restored buildings in the area. Today the Rocks area is predominantly a tourist attraction.

for visitors, creating a demand for similar 'rides' and 'entertainment' being added or appended to the urban 'experience'. As the 'vehicle' for a ride becomes more significant than the history within a museum or heritage centre, similar approaches are threatening to dominate urban culture. It must also be noted that the theme parks are attracting the desired wider market base of families with children and young people, but then theme parks are about the family and entertainment.

R. Harrison (1994a) reflects on a growing fashion in the UK for creating what he describes as '"oo-ah" experiences' which overpower the educational, recreational and inspirational aspects of interpretation. But even the ride, appropriate to the Jorvik Centre in York, has been much less effective when repeated elsewhere. A reality of the tourist industry is that people seldom return to a destination; having experienced a place, the wanderlust-driven traveller seeks different experiences and new destinations. While people are seeking new and novel attractions, they are also looking for convenience. A recent study in the Netherlands, for example, identified that visitors to the Netherlands Open Air Museum and Burgers Zoo were not travelling into the city centre of Arnhem, only 5 kilometres away (Dietvorst 1994). Towns increasingly dependent on tourism as an industry, and against strong competition to remain more attractive than other towns, out-of-town shopping facilities and theme parks, are obliged to seek a balance between the added value an attraction may bring and its impacts on the urban environment and its functioning.

Theming is a growing phenomenon as popular 'historic' images are transposed onto many aspects of life and leisure activity; shopping malls, for example, adapt heritage imagery for the themed retail environments they create, and holidays include themed coach tours and cruises (Boniface 1994). It is a peculiar search for an otherness assumed to be more acceptable, and with it a disregard for the qualities of local distinctiveness. A later-abandoned proposal for a tourist development on the Panama Canal was for a themed Mediterranean village, to be located at a point where the Canal meets the Caribbean Sea and to mark the national significance of the Canal returning to Panama's control in the year 2000.

Heritage from the past, museums for the future, cities for today

Museums for urban heritage
Parks created to preserve and display vernacular architecture otherwise in danger of being permanently lost are well established in Europe, the first being Skansen near Stockholm in Sweden; it was founded in 1891 and now attracts one million visitors a year. The Irish National Heritage Park near Wexford, or in England the Weald and Downland Museum in Sussex and the Beamish Open Air Museum in County Durham, are other examples. Many of these parks were established to exhibit salvaged buildings, but the Poble Espanyol in the Montjuïc Park in Barcelona, completed for the 1929 exhibition, was specifically built as a presentation of architectural styles from all over Spain. Open-air museums are not themed in the way theme parks are, but neither do they constitute a substitute for the urban heritage. Borley (1994) distinguishes between [genuine] heritage (historic properties) and heritage collections brought together to serve the industry (parks). The buildings themselves, if salvaged, are likely to be authentic but they are exhibited out of their original context.

Heritage parks, like museums, do not constitute urban heritage, and their aims and intentions must be clearly understood. The Weald and Downland Museum consists of over forty buildings set in 50 acres of parkland. The predominantly rural and agricultural buildings are representative of different periods and lifestyles and, most importantly, illustrate building materials and techniques of a past era. This aspect is emphasised by various means, including the establishment of a new conservation centre to make more of the museum's work accessible to the visitor. At Beamish Open Air Museum, a typical North Eastern market town is re-created and set specifically in time to 1913 wherever possible, including a railway station, a home farm, a colliery and associated pit cottages. The open-air museum uses salvaged buildings from the region, early twentieth-century transport and real artefacts to create a story around the chosen theme. The approach differs in the more recent Highland Folk Park in Scotland, which aims to combine leisure and learning, promoting the link of traditional crafts to present-day living. The activity is described as heritage in action, where the heritage is the craft and not the buildings, which are replica structures so that they are perceived as they would have been in the past rather than as museum objects.

A less authentic museum-based approach is the re-creation of street scenes, shops and urban life from the past, such as the Castle Museum in York or the Craft Museum in Delhi. The aim again is to portray and display a way of life gone by depicted as an urban environment at a given point in history. But it is difficult to re-create human presence, a vital ingredient of urban life and, however much

Fig. 3.7 The Craft Museum in Delhi, where, despite the authentic architecture, the smells and atmosphere of Old Delhi cannot be re-created.

the animation, the Craft Museum is by no means able to capture the smell, noise and the street life of Old Delhi. Human beings must be recognised as the vital constituent of urban character. A museum approach may be identified as an architecture collection or heritage park, but it is unable to replace the urban environment because of the absence of the social structure in the spatial re-creation.

Urban heritage is not a return to a certain period in history; on the contrary it is a cultural framework for present-day life. Historic buildings are part of human, urban and social history and form part of a common heritage. At times pressures for development, growth, modernisation and continuity of the urban environment make these buildings redundant and obsolete as they become obstacles to continuity, and the need for development becomes greater than the value of the vernacular. The collective loss of this heritage is an historic and cultural loss to society today and to future generations. In such circumstances the heritage museum can act as a saviour of physical fabric, providing more material evidence than would be possible through recording, even if only through a select number of examples.

The Soğukçeşme Street project in Istanbul (see Figure 3.3) may be criticised for creating a fake, but considering the loss of the urban vernacular on the historic peninsula, the tourist-centred approach, approved in 1977, was at the time one of the few means of protection possible (N. Eldem *et al.* 1978). In the nearby neighbourhood of Zeyrek, the old wooden houses are rapidly disappearing. Accelerated urban growth, an increase in land values and changes in social structures mean that the traditional timber-framed buildings are being replaced with concrete apartment buildings providing a flat for each son – an unsightly yet contemporary evolution reflecting changes to family life in the second half of the twentieth century. Nevertheless, it is a social and economic response which has to be recognised, even though it is not a desirable scenario for heritage, nor does it create favourable urban surroundings. Where an historic street or area has become isolated from its original context, an appropriate museum function is one way of saving and utilising buildings. However, re-creation of a past time for visitor appreciation cannot be seen as a universal solution to the conservation of the historic urban fabric.

While the Weald and Downland-type approach sets out to salvage material which would otherwise be lost, and uses it as an educational tool of history, heritage villages built merely as tourist attractions are closer to theme parks but with the added danger of promoting false historic and cultural assumptions. Heritage museums, even though separated from the urban context, must remain truthful to their subject and relevant to place and time. In Dubai the historical Hatta village has become an isolated 'tourist' place, specifically rebuilt and furnished in the traditional way as a 'place of heritage'. At the archaeological site of Great Zimbabwe, on the other hand, a nineteenth-century model village as a 'live museum' of the local Shona people has been built to add to the attraction value of the archaeological site, which dates from AD 1100–1450 and furthermore is a World Heritage Site. The village is not authentic in location or form and is more an 'artist's impression' than a factual re-creation, and Ndoro and Pwiti (1997) report confusion among visitors. The village gives out false information, on its location, its authenticity and on the Shona, including erroneous stereotyping, while also detracting from the World Heritage Site. The thinking behind the village is that visitors, not finding the archaeology sufficiently enthralling, will need an additional attraction in order to be induced to visit the site. Not only must the aim and intention of a museum or heritage park be clearly established and communicated to the visitor, but the boundaries between what is real and what is fantasy must also be made clear.

The town museum

Dubai's Hatta village or Zimbabwe's Shona Live Museum are attempts to re-create an urban, living environment of the past predominantly for an outside tourist market. Colonial Williamsburg, in the United States, is the epitome of the town museum concept and one of the most widely discussed. The re-creation of Williamsburg, capital of the eighteenth-century colony of Virginia, is one person's vision, that of Dr W. Goodwin, rector of Burton Parish, made possible through the auspices of John D. Rockefeller Jr. One of the 'most important centres' of white American history has thus been re-created and restored to 'its former glory'. The 'park' re-created streets and open spaces, and contains up to 500 reproduction historic buildings and gardens, of which only eighty-eight were partly original. It reflects in a typically North American fashion a 'grand' concept, and the selective reinvention of urban heritage, to provide an 'experience'. Nevertheless Williamsburg is a well-managed site

> dedicated to providing a believable experience in American Heritage. . . .
> All the buildings in Williamsburg's historic area are fully used, lived in daily
> by people of this century, who conform to the custom of another. They are
> people living between two centuries and adding life to our outdoor museum.
> (McCaskey 1975: 156)

Williamsburg is a museum, a museum reinventing and in the process glorifying and idealising a past era of urban life. The town is visited by one million people each year and although originally only a town of 2,000 people, today it provides employment to 4,000 (Tramposch 1994).

The pressures on a 'real' historic town are eliminated through planning and management, and tourist damage or erosion to 'historic' fabric is simply repaired or replaced. The museum town can potentially eliminate many of the problems faced in historic towns and provide the benefits of adequate facilities, a reception centre, guided tours, a movie theatre and craft shops. Pressure is also planned for, sufficient car parks are discreetly placed on the outskirts, and comfort requirements and technology can be easily accommodated; high-spending conferences can be attracted to state-of-the-art convention centres which are also in desirable surroundings, but where wear and tear on the 'historic' fabric are easily dealt with. In Colonial Williamsburg even the cultural difference or communication between host and guest is being taken care of. Furthermore, history has been selective and idealised in portraying a chosen, cleansed and sanitised theatrical description of events, while the less desirable parts, such as the slave quarters for example, have been conveniently forgotten (Appleyard 1979); a black history was not introduced into Colonial Williamsburg until the 1970s.

Like 300 other American outdoor history museums, including Greenfield Village in Michigan and Old Sturbridge Village in Massachusetts, Colonial Williamsburg is a recognised and valued educational and 'entertainment' destination for the user market. Nevertheless,

> Foundation-owned hotels and restaurants appear inside and alongside the historic area, and in this regard the site resembles the extensive service-oriented work of Disney more than the work of any other outdoor history site.
>
> (Tramposch 1994: 31)

With the addition of 'complementary' attractions such as sports, air-conditioned hotels, golf courses, a wide range of entertainment opportunities and comprehensive conference facilities, a steady flow of visitors can be ensured to what has become a successful business venture responding to a demand in the marketplace.

In the knowledge that heritage and culture attract tourism, a chosen culture and at times imported culture is being freely implanted in the urban environment for marketing purposes. Chinatowns, for example, are not only the expression of a minority culture, but nurtured by local authorities seeing the potential in the visual and cultural qualities of an added attraction in the urban environment. Commercialism has meant that combinations of real place, historicism, vernacularism, and existing and imported culture are being assembled as retail opportunities. Santa Fe in New Mexico, for example, is a Mexican 'pueblo' setting adjoining a Native American reservation combined with a European historic town formula of craft and gift shops, French cafes and a Swiss creperie. Described by a British travel journalist:

> the adobe buildings squatted like great Christmas cakes, the walls the colour of marzipan, flat roofs with smooth royal icing and thousands of candles on top.
>
> (Herbert 1998)

Nonetheless, it is a successful tourist destination, because the marzipan 'pueblo' style appeals to Europeans, and the European historic town formula to the Americans; while the Native Americans try to make a living selling crafts.

Colonial Williamsburg must be viewed as a unique example of a museum rather than a generic model for urban heritage, for it represents a realised vision of a conscious return to the past, not an imposition onto an existing situation. Like a museum, it does not involve an existing community, their contemporary lifestyle or aspirations. However, the honesty in location and research in rebuilding must be recognised, as in the Jorvik Centre in York. Now referred to as the Jorvik approach (Breeze 1994), the 'formula' has predominantly failed elsewhere because it has been copied rather than understood in its approach and in the planning process behind archaeological rebuilding and interpretation. Tramposch (1994) reports that the heritage language of Colonial Williamsburg became so popular that it was borrowed and copied for numerous locations and buildings, often with no historic precedent. Building replica pueblos or Arab towns in the desert is closer to theme parks in terms of urban and historic (dis)honesty, yet many have much to learn on visitor management and profit making from Colonial Williamsburg and the Disney Corporation.

In the early 1970s, when Tanzania was developing a tourism policy, Gordon Fair, a policy maker, in a debate on the image Tanzania would portray to the outside, was quoted as saying:

> 'How do you get the tourist to meet the people without them becoming absolutely obnoxious? The people the tourists want to see are usually the most primitive in their most primitive state. These are the people that emerging nations are not likely to want pushed as representatives of their countries, and for a good reason. I'm sure Tanzania wouldn't want a bus load of tourists to descend on a ujamaa (self-reliant) village for a snapshot session. They don't want tourists disturbing their normal way of life. We suggest isolating tourists . . . we've got to set up artificial villages so that the tourists can have something to see when they arrive, and not disturb the people. It may be contrived – it may be fake – it is fake – but it's a lot less aggravation on both sides.'

(Shivji 1973: viii)

The question is: would a replica Venice, 'The Venice Experience', really ease the pressure on the historic island and make it Venetian again?

And the issue remains: while it is common and acceptable for museums to borrow from the urban language, how much can urban environments afford to borrow from museums? Williamsburg apart, real towns are being turned into museums or theme parks in a competitive market. On arrival at what appears to be an entrance, it is difficult to know whether Old Rauma, one of Finland's oldest surviving settlements, is town or museum as guides await visitors to a backdrop of freshly painted and brightly coloured timber houses.

Fig. 3.8 Old Rauma in Finland: a living town, but where the first impression is of a museum.

The city as museum?

The question: can a city be both museum and town?, the commonly voiced opinion: no. The city is a living, dynamic environment where cultural heritage is only part of a complexity of relationships. A museum on the other hand is an organised and managed environment, not necessarily static, but one which creates a framework for the presentation of cultural heritage. The remit and aim of the museum interpretation are to open a window on the past, encompassing education, instruction and enjoyment. But at a time when museums themselves are no longer just in cities, but are of cities, entering a dialogue and playing a proactive role in the urban environment and its development, cities pursuing a museum role can only be short lived.

Two prerequisites for urban conservation have been identified: the will and interest to conserve and the financial backing with which to realise it. The power behind a strong conservation movement in Europe has been the people – residents valuing older quarters as places to live. The financing of urban conservation has often resulted in the gentrification of areas, and is increasingly being motivated by tourism which in turn is turning historic towns into stage-set imagery, 'freezing' them in time. It must come as no surprise, then, for tourists to treat these fairy-tale locations as if they were museums. As a museum, the city gains a singular identity in contrast to the underlying complexity of urban life. Colonial Williamsburg may claim to be a living museum, but the 'life' is merely a theatre. Roy Worksett (1978), in referring to Bath, points out that if the city is an organic system inbuilt with continuous change, then Bath would have to be classed a museum, with 5,000 listed and protected buildings; it is static 'like stuffed animals in a display case'.

Cities like Bath or York are being turned into museums through conservation attitudes. The fear that their attractiveness will be lost because of new developments, the recognition of a winning formula, mythical date lines to which everything

Fig. 3.9 The use of fake history in the Swinegate development in York contributes to the 'museum' and 'model town' image of the place.

adheres, and planning control mechanisms which impose restrictions, serve to encourage appearances of periodism. Conservation area boundaries established in order to maintain the character of a certain area of historic significance are becoming the ring fence within which only a certain style of development is being permitted. Larkham (1996: 131) argues that there has been an over-designation of conservation areas in the United Kingdom, especially as available funding and support have become limited, and they have thus come to serve as boundaries for development control rather than encouraging active development initiatives.

As a museum, the city becomes static, a quality which over time becomes stifling for users and the local community. Business expansion is limited and valuable businesses may eventually decide to relocate to a place where there is more potential for expansion. A freezing-in-time attitude to conservation restricts urban growth and restrains a natural dynamism and an inborn urban tension. Walled cities in particular become a totality in protection and in the way they are considered a tourist attraction. The small walled town of Mdina in Malta is frequently mistaken for a museum as tourists are bussed in from surrounding resorts. The pressures of tourism have reached such levels that charging an entrance fee to offset increased service costs has been considered. The proposal was rejected by residents, afraid that it would only give visitors further liberty to act as if everything were a museum display or show, and contested by other citizens arguing that Mdina belonged to the nation.

The city as a living environment must continue to develop and grow. As in Cannigia's paradigm of the leading type being introduced on the periphery and gradually penetrating the existing, contemporary architecture and contemporary styles must also be permitted into the development of the historic environment. However, it is a high-quality contemporary rather than replica pastiche architecture which is clearly a new link in the chain and the best way to avoid a static historic image. It is often the case that grand and high-quality architecture of a past period was built at a time of affluence and attracted well-known designers and builders, whereas the present-day situation may be one of decline where cheap solutions are more likely to be sought (Worksett 1978). Moreover, it has been this appearance of poor-quality modern buildings in the past that has increased the pressures for preservation and the refusal of the new. The question of contemporary architecture in historic settings is one of quality. The control of aesthetic quality is a much debated issue of differing opinions, one of commissioner, planner and designer and decision makers in the urban environment. Sensitive yet celebratory additions to old towns are called for, simple, truthful and in harmony (Warren 1998).

There are many successful examples of historic towns where high-quality contemporary architecture is being welcomed and successfully incorporated into the townscape. In Oxford and Cambridge funds available to colleges and enlightened patronage have resulted in some very successful modern additions to the historic fabric. Bruges is another example of successful modern intervention in the old town, domestic in scale but clearly visible from the historic canals (see Figure 1.6). The Rocks area of Sydney also successfully incorporates contemporary structures within the old fabric.

Summary and conclusions

The common outcome of the specifically tourist historic town has become something that looks 'picturesque' or 'exotic' in appearance, but remains superficial in content. The sought-after realness of character is lost as historic towns become generic global products, as market planners and developers trying to retain a visitor base turn to short-term and short-lived solutions and a bland response to post-modern 'experience' seeking. Presentation and interpretation decisions as an outcome of management, marketing and short-term financial planning are jeopardising future sustainability and displacing the irreplaceable qualities of identification, sense of belonging and local distinctiveness.

'In addition to the "surface appearance" . . . we must understand that good urban places have a structure and an underlying dynamic of activity' (Montgomery 1998: 95). Historic towns are not museums, they are alive with culture and community, and the 'history' is only a modern-day interpretation. The boundaries between urban and museum are being lost, in some cases positively but also at times dangerously.

Museums are becoming part of urban life, actively involved in the regeneration and the cultural activity of the place they are of, as well as providing the medium for reflecting on a past urban life which is no longer possible. Meanwhile, the development of technology and its application to interpretation, coupled with increasing competition between towns in the tourism market or the desire to gain a bigger share of the 'leisure' market, mean that the museum historic town is being created. The following case study on Mdina in Malta discusses how a community is being turned into a museum exhibit by tourism promoters.

The preservation and continuation of urban heritage are a complex issue and involve a large number of players, as well as constraints and conflicting priorities. There is the residents' desire for better living conditions, communities' desire for the protection of heritage and the tourism planners' desire for attractive heritage and visitor potential. Often these desires are in conflict rather than in harmony with one another. The next chapter considers the roles of key players in the decision-making process for the future of historic towns.

Case study
The walled town
of Mdina, Malta

Although planning or conservation in Mdina has not been a preservationist museum approach, the small size of the contained walled town and the heavy influx of visitors make Mdina residents feel as if they are a museum display.

The place
The small walled town of Mdina is located on a hilltop in the centre of the island of Malta. It was the capital of the island until the arrival of the Knights of St John in 1530, Mdina was built under the influence of earlier Arab occupants and takes its name from the Arab *medina*, meaning city. The fortified town is Islamic in character, with narrow and angled streets shaded by the high walls, overhangs and projections. The walled town contains a mere 69 households and 368 residents according to the 1995 census (Schembri and Borg 1997). It is the home of some of the oldest Maltese families and nobility with their grand and historic residences, alongside the exquisite Romanesque cathedral. The town is also known for the Cathedral Museum, the National Museum of Natural History, numerous churches and excellent views over the island from Bastion Square. More recently these cultural attractions have been joined by the 'Mdina Experience', a multi-media and film show.

For the residents the walled town represents a valued and peaceful environment of architectural and social quality. Most buildings are being well cared for, and the problem is not so much the conservation of the physical fabric, but the conservation of the values and atmosphere of the town, the conservation of place and identity against a growing tide of visitors attracted to Mdina's picturesque appearance.

Tourists in Mdina
The Maltese islands are a popular tourist destination for the Mediterranean tourism market. To the small island economy, tourism is a major source of income, accounting for as much as 40 per cent of economic activity. Traditionally much of the tourism to these islands has been coastal resort-based beach tourism, with the rich cultural heritage and landscape being seen as secondary attractions. The National Tourist Organisation, in a drive both to increase tourism potential and

Fig. 1 (a) and (b)
Mdina is still a typically
Islamic town in its
urban morphology,
with high walls and
narrow winding streets.

(a)

(b)

to reduce pressures at high season, has started promoting culture and nature attractions of the islands and associated all-year-round travel. Consequently a longer visitor season has been established, and a greater interest in other attractions such as village feasts (festa), cultural events and heritage has been developed.

Mdina is part of the highlight history presented to tourists and is one of the most popular sites, visited by as many as 750,000 visitors in 1992, and according to Boissevain (1993: 3) it had become so popular that three out of every four tourists visiting Malta went to see Mdina. The growth of year-round tourism has increased the pressure on Mdina, especially with the new emphasis on cultural tourism promoted by the government. Cultural activity, such as open-air concerts and colourful festivals, has been 'imposed' on the old town. In June 1993 for example a festival was held under the name Mdina '93, which included a wide spectacle of events from historical re-enactments to street theatre, musical events and exhibitions. Over the week the small town attracted tens of thousands of visitors, most of whom were Maltese. The residents of Mdina were reported not to be as joyous and many felt that they had simply been used (Boissevain 1994).

For the local residents of Mdina, the tourist or cultural visitor invasion has not been overly welcome. Complaints include the increase in retail simply catering for tourists and the inconvenience of tourists blocking the roads, polluting the streets, being noisy and dressing indecently. Moreover, some residents have expressed complaints that even services like street lighting are better on tourist routes. But most of all it is the spectacle of being a museum object and the invasion of their privacy that upset and at times anger local residents. 'They felt they were being obliged to sacrifice their privacy and tranquillity for the national good without compensation from either government or tour operators' (Boissevain 1993: 5).

Fig. 2 Tourist shops are taking over the main square.

Mdina is promoted as the 'silent city' because the narrow streets make it a predominantly pedestrian environment and only permit holders are allowed to use vehicles in the walled town. In reality it is far from silent, as noisy groups wander through the narrow streets, and the growing commercial activity serving the industry also contributes to the noise. For such a small town and tight-knit community, the carrying capacity for tourism is naturally very low. Furthermore it is not only the shops that have turned to tourist interests, but there is growing anguish that vacant properties, no longer affordable to the local residents, are being bought up by outside entrepreneurs to develop for tourism. The establishment of a longer tourist season, hailed as a good thing by the authorities, is viewed in Mdina as an even longer period of disruption, with no respite or quiet period for the residents (Boissevain 1996).

It is a common daily occurrence for tour buses to deposit tourists at the city gates where they enter the attraction for the specified period of time before they are collected again. In the face of rising service costs, the introduction of an entrance fee to the walled town was discussed. However, residents felt strongly that this would be a ticket for visitors to feel that they were definitely in a museum with the right to wander, peer and 'snoop' as they pleased; especially as residents already report frequent occurrences of visitors peering through open doorways. Boissevain (1994: 12) questions the ownership of Mdina: whether it rightfully belongs to the small number of people who reside there, or to the Maltese heritage as a whole, or to an even wider global heritage interest. It has been recently reported that some residents have also entered the tourism business themselves, maybe in the spirit of 'if you can't beat them, join them'.

Issues and options

Mdina is being treated as a museum by visitors and as a heritage park by the authorities, while the inhabitants strive to maintain a sense of place in a year-long succession of visitors and events. Tensions are clearly evident, between ownership as a place to live and ownership as a national monument; between residents' interests and visitors' interests; between residents and tourism developers, be it the entrepreneurs moving in or the authorities organising events.

How can Mdina remain a town and not end up a museum, especially as the effectiveness of tourism management will be very limited at the small and intimate scale of the walled town? There is nevertheless a greater need for local control and local say in decision making. Some options in considering Mdina's future could include:

At local level

- Control of opening times for tourist facilities, which can for example be determined by licensing agreements.
- Local power to make choices on events, and a proactive role in guiding such activities.
- Local presence and decision-making stake on organising committees for events.

At national level

- Ensuring tourism revenue returns to Mdina to mitigate environmental pressure and damage.
- Through marketing, distribution of interest to other walled towns or attractions on the island (although a popular attraction, Mdina is not a must-see destination and expected photo opportunity).
- Boissevain (1997) suggests a guide of dos and don'ts to be distributed to visitors and the guides coming to Mdina.

The future

The question remains as to whether Mdina will be able to remain a place for its residents or will simply be turned into a commercial museum for visitors.

4 Decision making for the historic environment

Introduction

Tourism and its management in historic towns involve two broad areas of expertise: the fields of tourism marketing and management, and those of urban planning, environment and conservation. Although closely linked in remit and areas of conduct, the two are often administratively isolated from one another, resulting in contradictions and conflicts. The focus of this chapter is decision making in historic towns for urban conservation and urban tourism, and the concern for the management of the resources which constitute the urban ecosystem, built, natural and human. Urban management encompasses planning, directing, organising (co-ordinating) and controlling roles (Page 1995). Management is defined as 'taking conscious decisions, with an eye to the future, about ongoing operations or the use of assets, or both in combination within a structured organisation' (Lichfield 1988: 38). The intention is to identify the key decision-making roles in the management and development of conservation and tourism in historic towns, and to address the time frame for which decisions are being made.

Government structure, both national and local, is different for each country, particularly in respect of the location of power, control and decision making. The intention here is not to discuss the variants of governmental models but to highlight common powers for decision making and the relationships among key players. The total cast of urban management points to a large number of players in a variety of roles, from a wide range of disciplines and backgrounds, and often with conflicting interests and agendas. Furthermore, the urban environment is only managed in part, and decision making emerges from ownership and key management roles. Core decision making is identified in order to understand both the process and areas of conflicts and tensions, and ultimately to establish the critical mass necessary for effective decision making which is representative of all interests concerned.

The relationship between individual or collective decision makers can turn to one of conflict or tension. Conflicts originate from known dichotomies and from differing objectives often closely linked to accountability structures. Larkham (1990) points out that the decision-making process involves outsiders (boardroom) and insiders, local agents of change with an understanding of the local environment. A delicate balance has to be established between insider and outsider so as to promote effective management and to maximise the benefit of development.

Three overlapping relationship paradigms appear. The first is a legislative framework, a distinctly top-down and established relationship among national, state and local government. The second is a participatory relationship between those initiating and those receiving development or change. The third overlying framework is one of finance, and involves most of the key players as well as the global tourism market. Each player within these frameworks has a policy, finance, implementation or control role.

This chapter considers the following questions:

- Who are the key players and at what levels are decisions being made?
- What conflicts arise in the decision-making process?
- What are the accountability relationships?

Key players

A framework for analysis
Unlike the more clearly defined aspects of building conservation, urban conservation is a complex and long-term process involving a large number of players, from public sector departments and the political forces that dictate to them, to private professionals and non-governmental organisations. Key decision making in this field involves most of the following:

- national government (policy);
- local government (elected or appointed);
- local public sector officials, local policy makers and professionals;
- professionals and consultants (employed by local government);
- non-governmental organisations;
- social agencies;
- the private sector;
- users (resident community).

The development of tourism in an historic town introduces further new players, including the influential and less accessible global tourist industry:

- global tourism market;
- national government (policy);
- local government (elected or appointed);
- local public sector officials, local policy makers and professionals;
- professionals and consultants (employed by local government);
- the private sector;
- users (resident community);
- visitors.

With each player in a policy, finance, implementation or control role, as more departments and players are added to the decision-making process, new agendas and objectives are also introduced. The complexity of relations is often compounded by a lack of communication and the absence of collaboration in similar areas of operation. Tensions arise between players' and participants' objectives and priorities, including within organisations providing services and the levels at which individuals interact. A well-established vertical or linear top-down decision-making structure is apparent in the government sector, but horizontal relationships among different government or local administration departments are often poorly established. A more confrontational relationship exists between provider and recipient at local policy and project implementation level. Political choices at national or local level influence decision making, as do financial and investment partners.

The global tourism industry

The tourism industry, alongside other cultural industries, has been one of the first to grow and develop at a global level, regardless of national boundaries. Connections and links among operating and managing companies frequently remain secretive and are often not clear on the local, high street level where a holiday is purchased. Significant power steering of tourism development is in the hands of large multinational operators having within their control a range of services from airlines to hotel chains.

Most tourism is generated and controlled by the developed world. The West is also responsible for the development of much of world tourism today through its agencies, operators and airlines. Therefore, decision making, coordination, destination choices and profits are being made in the West. Each year tourism from the West looks towards widening its horizons and discovering new and more exotic destinations. The international tourism business is consumer focused and often ahead of governments in market research and forecasting. Tourism today has become a worldwide phenomenon and most countries are competing for their share in the market.

A visitor typically purchases a holiday through a high street agent. The booking package may include an air ticket, accommodation and facilities at the destination. Both the agency and the airline are likely to be owned by the same operator, which has also come to an arrangement with a local accommodation provider at the host destination. Local owners of hotels and similar establishments often depend on the deals made with the operator's agents to reach a desired capacity. Over-supply on the market leads to price cutting which benefits the operator whose concern is to make a profit by delivering a desirable holiday to the customer. Tourism moves in cycles and there is little guarantee of its continuation at the same levels, as has been clearly demonstrated for coastal tourism in the Mediterranean. When a destination becomes popular, the operators with money want to invest in the area and the local hoteliers welcome it and start creating more space. It is 'at this time when the host country has to be very careful with the growth of tourism' (Josephides 1992: 53).

To remain competitive in the market, the operator, as service provider, seeks new destinations and newer and better accommodation at a competitive price. In times of crisis, war or unrest the operator pulls out, offering the customer an alternative and leaving the destination provider with at most a small deposit payment.

Similarly, an upmarket operator will move out of an area seen to be spoilt, while a more downmarket operator moves in, with even smaller payments to the local establishment. Once a destination has been flooded by downmarket visitors, 'you start getting ghettos, catering for a particular kind of tourist mentality' (Josephides 1992: 54). Interests or concerns at local level need not concern the global operator; and furthermore a very small proportion of the pre-paid holiday money reaches the locality.

It could be argued that tourism as a global industry sees the world as its asset, and much of the current approach is based on what is seen as a wide choice of worldwide destinations, with the false perception and attitude that there is still much more of the unspoilt yet to be exploited. Sustainability and long-term goals, much more common to other industries, are often overlooked in tourism in favour of immediate gain which may be at the cost of future gain.

Role of national government

The role of national government is one of *policy* and *finance*. National government, through legislation and subscription to international convention, establishes a legislative framework and is responsible for the safeguarding of law and con-stitution. Elected governments, both national and local, by the representative nature of their constitutions, have a priority to support measures that are consistent with the values of their electorate, but at the same time they must adhere to the values and ideology of their party (Corina 1975).

Policy and law relating to historic towns are likely to be dictated by a number of different departments or ministries such as those dealing with culture and antiquities, environment, tourism, transport or housing. One of the main targets of national governments is the furthering of development and increasing foreign revenue, for which tourism is seen as a prime resource.[1] National-level decisions on tourism growth targets or road and rail networks have a significant impact on the development of tourism in a given locality, but the political nature of national or state governments can also lead to short-term policy decisions and targets, including those concerning tourism development and economic growth. Inter-national tourism promotion is also likely to be funded and therefore dictated at national level.

Governments have a clear role to play in the maintenance of the heritage and environmental assets on which sustainable tourism is largely based (Paszucha 1995: 40). National-level links to conservation often start with the acknowledge-ment of international charters, and the designation or listing of historic buildings and the protection of major monuments may be the responsibility of the national administration. When the listing of historic buildings is undertaken centrally, heritage as seen at the national level often concerns monuments and archaeological sites rather than urban environments. In developing countries, for many over-worked and underfunded heritage departments, historic buildings become a name on a protection list rather than a cause for action. Authorities are often concerned only about monuments and sites with tourist appeal in bids to increase visitor numbers, thus revenue. In most countries, the state is responsible for the determination of cultural policy,[2] linking at times with the choice of iconographic repertory to be the representative of national culture for both national and

Fig. 4.1 In Plovdiv, Bulgaria, it was the former Communist government who took on, paid for and controlled the immaculate restoration of the historic fabric, which also involved the decision to relocate residents.

international consumption (Canclini 1998) – an iconography which is heavily used by national tourism boards in tourism promotion campaigns. Similarly, the state exercises social control over minority culture, and the more equitable dissemination of cultural goods must be seen as a leading role for the state in determining cultural policy (UNESCO 1998). More recently, however, there are greater opportunities for places and regions to embark on promotion, especially through the possibilities offered by information technology.

National governments play a critical role in cultivating slow and selective growth (Bodlender and Lickorish 1991). Where tourism is a new industry and the local private sector lacks experience and capital, national government investment in tourism will set an example and a standard for future developments and it will avoid domination by external investment. In India for example, the government has set up a successful chain of guest houses and related tourist facilities in order to encourage private sector development, and to establish the desired standards.

Role of local government

The role of the local government involves *policy* and active *implementation*, providing municipal services and managing development. As an agency of national government, local government is responsible for implementing nationally or internationally agreed law. The remit of local government can range from a large metropolitan authority to a village council, with varying degrees of autonomy and authority which are assigned and regulated by national government. A local government or administration is controlled and regulated by national or state government in varying degrees. Local governments are responsible for the management of urban systems, and planning in urban areas is undertaken to achieve many of the goals associated with urban management (Page 1995). The focus of local governments is the management of urban growth and development. Lichfield (1988) draws the comparison between an estate managed by the owner, be it a private individual or an organisation, and the urban totality which is managed only in part by the local government, leaving many components which are not and cannot be managed. The role of a local authority is to manage urban resources; this involves maintaining designated services (transport, schools etc.) and their associated relationships, based on economic and market choices.

Local government may be fully appointed by central government, or it may be an elected council and mayor. The decision-making and regulatory power of local government varies according to the links and relationship to national or state government. The institutional characteristics of the urban government, however, play an important role in determining its effectiveness (Davey 1993). Paszucha (1995) points out that the importance of the local is being recognised, as a trend towards regionalism and enhancement of local political power in former communist countries. In many such countries today the power of local government still remains minimal, in what is a transitory period establishing new planning systems and introducing urban management. For some historic towns this period has unfortunately come at the most critical point of developing and managing tourism. Local governments also have direct links to local interests and businesses, chambers of commerce, and the like, by which they are influenced. An elected council is accountable to the voting public and at local level faces greater political risk and exposure than a national government does.

D. Harvey (1997) points out that twentieth-century urbanisation has resulted in a massive reorganisation of political structures. Generically, urban government provides services and regulatory functions within the boundaries of its jurisdiction but is prone to overmanning, which leads to inefficiency (Davey 1993). Privatisation of municipal services means that the local authority is no longer the only provider of all functions; however, an imbalance may appear as unprofitable functions remain within the authority. Professional representation within local administration is becoming a managerial role, judged on the quality of service management.

The task and responsibility of the local administration in the historic urban environment are wide ranging and may be controlled by a number of departments, the interests of which overlap:

- economic regeneration
- planning and conservation
- housing
- tourism
- traffic
- public health
- city engineers (infrastructure)
- social services (including disability, access, etc.).

Each of the departments within the municipal organisation has a separate agenda, development priorities and budgets to realise its objectives. While the jurisdiction of heritage may lie with a planning department, conservation plays an important part in tourism promotion. The local authority is also likely to be responsible for the activities of the local tourist board. Establishing cross-departmental teams is a major task (M. Middleton 1982), but the integration of services among departments is essential, as 'effective urban management requires more than competence in running individual services' (Davey 1993). Planning involves the management of resources and balancing public and private sector interests, and may be reactive (development control) or proactive in encouraging and initiating development. In Lyon, for example, local government was influential in setting a precedent for conservation in the 1960s, when the old centre came under a protection order, by upgrading several courtyard-type buildings to demonstrate what could be done with buildings that had previously lacked indoor bathrooms or proper kitchens, but contained artistically attractive courtyards. Through tax incentives the entire area was restored and by the late 1980s it had become near impossible to find an apartment in the old town (Repellin 1990).

The development and planning of tourism are directly linked to the community through the local authority. A balancing role is evident, between the needs of existing users and those of future users – such as a new cultural activity that not only is going to attract tourists but also is desired locally. The conservation of urban areas cannot be divorced from political interests and it is part of the political game that solutions with higher vote-winning potential are favoured. An active role for local government is through the purchase and restoration of redundant historic buildings, setting an example for conservation and a standard for works to be undertaken. Municipal interest in an historic quarter will raise awareness and will encourage residents to invest in and upgrade their properties, as was illustrated in Lyon. The local authority also has an important function of training local business in tourism.

By buying in services, the local administration becomes a client to the private and professional sectors and takes on a new control role compared to a previous one of implementation. As local government is moving from a professional to a management-oriented service, Ashworth and Voogd (1990) argue that the goal of urban planning is no longer the production of a well-organised urban liveable space, but for a well-organised public decision-making system. However, bringing planning control closer to city management creates a new tension between design and control. Planning departments in the UK, for example, are predominantly involved in development control, which is both a sophisticated process and a political necessity. But Whitehand (1990) questions whether authorities are simply responding to pressure from other parties or actually exercising a townscape management role. Similarly, A.C. Hall (1997) argues that alongside planning policy there must exist design objectives for specific design areas. Unless it is commissioner of a building, a local authority does not have full power to control aesthetic quality (Larkham 1996). For many western cities development control based on accepted and established plans and policy is in danger of becoming too rigid and thus losing an innovative edge, to the extent that in places continuity is jeopardised. There are now examples of residents moving out of historic areas not because these are undesirable places to live, but because they feel constrained by the controls imposed by local planning and conservation authorities.

Professional roles

The local government within its organisational structure both employs a wide range of professionals and outsources tasks to professionals operating within the private sector. The task of the professional within local government ranges from the direct execution of works to more distant quality control, management and regulatory duties. The role of the professional is based on *implementation*. Larkham (1996) identifies direct and indirect agents of change on townscape, whereby architects and designers are seen as the professional group most influential in making changes; local authority planners and amenity societies on the other hand become only indirectly influential in their role of development control and processing of planning applications. The quality of professional expertise is vital to sensitive development and to effective management.

Even within each broad professional group there can be limited overlap and communication. Planning itself has a broad agenda of which town planning and urban design are only a small part. Planning concerns itself with a variety of roles including legal, managerial, design and implementation; it covers areas as diverse as landscape and transport, and it reflects the planning system in each country, which in turn is closely connected with the country's political, legal and administrative systems (Orbaşlı and Worthington 1995). Urban design is a pluralist activity involving negotiation between many parties and the general public (A.C. Hall 1997). Townscape management, conservation and development are all important social tasks of spatial planning (Conzen 1981). A planner–designer duality emerges and Sammuels (1990) points out the importance of a morphological study of the urban form being carried out by designers, who will provide inspiration, rather than its being left to planners. It is also likely that different professionals (architects, designers, planners or managers) and teams of professionals will be appointed to different projects, with few formal links to other teams working within the same townscape. In local authority-financed projects, the authority may enter into a relationship with a professional service provider, but it still has responsibility for establishing a brief, securing funding, managing finances, monitoring and controlling quality.

Another key role is in the appointment of professionals to projects. With decreasing in-house expertise this is increasingly the role of the local authority, but in the case of privately funded developments it rests entirely on the developer's or investor's choice of appointment, over which the authority has limited or no control. Poor-quality restoration for example can be equivalent to demolishing a building, and although the recognition of the specialist expertise is central to the project, it cannot be enforced, only controlled. In the case of developing countries, obstacles to planning and running conservation programmes often stem from a lack of qualified or expert staff, combined with limited resources to finance projects or control implementation. Training of local professional expertise must, however, be seen as a priority over importing high-fee foreign consultants. For the outsider specialist, it is equally important 'to provide advice for the specific needs and capabilities of governments, usually within their own tradition, instead of imposing a Western pattern for control and development' (Antoniou 1981: 12). In most cases, professional activity is a balance between outsider and insider, valuing the knowledge of the outsider but identifying the needs of the insider by establishing expertise for long-term and overall cost-effective solutions. Poor administration in the public sector is a known problem, and complicated bureaucracy for the simplest action is common to most places. In an effort to avoid a lengthy and expensive process, owners continue to repair, change or demolish historic properties without official consent.

Physical aspects of development are influenced by urban and spatial planners, regional planners, urban designers and architects, whereas economic development and tourism are overseen by tourism management professionals, often independently of the physical planning process and professionals. The two areas are frequently controlled by different departments, funded from different sources and run under different legislation, and therefore may have within their brief only minimal opportunity to communicate with each other.

Role of other organisations
The role of non-governmental organisations and social agencies, depending on their size and constitution, involves *funding*, *implementation* and *control*. They range from established international or national agencies, to short-term issue-based community groups. The non-governmental or charitable sector is apolitical and non-profit-making with an interest in a chosen cause and community benefit. The influence of this sector is wide ranging, including campaigning, control over projects and developments, promotion of good practice, awareness, education and training, and financing. Control over finance, in particular, leads to an important decision-making role.

In Western Europe there is an established tradition and a strong network of conservation bodies, amenity societies, advisory groups and network associations to provide assistance to projects and local governments. In England, for example, the Civic Trust and the English Historic Towns Forum are directly involved with historic towns alongside numerous other smaller or locally based organisations. Both larger societies and smaller pressure groups depend on support from volunteers and moreover acceptance by the authorities. Some conservation bodies are also important in awakening and promoting interest in the rehabilitation of the existing urban fabric. In developing countries many amenity societies are still only in the pioneering stages, and they often lack the power and financial backing their western counterparts enjoy. They do, however, play a potential role in education and as intermediaries between inhabitants (owners and users) and the authorities (bureaucracy).

International organisations, from the Council of Europe to the World Bank, and United Nations agencies such as UNESCO, alongside aid agencies play an important role in the funding of urban development projects, in training of professionals and in monitoring programmes. The significance of cultural heritage for development is being recognised widely at this international funding level. The World Bank, which (for example, through its Urban Initiatives programme) focuses on culture as a trigger for regeneration, states that

> The World Bank increasingly appreciates the role that culture can play in urban development whether through sustaining built and lived heritage, encouraging the contemporary cultural industries or recognizing the impact that culture plays in defining identity, generating motivation, civic pride and fostering a sense of empowerment.
>
> (http://www.worldbank.org 1998)

Nevertheless, the funding organisations control where and how the money is spent and they exercise control over action.

Role of the private sector

'Private sector' is an umbrella term for a wide range of interests and activities, from multinational hotel chains to local shopkeepers. The role of the private sector revolves on *implementation* and *financing*. Middleton and Hawkins (1998) identify three areas of private sector involvement and decision making in tourism. The first is destination based, providing visitor services; the second is directly involved in the marketing of destinations – it has its base outside the destination and involves tour operators and agents; and the third includes the investors, developers and banks providing the capital for tourism investment. The informal sector in developing countries as an entrepreneurial force must also be viewed as part of private sector activity. In the absence of grant aid or similar funding, the financing of building conservation falls to individual owners and occupiers of historic property. Private sector involvement is motivated by potential profit and tourism is often the carrot that makes building conservation attractive and profitable to the private investor.

In emerging markets the private sector will be seen as an important financial resource. High start-up costs and immaturity of the business sector, however, restrict the number of potential suppliers. Insufficient controls in changing planning systems present the danger of developers cashing in on the historic past, often with little concern for its future integrity. Under former communist administrations, popular historic towns are suffering, as the subsidies which were previously enjoyed are no longer available, and as ownership and responsibility for buildings are being contested and planning systems are in the process of being overhauled or reinvented while commercial tourist development has escalated beyond expectations. While the former socialist planning system has been disregarded, limited experience of the rapidly emerging market situation has resulted in the market dominating decision making.

Tallinn in Estonia, dependent predominantly on day visitors from Helsinki and Stockholm, has experienced retail-driven development in the old town, much of it closely linked to corruption, with little margin for urban development or planning due to the lack of expertise and governance (Jaakson 1996). Paszucha (1995) notes that the unique position of the private sector in securing tourist development is becoming recognised by Eastern European governments, but he stresses the importance of small-scale, manageable private initiatives which are possible to realise, over large schemes with unknown prospects.

Private sector businesses can provide the practical influence to local-level tourism, including sustainability, though as Middleton and Hawkins (1998) point out, this is commonly ignored. Although the private sector is looked on as a

Fig. 4.2 In Quedlinburg, following German unification, the financing of building conservation has had to heavily rely on owners' own efforts and the private sector, with only limited grants available from the local government.

financial provider, the investment is based on economic gain potential. In developing countries, with reduced public funds for conservation and a competitive market-led economy, there is a wider role for the private sector, but equally the local private sector is unlikely to provide the much-needed capital. Another inside–outside dichotomy appears as the need is met by the outside investor, not only transferring benefits out of the locality, but also permitting the outsider to enter the decision-making process by virtue of holding the purse strings. Larger organisations are significantly more powerful and it is not unknown for potential investors to levy political pressure at both local and national government levels. As initiator and investor, the private sector participant also plays a significant decision-making role in identifying and appointing other decision-making participants such as architects or construction firms (Larkham 1996).

The private sector is also emerging as a service provider, especially in the West, where local government services are being sourced out to private operators, potentially introducing dynamism and buoyancy. However, the private sector will only provide the services for which there is a return, leaving less profitable services to local government.

Role of the users

The role of a user or resident, often considered under the collective identity of community or society, is more difficult to define and can be very varied. The resident community is collectively the recipient of local government services. The local government has a duty of 'delivery' to residents, and residents may or may not have the right to vote for a local governing council, but do maintain citizenship rights. At times citizens who have fought for the conservation of their towns have become alienated as the old towns are transformed into tourist attractions, with the focus on visitor, 'outsider' needs rather than those of residents. In York and

Canterbury, commercial interests and tourism have almost taken over the historic centres, both town centres having been 'saved' from development in the 1960s by residents campaigning and taking action.

Towns and cities belong to the people who live in them and must reflect their desires (Worksett 1978). Providing for both the local community *and* the tourist industry is a balance of investments. While images and facilities are being created for the visitor, residents are ignored, as planning and conservation become professional activities isolated from society. The resident community is not simply a recipient and users must be recognised as key players in shaping the future of a place. Society is not motivated by public roles, political futures or profitability, but by the desire for a better quality of life. Community action, either actively or passively, has an influence on projects and planning. The future continuity of an historic town as a living environment is only possible if the resident community is identifying with its historic and cultural values, and the development of cultural tourism, for example, must respect the cultural values of the community.

Citizen or community participation remains a favoured term, and an idea conveniently exported to the developing world, while resident communities continue to be displaced in favour of smarter city centres and community schemes give way to market forces. Today historic towns have become gentrified centres of tourist interests, where citizen participation often means the public contributing to decision making for communal spaces, or simply the availability of information

Fig. 4.3 In the absence of grant aid, and to avoid the bureaucracy associated with planning applications, citizens, as in this example from Bergama, continue to 'repair' and alter their properties, not necessarily in the best interest of historic building.

on local council activities on town hall notice boards. City authorities are not isolated from the market, and decisions are often influenced by economic gain and market pressures.

The idea that conservation and architecture concern both buildings *and* people, from the architect and the sociologist to the layman and the tenant, may be relatively new, but it is central to long-term sustainable development. There is an important role for individuals in the conservation of their environment. In conservation, it has been argued that 'attachment to historic buildings and town scales is stronger among local residents than among administrators and politicians, whose job it is to oversee environmental matters. In this sense conservation is a popular and non-establishment movement' (Butt 1988: 1). Better communication is needed, using a non-professional language which is understood by all, ensuring that everyone can identify with, and feel responsible for, the environment.

Visitors to historic towns also play a role both as users and as financial benefactors. As users of the urban environment they become recipients of the services provided, but they are not linked to city government in the way that residents are. Visitors, in choosing destinations, not only look for the best deal, but also seek quality, and visitor satisfaction is an important aspect of visitor management as it ensures the continuity of visitors to a locality.

Conflict and contradiction

The chapter has thus far identified key players in relation to conservation and tourism in historic towns and town centres. These players approach issues from a multitude of directions, priorities and agendas where at times conflicts and tension are inevitable. Common incidents of conflict occur:

- between central and local government (policy and control);
- between political and professional priorities in local government;
- between different departments of government (at national and local level);
- between the public and private sectors;
- between the local market and international operators;
- between community and local administration;
- within the community itself;
- between community and visitors.

Conflict between central and local government

The relationship between national or state governments and local government is based on central and local control of services and the distribution of tax revenue. A significant cause of conflict is financial as local administrations are dependent on national governments for the budget allocation on which the financing of initiatives depends: if revenue simply returns to central coffers, the incentive at local level is lost. On the other hand, large-scale development projects are likely to be dependent on capital funding provided by central government. Another cause of conflict between national and local administrations is one of policy and targets at national level, and priorities at local level.

Municipal boundaries, determined by central government, ascertain the extent of municipal service provision and the remit of their jurisdiction. Contradictions may arise between project areas determined at national level and actual municipal boundaries; even conservation areas at times fall into two different municipal areas. Implications are greater when development is large scale or tourism concerns are regional, such as in a national park. Where national, urban and rural authorities are involved in a project, there is room for disparity, and disagreement can arise over who controls development. Further conflicts are experienced where conservation areas are under municipal legislation, but historic buildings and listing are controlled at national level through departments of culture or antiquities. Municipal powers may be seen to be levied for redevelopment of an area at the cost of historic buildings, or national policy may be seen to be hindering development or not being responsive to local need.

Conflict arises where tourism development and promotion policy contradict principles of conservation. A locality is often dependent on national tourism promotion for attracting visitors and has little input into economic and tourist number targets being set at national level, and promotion, planning and development policy are usually imposed from the top down. Local government loses control over even environmental matters, when central legislation overpowers local initiatives. In a series of recent examples from Turkey, national legislation on Tourism Development Zones[3] has meant that special zones designated at ministerial level not only were attracting low-interest government loans for development, but also were exempt from planning legislation. This law has led to the undoing and despoliation of natural and coastal areas, which were given over to multi-storey hotel buildings, while similar structures were inserted into the historic urban fabric, including the construction of high-rise hotel developments in historic parkland and in the heart of a residential neighbourhood of Istanbul, where the scale of the surrounding traditional urban fabric and their potential environmental impact was completely ignored (Ekinci 1993).

National governments may sometimes be more damaging than helpful to local problems and lives. National policies for development with short-term results, often closely linked to election dates, can potentially overpower the interests of small communities and the economies that support them. Tourism, favoured at the national level as a source of foreign income and even as a solution to historic building conservation, holds within it the threat of displacement at local level. Therefore, the role, involvement and commitment of the local governments are perhaps the most important agent in the development process and the local citizens must be agents of conservation. In many developing countries, however, local authorities do not appear to play a significant role in the decision-making process on issues where the health, wealth and growth of old towns are concerned. Middleton and Hawkins (1998) point out that the traditional macro-level approach is too generalised and outdated for present-day realities. To be effective and sustainable, a visitor management strategy must be generated at local level.

Political and professional conflicts

Within the local administration, the highest level of decision making is by elected members. However, initial information and guidance to the members are provided and then implemented by the body of professionals employed within the council administration. Execution of local government policy and duty, meanwhile, has moved from local administration to professional autonomy, reflecting the increasingly technical complexity of the job. This predominantly professional group is apolitical but can become significantly influential in decision making.

In the case of elected local governments conflicts and power struggles are likely to arise between professional duties and political aims. Page (1995) points out that it is not that simple to identify the local government organisation responsible for urban management. Most notably, political choices are more likely to be short term, aimed at quick and visible results, depending on the power available to each post. On the other hand Corina (1975) points out that the council officers (professionals) may be selective in the options they present to elected members, though where a professional seeks a direct solution to a specific problem, the politician is more likely to opt for more global criteria or policy. Another conflict arises between the intelligence of professionals and their perception of politicians' intelligence and understanding of a situation. As elected members often depend on professional judgements to make their political choices, Corina (1975) also notes the importance of elected members understanding the decision-making process within their administrations. An elected mayor, or equally the city architect, may become a powerful decision maker, and 'political authority needs the support of strong administrative leadership' (Davey 1993: 18). The role of local government as client to the professional sector means that the professional input is more efficient, but removed from local authority objectives. Exposed to only a small section of development, professional choices may ignore other or longer-term goals, due mainly to a lack of communication.

Corruption, also a decision-making mechanism, is closely linked to governments, more often, though not exclusively, to those in developing countries. Although disruptive of sustainable objectives, corruption in many places has become an accepted part of the development process. Corruption ranges from small tips in order to complete or circumvent a tedious bureaucratic process, to the determination of land use plans to suit the interests of the ruling classes, against professional advice and often at the cost of the environment. Citizens' lack of confidence in the authorities often stems from stifling application procedures, complicated paperwork and known cases of corruption.

Conflict between government departments

The first section of this chapter listed local government departments which play a part in historic town conservation and tourism development. Each department is likely to have or be given its own agenda, policy and priorities as well as adhering to national policy and legislation issued by different government departments, and it is not surprising that conflicts arise. For example, health and safety policy or legislation will be more concerned with proper sanitation than with the safeguarding of historic property, while conservation work approved by the historic buildings department may not comply with building regulations. An obvious conflict arises between urban planning departments concerned with conservation and economic development, and tourism departments aiming to increase income potential. The major source of conflict is between tourism promotion, which views the historic town as a 'product' with an image, and conservation work responding to urban and community needs.

In the field of urban planning alone, policy planning, transport networks and listed building legislation are likely to be controlled by different players. In historic town centres, for example, policies for urban development and legislation concerning conservation areas may be contradictory. A planner responsible for a conservation area may not be aware of a city-wide transport policy; or the transport planner may not realise the level of damage caused by traffic in an historic environment. Conflicting national policies and the ignorance of local governments form a major administrative block; they may hinder the conservation process and proper planning for tourism development.

Often those entrusted with safeguarding heritage are not given sufficient legal status or leverage to carry out their mandate effectively and control conservation. This was the experience of the Zanzibar Stone Town Conservation and Development Authority in the 1980s when the piecemeal work being undertaken was uncoordinated and a lack of development control was evident as conservation work was being carried out by a complexity of departments and players, each being individually exploited by developers (Meffert 1995).

The key role of local-level administration has been stressed. In many countries the power and influence of an elected mayor are seen to be significant for development, and a well-informed cross-disciplinary vision can be highly influential in the realisation of developments. However, a powerful ego or corrupt personality could be just as damaging to the position, the outcoming development, the future of the place and the trust of the people. However, the urgent need for better coordination and collaboration between departments is apparent and can be met either through a visionary decision maker or through better communications and working arrangements, including partnerships on projects as well as in day-to-day work.

Conflicts between the public and private sectors

Traditionally the relationship between private and public sectors in urban management was seen to be one of friction, a 'them and us' attitude to the imposition of legislation against a desire to maximise profit. A breakdown in relationships is apparent when commercial developments either pull out of town centres or, on the contrary, completely take over historic town centres, dominating shop frontages with inappropriate signage for example. A lack of commitment and encouragement by the authority deters private initiatives, but an absence of professional control imposed by the authority results in the built heritage being destroyed by speculators or contractors selected on a cheapest tender basis for restoration projects. Much damage can be done in what becomes a transitionary period in the legislative framework, especially at a time of unexpected tourism growth. In Tallinn in Estonia, the loss of the once powerful city architect of Soviet times, the as yet 'unestablished' power of urban government, combined with insufficient market experience and the continuation of a bureaucratic process, have awarded power, through corruption, to the private sector, to the detriment of the old town. Jaakson (1996) notes how a McDonald's restaurant has been able to secure a prime and historically significant location within the city walls without the decision being questioned.

The public and private sectors have very different agendas and until recently they have remained distinctly apart. However, as the two spheres overlap and

Fig. 4.4 Inappropriate shop frontages in the historic core are often an outcome of private sector domination and an absence of regulatory control from the public sector (Çeşme, Turkey).

boundaries are blurred, they constitute two important players in the provision of services, development and balance of payments. Nevertheless, within the marriage is an underlying tension created by differing objectives. Also, as diverse as the local authority structure has been demonstrated to be, it is still a team with a collective identity following a certain political line, which can be governed. The private sector, on the other hand, is not a totality of parts, but a disjointed distribution of interests with no common representative.

Partnerships establish a working relationship between the two sectors. In public–private partnerships the objectives of both parties are different and the partnership needs to remain efficient and accountable, with both agendas being represented (Jewson and MacGregor 1996). The public–private partnership is regarded as a strategic question for countries entering a stage of transition to a market economy and where previously the relationship was seen only as one of conflict. In developed countries there has been a longer tradition of partnership between the public sector and private funding. The increasing collaboration of public and private sectors in urban management and in tourism development has to consider a wide range of variables very carefully, from the profits of the private sector partner to community approval and the support of public authorities. Unlike the marketing of products, the marketing of an urban environment is often the remit of government, for whom there are priorities other than achieving a financial profit.

In the case of developing countries, the private sector often does not have the necessary resources to invest in tourism. In such cases, partnership is led by the government, in the form either of incentives or of direct investment into projects, as has been the case in the early years of tourism in Turkey and India. On the other hand, in many communist countries tourism investment was solely government controlled, and a slow and sometimes painful process is under way as the private sector takes over in a field where it has little experience and any previous model was based on government subsidy. The question of state and private ownership may also play an important part in the nature of public–private partnerships. High levels of state ownership bring a different approach to conservation and the decision-making process. In post-socialist situations the question of ownership, and therefore responsibility, has at times been a hindrance to conservation.

Conflict between the local market and international operator

Josephides (1992), in referring to Corfu, describes how this most beautiful island has been made so popular by the operators and the press that its capacity has been eventually overstretched and the island overdeveloped into a downmarket holiday destination; and how the operators selling 'a dream' or 'a fashion' have eventually found it too difficult to 'sell' Corfu (Josephides 1992: 54) . The conflict is between insiders and outsiders and takes place at two levels.

The first is a cultural conflict; as culture becomes a performance, art and crafts become souvenirs. It is often a myth that tourism enhances craft traditions, because it is more often the cheap and tacky that becomes popularised alongside imitation antiques. But more important is the second, the economic conflict, initially a question of who can afford to take the risk and then of related profits. Resentment is immediately felt if the outside operator appears to be making money at the locals' expense and a quick profiteering racket follows at local level. If locals see the riches of tourism going elsewhere, they are unlikely to wait for trickle-down effects. Middleton and Hawkins (1998) point out that the international investor is rapidly followed by local entrepreneurs not wishing to miss out; these are mainly guided by quick riches rather than concern for the environment they are ruining. The perception that there is no repeat buying in many cases cheapens the product and the quality of service.

In many places, and particularly in developing countries, tourism is ruled by outside tour operators, who demand that the culture fit in with their timetables and visitor schedules. 'Tourism manipulates the tradition and customs of people to make the tourist experience more interesting and satisfying' (Negi 1990: 37). If the tourists want to see the local villagers in mud huts using primitive farming methods, that is precisely what the tour operator will demand, even if the society has changed in its lifestyle and farming methods. In many cases, events, dances, religious ceremonies and festivals are being performed purely for tourist interests, having lost their original meaning or sequence in the year. The Spanish tourist authorities have not only marketed local festivals as tourist attractions, but ultimately humiliated locals by offering to pay for performances.

'In the *realpolitik* of achieving inward investment and of earning foreign currency, however, national governments of smaller countries have little real power against multinational corporations with choices to exercise' (Middleton and Hawkins 1998: 91), while Krippendorf points out that

Fig. 4.5 A fiesta in Granada's Albaicín quarter is a local event and not merely a tourist attraction.

Efforts are being made to win back the decision-making power in essential matters rather than leaving it to outside people, companies and institutions which are mostly in the cities of industrialised nations (transfer back of decision-making process). The will of the local population to participate will not only manifest itself in the tourist areas, but also find its way back to the countries of the tourists (marketing channels).

(Krippendorf 1995: 313)

Conflicts between community and local government

In order to secure its political future, an elected local government has to command public respect determined by a 'culture of performance' and 'efficiency' of the service provided (Davey 1993). The public as resident is the user of public services and pays for the privilege through taxes, and will challenge the provider when service standards fall, there is a decline in environmental quality or when it is felt that development is not in their, the citizens' or the tax payers', interest.

In the glamour and speed of 'product' development and tourism growth, a rift appears between the community and the authority if the authority is seen to ignore local concerns. A survey in Antalya, for example, revealed quite clearly that there were significant differences between the residents' and the administrators' perceptions and attitudes towards tourism impacts and development (Korça 1993). In Sardinia a proposal to floodlight an archaeological monument was met with outrage by a nearby village still awaiting lighting for its streets (Oddermatt 1996).

Similarly, the residents of Mdina have complained that tourist streets have better lighting. In the town of Salt in Jordan, described previously, the local residents and shopkeepers of the historic town are ignored by the governing bodies in Amman, who favour an imported approach to present the town as a tourist attraction. The absence, also, of a local government and local-level decision making means that decisions concerning the town are being made externally in Amman, where Salt is being evaluated for its historic importance and tourism potential only.

Two issues need to be recognised: that the local community has to have a say in conservation issues and planning for tourism, and that local involvement in planning will actually optimise a town's development potential.

> In the deteriorating climate, outside planners and conservationists, who depend on appearance, too easily mis-perceive the concerns of the residents. Conservationists see the need for salvaging the physical heritage, the elegant but decaying façades, the wastelands and the scruffy back-yards, while the residents are concerned about jobs, sanitation, traffic and safe places for children. Cities in some cases, see the population itself as a detriment to the area, particularly new, poor and foreign immigrants.
>
> (Appleyard 1979: 30)

Wates and Knevitt (1987: 5) point out that 'The environment works better if the people who live, work and play in it are actively involved in its creation and management instead of being treated as passive consumers.'

Foremost, a local authority has to be interested in development and the potential of conservation. The aims of development planning can then combine with conservation to provide a better living environment for residents and encourage visitors, through involving the local community in the decision-making process. A local authority is the first direct contact between the local population and administrative decisions and laws governing conservation and intervention. Nevertheless, in public participation, the residents' role remains consultative and not decisive. Government grants for conservation are a luxury available only in a select number of western countries, where they are rapidly declining as a source of funding. Tourism increases awareness and provides commercial income, but not the direct cash benefit or funds to pay for the upgrading of housing. As catalysts for development, local governments can play an important role by:

- establishing a working partnership with the community;
- promoting tourism which is based on local initiatives and which benefits local interests;
- valuing and supporting planning and conservation policies that encourage investment in upgrading the houses of local residents;
- providing locally available expertise to maintain quality of conservation;
- establishing or supporting existing conservation associations.

Community: conflict within

The ruling classes control and impose their own socio-cultural values on the past. An internal tension of ideology and power relations arises, over the qualities of place and representations of heritage. Each section or class of society has different links, identifications and associations with history and the environment. A so-called reclamation, more commonly known as gentrification, of an area by the middle classes is likely to remove a later layer of history and identification with an immigrant population maybe, to 'return' to an idealised one based on the cultural values of decision makers or influential classes. As historic town centres become gentrified, the middle classes are seen at the forefront of heritage interpretation. Although public interest and pressure groups continue to play a very effective role in challenging decision making, through campaigning or by imposing pressure on national and local authorities, citizens' groups often constitute, and therefore represent, the views of a minority of educated people, at times members of quasi-political groups, and they do not always express the ideas and thoughts of the majority.

Another source of tension between owners, landlords and tenants is tenure. In an upgrading programme where property owners in a district benefit from the works, tenants invariably lose their accommodation as higher rents are demanded for the improved properties. As tourism takes over an old quarter, it is the tenants who are first to be displaced. Especially in projects that directly involve willing residents and existing social organisations and which depend on local skills, it is important to recognise that occupants who have contributed to the process will need the security of a long-term rent tenure for the process to which they are contributing to benefit them.

Fig. 4.6 This guest house, located in a residential neighbourhood in Bergama, may be a local entrepreneurial activity, but infringes on what is deemed to be a 'private' street by local residents.

Conflicts between community and visitors

Most tension with tourism in historic towns results from overcrowding, increasing prices and the crossing of cultural boundaries. The local response to tourism is going to reflect social, cultural and economic factors. While residents often start off by being hospitable and welcoming towards visitors, once there is a feeling that their hospitality is being exploited by operators and excessive numbers, and that their privacy and lifestyle are being invaded, hostility sets in and tourists are seen purely as an element of economic gain. Boissevain (1996) is concerned that cultural tourism can be even more demanding when locals are perceived as part of the sought-after culture, and greater tensions are created as tourists cross thresholds and boundaries in search of a 'culture' they have paid for. A response from residents may start off as silent resistance, but can build up into organised protest, as was the experience of Bruges in the early 1990s for example, and finally to aggression.

In the tourism marketplace, the visitor represents the demand, where the supply side involves the residents' interests, and the lifestyle of the resident may even be the primary attraction to the visitor. The host and guest analogy of resident and tourist in historic towns often ignores the simple fact that while guests have chosen to visit a location, the so-called host has not necessarily made the choice of hosting. Second, the guest is at leisure, at a time when the host is working, including in jobs which involve servicing the guest. Cultural differences, rich–poor divides and differing attitudes create conflict and eventually lead to the common two-way

Fig. 4.7 Understanding local life and priorities is essential before developing a tourist product (Simla, India).

perception of tourists abusing locals and locals cheating tourists. The notion that Western tourists are rich results in price increases or double pricing as tourists become dehumanised objects of economic gain and any social interaction between the host and the guest is likely to be lost. In the West, where the guest and the host share similar cultural and economic backgrounds, the leisure experience is more easy to share and tourism developments frequently also serve local needs. The local lifestyle of the Mediterranean, for example, involves whiling away time in outdoor cafes.

Extreme but increasingly common occurrences in poorer economies of people being moved away from their livelihoods for tourism have serious social and economic consequences for their community. Tourists at leisure in Caribbean or similar 'paradise' resorts are often unaware of a fishing community which has been displaced from their 'exclusive' beach. A commercial balance between local interests and tourist interests needs to be maintained. The hostility of the host is also a conflict with the local administration, which is seen to encourage tourism at the locals' expense. Eventually overcrowding and elevated prices not only marginalise locals but also deter tourists.

Conflicts of accountability

In a scenario where a professional is appointed and thus employed by the local administration for the implementation of a project, the work is overseen, controlled and possibly managed by a local administration representative, reporting back to a department which is guided by policy and political preference. A complex relationship emerges: the professional is only directly accountable to the local authority as employer while the authority, through commissioning the service from the professional, is providing the community with a service it is contracted to provide. The community is the recipient or beneficiary and not the client, and only in the longer term may it express support or concern through voting for or against elected council members.

In another scenario, a visitor purchases a holiday from a local or national agent. The purchase is for travel to a destination, accommodation and possibly an element of service at the destination; but, contrary to common perception, no purchase actually concerning the destination has been made. Complaints on accommodation standards can be directed to a hotel manager and likewise to a transport provider and ultimately to the agent from whom the purchase is made, as all have a direct and defined contract with the customer, though in the global travel marketplace, the buyer is often ignorant of the ownership of the purchase. The city as a destination is party to no direct agreement with the visitor and therefore it is not directly responsible for the visitors' experience, but depends on the satisfaction of the visitor to improve and sustain the 'product'.

Political accountability is achieved through votes; it is not direct and it varies according to electoral systems. Municipal government is more open to corruption but also more exposed than central government is, but accountability can become very narrow and linear. A professional undertaking work for a local council is accountable to the commissioning department, the department to the elected committee and they, through the political interface, to their electorate. A funder, by virtue of providing otherwise unavailable investment, will make demands on local government which must be fulfilled before development commences. This typically may be a scenario from a corrupt underdeveloped economy, but it has also been the experience of authorities in Florida and Paris with the Disney Corporation (Ghirardo 1996).

Summary and conclusions

The urban 'product' does not have a single owner; there are many owners, users and claimants to urban space, linked or conflicting through a complexity of relations. A town or city is only ever managed in part and key players emerge from these ownership and management patterns. The local administration remains in an important position of being the representative of all interests. The role of the state is to break the boundaries for trans-regional and multi-level cultural policy. Most important for policy and understanding is to encompass both conservation *and* tourism.

The total cast of players is in a variety of roles, from a wide range of disciplines and backgrounds, with at times conflicting interests, agendas and accountability structures. One of the main conflicts arises because tourism and heritage are regulated by different government departments, controlled by different local government sections and administered by different professional fields, none of which traditionally work together. Heritage can enrich the lived-in environment, as long as a delicate balance is reached between tourism development and conservation priorities. Success will depend on attitude, support and investment from the local governing powers, private and public initiatives and the industry at large. The following case study on Antalya examines the failure of the decision-making mechanism in safeguarding the old town.

The task of successfully managing the urban resources, built, natural and human, has to depend on a collaborative model and new ways of thinking and of breaking boundaries of decision making through:

- more local-level decision making;
- strategic thinking;
- partnerships;
- an active role for the community in decision making.

The next two chapters analyse the planning process and the management of tourism in historic towns.

Notes

1 For example, tourism finances accounted for 40 per cent of Kenya's and 34 per cent of Nepal's export earnings in 1988 (Erlet 1991: 2).

2 The exception is the United States, where private initiatives are highly influential in determining cultural policy.

3 Tourism Development Zones, introduced under Tourism Promotion Legislation (Turizm Teşvik Yasası) of 1982, were intended to promote tourism investment. An area, once designated a Development Zone, was exempt from planning legislation and furthermore the owner benefited from tax relief (Ekinci 1993).

Case study
The old town
of Antalya, Turkey

In Antalya, situated on Turkey's Mediterranean coast, urban conservation has become a victim of tourism and associated commercial growth, whereas it began as a response to a growth in tourism.

The place

The known history of Antalya dates from the second century BC; it was an important military and trading port under the Kingdom of Pergamum, and thereafter under Roman rule from the first century BC, and it is to this latter period that most of the earlier architectural heritage is due. Following a period of decline it was revived under the Seljuk Turks in the twelfth century, when a breakwater, dockyard and quay were built. By the fifteenth century it had became an Ottoman port town with a predominantly Turkish and Greek population alongside a small Jewish and Armenian community. Following a more turbulent period at the start of the twentieth century with the two-year Italian occupation from 1919 and with the declaration of the Turkish Republic in 1923, the Greek population was exchanged for Turkish immigrants from Greece.

Today Antalya remains an important port, but it is also the tourist hub of Turkey's southern coast, with its international airport, close proximity to favourable beaches and location within an area of historic antiquity. The city has experienced rapid urban growth since the 1960s and high-rise concrete buildings have surrounded the historic core, and as with most developments of the period, serious traffic and infrastructure problems have followed. The city walls and the designation of Conservation Area status in 1973 were able to protect the old town from this ensuing development, while the old harbour had long since been replaced by a modern port further along the coast.

The walled town is located above the old harbour, connecting through with steep and narrow streets, while the grander mansions sit proud above the harbour walls commanding some of the most desirable views. At its north and east sides, the walled town connects to the main thoroughfare of the modern city through several city gates, including a Roman portico, highlighting the earlier origins of the area and the city walls. The extremely hot summers are counteracted in the old quarter

(a)

(b)

Fig. 1 (a) and (b) The lack of sufficient control or enforcement has resulted in many timber-framed buildings being replaced by so-called 'replica' concrete ones serving the needs of the new owners. This new architecture is pastiche rather than historic, and has developed at the expense of the genuine built heritage.

through streets shaded by overhanging projections, inner courtyards and terraces (sofa) capturing the sea breezes – in stark contrast to the overheated concrete apartment blocks lining the causeways of the modern city.

Conservation and tourism

The old town of Antalya is an early example of conservation planning; the project launched in 1973 was also one of the earliest tourism development projects in Turkey and the first to consider an historic urban area of this scale. The project involved the rehabilitation of the redundant harbour to create a marina complex and recreational area, and the restoration of some of the larger houses forming the 'backdrop' to the harbour, for use as guest accommodation, with a future objective of supporting building conservation in the residential neighbourhoods. In 1977 the harbour and old town scheme was incorporated into the Antalya Tourism Development Project,[1] which aimed to provide high levels of infrastructure and control over tourist facilities. Conservation in the harbour and old town has been clearly influenced by tourism growth, and much of the outcome has been the result of tourism-centred decision making.

The first-phase plan was initiated by the Ministry of Culture and Tourism and funded by the Tourism Bank. A team of seven architects and planners was appointed to the project, and with the backing of the Bank the project was quickly completed. A new infrastructure was provided for the 5.5-hectare area and the harbour was developed into a marina, allowing space for local fishing boats as well. Derelict buildings were converted into shops, cafes and restaurants while a four-storey warehouse was converted into a medium-sized hotel, run by the Tourism Bank. The harbour area was landscaped and an open-air amphitheatre was created to encourage cultural activity. Restaurants and outdoor cafes catered for a capacity of 4,000 people, and parking space was provided at the harbour entrance (Bilgen 1988). A total of US$4.5 million was spent on the first phase, including the infrastructure, but this was balanced against rental income from the shops and the hotel[2] (Güney *et al.* 1986). Critics praised the project and it was awarded a Sedat Simavi award for Architecture and Urban Design, and a Golden Apple by the International Federation of Tourism Journalists (FIJET). Observations at the time included the following:

The architects responsible for the restoration acted sensibly, without 'fanfare'.

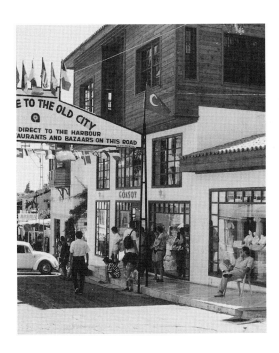

Fig. 2 The old town of Antalya has become a shoppers' 'paradise' and retains very few of the qualities that made it a 'neighbourhood'.

They did not beautify, but did prefer a direct expression of local tradition. For the first time in Turkey a comparatively large site of conservation has been restored and renovated.

(Kuban 1985: 54)

Another prominent architect, Cengiz Bektaş (1992), on the other hand, commented that from a social point of view the harbour, which was part of the everyday life of the city, had become an exclusive upmarket area. Cafes that replaced the local tea houses were too expensive for the residents, particularly the lower-income groups living nearby or the fishermen who had always used the harbour.

The harbour opened in 1985, a period of rapid growth in mass tourism in Turkey, with the market gaining confidence after a period of military rule and a national political agenda aimed at seriously increasing tourism capacity. Tourism revenue in 1985 had more than tripled since 1983 and in Antalya the 25,000-bed target of 1977 had more than doubled to 66,000 by 1992, turning it into yet another 'concrete coast' with insufficient infrastructure.[3]

Following the harbour development, the planned second phase of the project was to assist residents in restoring and rehabilitating their houses. However, in 1985 the conservation funding to the project was stopped, and even more dramatically the professional team was dispersed in 1989. By this time only the occasional house had been converted into a guest house (pension) or a shop. The area remained a predominantly residential neighbourhood with friendly inhabitants and children playing on the streets, but many of the houses were in need of repair and several had been poorly restored. The disregard of established intentions and the absence of a professional team in the late 1980s had serious implications for the future development of the old town. Kuban commented that the strength of the project lay in the fact 'that those responsible for the project were also given full control of its implementation' (Kuban 1985: 54). Although the original town plan had aimed at keeping 75 per cent of the old town residential, this was ignored and with the withdrawal of control, properties were being haphazardly and poorly 'restored' or rebuilt as concrete so-called 'replicas' for use as guest houses, restaurants and shops (Mercangöz 1991).

The evaluation of the planning phase shows an enlightened commissioner and a sustainable approach, most notably by:

- employing a multi-disciplinary professional team of architects, planners and economists;
- sound financial planning with finances secured for the harbour and income generated targeted for further improvements and to support conservation in the residential areas;
- professional and sensitive conservation and development in principle and in implementation setting a good practice example;
- showing consideration for the local community.

The five-year period between 1985 and 1990 saw a flurry of activity in the old town, which not only was contrary to the objectives of the project but irreversibly destroyed the old town and displaced its resident community. Today, the area has been transformed beyond recognition, in a rapid and uncontrolled conversion into pensions, bars, restaurants and carpet shops, with poor-quality and insensitive alterations, the peace replaced by shopkeepers shouting out to attract tourists, while local establishments like the bakeries and tea houses have altogether disappeared.

Conflicts in decision making

The growth of commercialism in the old town reflects the growth of tourism in the region and is a blatant reflection of commercial pressure in a market economy. The commercial pressure is not, however, from a multinational organisation, levering favours at national level, but a series of small, independent establishments which have been able to convert houses into shops and restaurants and have been allowed to rebuild historic properties in reinforced concrete. It is not simply a commercial issue and there are a number of reasons, including:

- conflicts between national policy for rapid tourism growth (mass tourism), regional policy for infrastructure works and local development objectives for the renewal of the harbour and the old town;
- conflicts between local-level growth objectives and national development targets;
- a loss of communication between political decision making and professional advice;
- the power of commercial pressures over planning objectives and architectural integrity;
- short-term political decision making ignorant of long-term development and sustainability targets (possibly in alliance with national-level political objectives);

- the exploitation of loopholes in planning and conservation legislation;
- the failure of local-level planning and land use control, including the absence of an established control mechanism to deal with the volume of change, and probably pressures from political powers;
- corruption at various levels.

Antalya illustrates both the importance of the control mechanism in planning for future sustainability, and the power of the market. In a period as short as ten years the entire neighbourhood has been transformed into a tourist shopping 'experience'. The people who made the historic quarter a living environment have left and a relatively well-preserved heritage asset has been destroyed. Furthermore, the piecemeal nature of the development has meant that the existing infrastructure is unable to cope with the new uses and imposed capacity, while a rapid rise in the provision of bed spaces in the immediate region has reduced the demand for accommodation in the old town. The built heritage and good-quality architecture has been lost, as has the urban quality in what has become a 'quaint' concrete jungle. The harbour has also been subsequently overdeveloped, losing the 'quality' that had set it apart. Tourist perception of the area is poor and cultural understanding even poorer.

Unfortunately, Antalya is not an isolated example and the significant growth of coastal tourism in Turkey from the 1980s has had similar impacts on numerous coastal historic towns. But whereas in many Turkish coastal towns unplanned and unregulated developments have overwhelmed small coastal towns and fishing communities, Antalya had had the opportunity and foresight for success.

Notes

1 A masterplan approach following the designation of Tourism Development Regions to 'absorb mass tourism' in 1969 (ECE 1976).
2 The rental income from the thirty-six shops provided US$30,000 a year with a further US$350,000 annual contribution from the hotel, which had cost a total of US$500,000 to restore and refurbish (Güney *et al.* 1986).
3 Figures from the Turkish Statistical Institute.

5 Planning for tourism in historic towns

Introduction

Tourism may be regarded as an environmental and social imposition, an accepted reality or an economic opportunity. Tourists have the potential to benefit a place, and also the destructive potential to ruin it. Whatever the opportunities it offers, some truisms of the tourism industry must also be considered: the first is the well-established fact that tourism is volatile, unstable by nature, fashion driven and plagued by political conflict, natural disaster and perceptions of security. Second, tourism is a consumer of natural environments, historic buildings, urban spaces and local culture, all of which, once they have been spoilt by overcrowding and overdevelopment, face the danger of being abandoned in favour of fresh and unspoilt destinations. A common cycle occurs in tourism: from discovery of a destination to subsequent tourism development; success, followed all too often by oversupply and overcrowding, 'visit it before it sinks' (Venice) or 'visit it before it is spoilt' (Dubrovnik) attitudes, and a lower and less profitable class of tourist taking advantage of the lower prices of oversupply. Not only parts of the Spanish coast, but entire islands have been consumed and reduced to nothing while their communities are left with few alternatives for their livelihood. There is a delicate balance between sustaining environmental quality and maximising tourism potential and benefit.

For the tourism industry historic towns are a consumer product, often identified as an image – a product, which nevertheless continues to be a living environment for a resident community as part of a larger urban mechanism and a complexity of spatial relations. Society is a socio-geographical group responsible for the existence of a town or part of a wider social, cultural and economic system (Conzen 1981), and urban morphology is a functional response to the requirements of a user society. The dichotomy of city as object (a consumable product) and city as subject (place of living) also represents the objective views of planning and the subjective views of society.

In the historic environment the decision-making process highlights a dichotomy of insider and outsider. The outsider is concerned predominantly with developing a product to respond to the market (potential visitors) while the insider is more concerned with place, locality and community. The dichotomy, however, is one of outlook and perception rather than one of the position or location of the decision maker. The energy of tourism, which can destroy a place, can also feed development and ensure continuity if it is properly channelled; this can be achieved through planning, management and creative intervention. This chapter evaluates the process of tourism planning and the objectives of marketing for historic towns. There are three basic components to the approach: the first is an understanding of the place and its needs, in the case of historic towns not only their spatial and morphological qualities, but also the community and the conservation process; the second is the projection of a place to a targeted visitor market; the third is planning for tourism, which encompasses the common objectives of long-term sustainable growth, maximising local income and achieving cultural continuity.

This chapter considers the following questions:

- How can tourism benefit urban development?
- What is the role of marketing?
- How can planning contribute to sustainable tourism development in historic towns?

Historic towns: conservation and tourism

The tourist-historic town

The tourist-historic town has emerged as conservation and tourism growth have started to take shape concurrently and tourism has become a major economic factor for historic towns. The growth and development of tourism are different for each town, as are the development and pace of urban conservation, and several scenarios can be discussed, based on variables of location, physical attributes, associated benefits, and key roles in developmental, economic and managerial decision making; the scenarios include:

1 Recognised and well-known historic towns where conservation is established, as are tourist interests. The visitor management need is immediate and there may already be resident unrest caused by the impacts of volume tourism. Planning aims to sustain the quality and attraction of the environment, and at times increase the attraction base to remain competitive in the market. The focus of planning is the improvement and maintenance of quality for residents and visitors.
2 Historic towns that are new to the tourism market where there is still a noticeable need for conservation and an increasing interest from tourism. Tourism and associated commercialism are likely to be leading conservation, and urban management has to cope with often unexpected pressures. Planning involves the demanding task of balancing the development of a successful tourism base with good-quality conservation. Planning is faced with a number of competing demands and even contradictory objectives.

3   Towns not known on the market, developing a previously little known historic
    area, industrial heritage or a history of association into a tourist attraction.
    The emphasis is on product development, planning for tourism and marketing
    the place-product. Pressures for management are secondary, and heritage re-
    creation may be considered more important than conservation. The objective
    of planning is to develop a market value for the place to aid regeneration.

Fig. 5.1 The main issue for Bruges authorities today is coping with the thousands of tourists descending on the town each year, attracted by the medieval architecture and waterways of the old town.

Fig. 5.2 Prague has had to cope with a sudden growth of tourism, especially as everyone wanted to see it before it was spoilt or became too expensive.

Fig. 5.3 For Quedlinburg authorities, attracting more visitors is seen as a means for reversing a downward economic trend.

The role of conservation

In historic towns urban conservation is often closely linked to the planning process, but with tourism development, conservation can take on a new product-led dimension. The previous chapters have outlined a West European approach to conservation in historic quarters where 'technically' balanced intervention and facade preservations have created favourable settings for tourism and shopping, but have alienated local communities and users. Urban conservation, in connection with the growing influence of tourism, is resulting in:

- gentrification of residential areas and shopping facilities;
- local alienation or feelings of loss of privacy;
- loss of community spirit;
- changes to urban space use, physical urban pattern and subsequently urban character;
- a freezing-in-time approach and a re-creation of past times, compromising the continuity of the urban environment.

The integration of conservation with tourism has been such that tourism is no longer an outcome of conservation but conservation is increasingly a product of tourism, resulting in:

- a hurried attempt to re-create or even invent history;
- facadism and 'pastiche' streetscape re-creation;
- over-sanitisation of both history and the life of a town;
- theming.

Thorough yet sensitive urban conservation as prescribed by international charter is only realistically possible in a select number of western developed countries.

For much of the world's historic towns it is either impossible to achieve or, more frequently, not desirable. Urban values and associations, and the character hidden in urban life often conflict with the 'sanitarian' ideals of urban conservation. It has been argued that an 'idealised' western model of conservation may not necessarily be relevant to non-European cultures or developing economies where:

- sufficient funds and commitment are not available for urban conservation;
- political preferences and even corruption are unavoidable and can play a significant part in conservation and planning decisions;
- inhabitants are often unaware of 'historic value', but desire better living conditions, modern amenities and services;
- historic value may not be regarded with the same 'object'-based values as apply in the West.

When the predominant objective of conservation is tourism development, it is in danger of becoming a superficial exercise devoid of cultural significance. Dilapidated and previously ignored historic quarters, gaining new value as assets, are hastily restored, done up or reduced to a series of pleasing facades with the prospect of commercial gain. The uncontrolled pace of this development has at times been sufficient to render the historic environment a worthless victim of commercial exploitation, as has been the experience of Antalya. The achievement of conservation and environmental objectives is integral to sustainable tourism development.

Heritage tourism involves place politics. Local distinctiveness is easily lost as planning policy sets out to differentiate, but implementation continues to side with the 'tried and tested', resulting in familiar results and the growing homogeneity of historic towns. 'The organisation of history in tourist settings transforms the cultural and historical life of communities and, hence, transforms place itself' (M.C. Hall 1997: 96). Even sanitisation may lead to the irrecoverable loss of distinctiveness. When a fishing village sea-front is tidied up into a promenade, the 'smelly' fishing activity is removed, rendering both livelihood and the 'authentic' redundant; yet the same feature is used to portray a romanticised image to the market, as in the case of the 'fishing' village of Kalkan in Turkey.

Urban conservation is fundamentally based on an understanding of a place, not only its spatial and morphological qualities, but also its community values. Feilden (1990) proclaims that civilising the city is about enhancing the quality of life of its citizens, and 'if a city is civilised for its own citizens it is more likely to get the right sort of tourists, and tourism should benefit the local people rather than international chains of hotels' (Feilden 1990: 14). 'Tourism is not called an industry by accident. Like steel and computers, it needs management, capital investment, manpower training and all the other activities associated with a major, competitive industry' (Turner and Ash 1975: 113). And like any other industry in an urban situation, it should be treated and evaluated as part of the economic and physical development process, notwithstanding environmental impacts and pollutants.

The process of understanding a place is one of looking, thinking and doing – surveying, planning and implementing for the professional planner. Insall (1999) advocates the importance of being imaginative at the thinking stage and picking up on opportunities to arrive at solutions. He also advises looking at the whole and then at the specific, in both space and in time. A comprehensive checklist for information gathering in an historic town should include:

- an inventory or database of historic buildings, their attributes and qualities;
- a classification of streetscape, morphology and understanding of open spaces and their uses;
- a condition survey of buildings (including a realistic evaluation of repair needs and costs);
- a survey of redundancy, reuse and reuse potential;
- an access and movement survey within the urban environment;
- a transportation survey.

An understanding of the present, then, has to be built upon with a forecast for the future in order to inform long-term planning. Simulation is a favoured tool of the planner, but as Floyd (1984) points out, urban growth and decay are not simply dependent on simulated models and may just as well be perceived through observation.

The financing of urban conservation

Securing a future for historic buildings is dependent on securing funds to enable their conservation. The historic towns conservation movement in Western Europe depended heavily on substantial government-generated budgets and urban grant funding. It was reported in 1990 that the annual conservation budget directly available to Edinburgh Council was £900,000 a year, part of which was made available in grants for the restoration of buildings and environments (Duncan 1990). In other examples subsidies were made available by socialist governments (Bulgaria) and directly by local authorities (Bologna). However, the completion of large-scale area-based conservation projects in recognised historic towns, the consequent refocusing of funding and the development of 'historic' towns new to the market have seen a shift in the way urban projects are being financed. Even historic towns in developed countries, once supported by generous government grants, are now facing cuts to their budgets. In England the Town Schemes funding for area-based conservation, begun in 1975, was discontinued from 1999. In latter-day examples, with reduced grant funding, the consumer-motivated approach to conservation has become more common, as has been shown by the regeneration in Dresden following German reunification.

The finance provider has clear objectives linked to the control of planning direction and implementation. Financial resources for historic town conservation are wide ranging, depending on the objectives of the funder:

1 Funding of heritage for historic value: specifically for the preservation or restoration of a recognised cultural object, a World Heritage Site for example. The objective of funding is clearly the safeguarding of cultural heritage, recognised as being of national or international significance. The source ranges from central government to an international donor.
2 Funding of heritage for regeneration: in recognition of the role of cultural heritage in area-based rehabilitation. The objective of funding is to support

regeneration and the source could be national regeneration budgets, public–private partnerships or international development aid.

3 Funding of heritage for economic development: a conscious use of urban heritage to develop cultural and tourism activity for income generation. The objective of funding is economic development. The sources of funding are various, including partnerships, local authority initiatives, the private sector and international investors.

4 Funding of heritage as a specific target for tourism: the use of cultural object purely for the purpose of tourism development. The object is profit, and funding is often from the private sector and externally generated.

The availability of finance for the preservation of national heritage, or heritage that is recognised as being universally significant, has a well-established precedent, and international funding in the twentieth century has frequently focused on major monuments and sites. Following conflicts in the 1990s, international aid was immediately available for the repair of the burnt-out library of Sarajevo and the war-damaged monasteries and paintings of Dubrovnik; but less was forthcoming for community-based projects and rebuilding the urban fabric. Part of the reason is the imagery attached to a major monument and the visual credit it will provide for the donor. Such is donor politics. Participants at a conference on reconstruction held in Dubrovnik in 1994, in the aftermath of the war, complained that much more rebuilding aid was directed to 'prestigious' and visually recognisable Dubrovnik than their relatively unknown inland towns.

Unlike their affluent counterparts, developing countries depend heavily on international organisations such as UNESCO, the World Bank and other agency funding to finance urban conservation and they depend on external loans or international investors to develop their cultural tourism markets. Yemeni authorities

Fig. 5.4 No sooner was the conflict over than scaffolding surrounded the monasteries of Dubrovnik, in projects made possible through international aid. The urban fabric, on the other hand, depended more on tourism growth before repair works could begin.

have shared the cost of rehabilitation in Old Sana'a with UNESCO, UNDP and several foreign (developed) country donors (al-Asad and Serageldin 1997), while the rehabilitation work in the Medina of Tunis has depended on a World Bank loan to support the government contribution; and work in the old quarter of Fez has been supported by UNESCO. Poor bookkeeping, uncoordinated projects and an absence of legal status, however, deterred potential outside funders in early attempts at the conservation of Zanzibar Stone Town.

The use of cultural heritage as a tool for regeneration is a more recent concept and a newer approach to development planning. The built environment, as property and commodity, is a resource (Lichfield 1988) which can serve tourism development, while income generated through tourism is potentially a resource for the conservation of historic buildings. In area-based conservation, tourism may not contribute directly to the balance of payments, but the upgrading of an area increases the economic base for future work and maintenance. Conservation funding must be towards long-term objectives and to the benefit of local interests. Investment through short-term but intensive funding must allow for future costs such as maintenance and obsolescence, particularly for technology-dependent projects.

The financing of area-based conservation is complex and will always be the domain of competing interests, not all of which can be regulated through the planning process. Developing tourism not only is dependent on townscape improvements and conservation but may necessitate heavy infrastructure provision. For example, a new transport interchange is a capital-heavy investment, with no direct return to a single funder, but it is potentially a long-term investment providing better mobility and improved communication, benefiting not only tourism but residents and other businesses in the region.

Private sector financing is increasingly essential for development but the power base created from private sector domination can be damaging as the authorities' role in development control is challenged. The increasing effect and power of the private sector in funding are apparent in East European historic towns which are suddenly facing the full impact of tourism and the loosening of controls. On the other hand, conflicts also arise when development control is seen to limit competition. While international aid helped restore post-war Dubrovnik to its former beauty, international investment in the form of hotel chains was seen at the forefront of reviving tourism. The opportunity for outside investment nevertheless lessened the sustainable development objectives which had been foreseen for future tourism in the immediate aftermath of the war.

Internal and external sources of funding have implications for the insider–outsider decision-making dichotomy. An 'outside' funder or funding organisation will invariably impose its control over projects, including the allocation and distribution of funds according to its priorities. While control of spending is necessary for the best use of agency sources, the level of control or the chosen direction of the awarding body may overshadow local planning objectives and long-term goals.

Sources and reasons behind the financing of historic building conservation are not mutually exclusive and are more likely to contribute to the conservation of an urban area simultaneously. However, the spreading of financial resourcing enables diversity and allows the local planning authorities better control. The underlying question is: 'Is tourism an effective avenue for conservation-led regeneration?' If it is, the realities must first be considered: first, that there is only limited funding available for the desirable conservation of historic urban fabric, and second, that tourism is increasingly becoming a significant alternative for urban economies. Conservation in the urban environment cannot be a museum setting to fulfil visitor desires and it must remain independent from financial direction, but at the same time there are also lessons to be learnt from towns where conservation took place well before the influences of tourism, but which were subsequently not only over-whelmed by the pressures of tourism but turned into museums as a result of it.

Urban planning and tourism

Ashworth (1989) points out that 'in 60 years of urban space modelling tourism is ignored' (quoted in Murphy 1997). Within the ongoing process of spatial planning, tourism is more likely to become an issue once a market has been developed and pressures are being felt rather than it having been forecast into early planning stages. Increasingly, conservation becomes the interface between physical planning and tourism.

> In modern society the variety of functional claims on the use of land, even that of the most basic ones, is great and many of them tend to conflict. Optimum success in spatial planning means an overall maximum fulfilment of these claims not as separate elements but as a complex.
>
> (Conzen 1981: 59)

As a spatial system, each town is a unique, 'open functional systems in space, albeit oriented towards, and dominated by, the needs of human society as these develop and change through time' (Conzen 1981: 77). The complex structure contained within the framework of a town plan includes the systematic distribution of building fabric and land use allocation and the dynamism of spatial relations between spaces and historical development. While research can identify the resource base, planning concerns itself with the utilisation and management of resources, community being an equally important resource for tourism (Murphy 1997). In tourism, forward planning assesses the level of new facilities likely to be needed, uses spatial models for development, evaluates empty and redundant sites and their best use for future development, and must consider the physical and cultural impacts of any intervention.

The knowledge and understanding of the resource are the basis for any planning intervention. Research creates the basis for the establishment of objectives, and both research and forecasting are used to test objectives. Setting objectives for tourism development is about establishing a delicate balance between environmental, socio-cultural and economic interests. The aim must be for sensitive development and an appropriate rate of growth for the improvement of the environment as a place to live in, work in and visit. Objectives for tourism planning in historic towns should be, among others:

- to ensure long-term benefits and sustainability of the tourism activity, while encouraging continuity in the urban environment;

- to develop and maintain a high-quality product;
- to develop a sustainable base for tourism growth;
- to market the product to the 'right' market effectively;
- to maximise benefits and minimise impacts through competent management.

Planning for the historic environment involves a number of different managers, each with a given set of objectives and a brief to work out ways and alternatives to achieve these objectives in a given time period (Lichfield 1988). Tourism planning objectives also differ according to the sector from which they originate: the politician-led targets of economic growth and increased foreign currency, the industry-based approach seeks direct economic gain, whereas the physical, spatial and land use approach looks to physical problem solving and finally to the interests of the user community. Ultimately, however, urban culture and heritage are being promoted, packaged and sold to the tourist as a 'product'.

Developing the historic town market

Marketing the historic town

The concept of marketing is relatively new to tourism, yet destination marketing has become the central force in the growth of the industry as destinations and service providers compete for a share of the market. Marketing involves an existing product or service which buyers are willing to pay for and sellers eager to trade (Laws 1995) – a balance of consumer satisfaction and profit, and of demand and supply. Destination marketers are in the business of attracting a sufficient number of visitors to provide for the economic demand. But unlike with most other products, over-promotion of a tourist destination results directly in environmental and social consequences.

The destination, or place-product (see also Ashworth and Voogd 1990), differs significantly from the goods and services for which modern-day marketing has been developed. The urban resource has more complex attributes and also limitations when subjected to the known concepts and theories of marketing. Unlike with most products, the purchaser (the visitor) does not see or experience the product beforehand and is simply buying a desired satisfaction at an acceptable destination (Bodlender and Lickorish 1991). A truism of the tourism market is that it is fragmented, complex and continuously evolving; customer loyalty cannot be depended on as repeat buying is rare, and the desire for new experiences will always be focused on the next and 'different' experience or destination. The sellable product is perishable in the short term; if a bed is not sold for the night it is lost as a resource.

The concept of product development is also difficult to apply to a complex urban environment, as it is only limited features or qualities that are actually being marketed, and furthermore urban cultural heritage encompasses not only the built heritage but also human activity (Lichfield 1988). Marketing uses heritage for economic and political purposes. Both the cultural asset and the inherent depth of historic towns are being overlooked when, as a product, they are simplified to become historic fabric, street patterns and selected history. The urban totality cannot be portrayed to the visitor, and expectations have to rely on the images and words which have been chosen to describe a place.

Defining the historic town 'product'

Tourism is selling a product, a destination and an associated service. The definition of the 'product', possibly more tangible in the case of a resort, is difficult to define in the complex and broad context of the urban environment. The key question lies in the ownership of the product, as it does with the ownership of heritage. The urban environment is the resource from which a product is developed, and the interpretation of place resources and the quality of the experience become the product (Page 1995; Bodlender and Lickorish 1991).

Market planning involves an understanding of the locality, informing its potential for tourism development and its place in the global tourist marketplace. Promotion is frequently seen as a national concern, where a place is formulated into a 'representative' image among many. 'Defining the image of an area is important to those who have to promote and sell the area for reasons of tourism business, but it is also important in attracting business investment across the board' (Fisher 1994: 147). Both the existing and the potential market are based on the product, defined through research with both its attributes and its recognised limitations.

Visitor and wider tourist pattern evaluation depends on the effective use and accuracy of both quantitative and qualitative data and observation. Destination-based assessment and information gathering in the tourism market to date remain elementary, and furthermore the images and perceptions of the visitor, along with fashions, are likely to alter frequently. Attempting to develop sustainable strategies for tourism without adequate management information reduces the process to political aspiration and guesswork (Middleton and Hawkins 1998: 82).

Meanwhile, a duality emerges between the historical attributes and cultural depths of a place and the market-research, product-based approach.

> The cultural pursuit has much to offer from rigour of scholarship and truthful heritage interpretation, but this must be balanced with the skills of the private operator who knows how to turn ideas into products with public appeal and how to market these effectively.
>
> (Fladmark 1994: xiv)

Sound market research is imperative for effective tourism planning when outcomes are accurately deployed in the development of both a tourism strategy and planning objectives. However, research, for an active and ongoing situation, must not be isolated from the present, and the development of an urban product for marketing purposes should be based on:

- a sound knowledge of urban morphology and spatial characteristics;
- an understanding of the existing users of the place and their needs;
- a realistic definition of the historic town as place, and only subsequently as a product or 'attraction';
- market research on the existing market and the potential of the future market;
- a SWOT (strengths, weaknesses, opportunities and threats) analysis.

An initial appraisal of the tourism potential of a place often uses a SWOT analysis, a commonly recommended planning tool for tourism development (Ashworth and

Larkham 1994; Dietvorst 1994; Page 1995) and also for the development of a place image (Laws 1995; Page 1995). The identification of the strengths, weaknesses, opportunities and threats is an important first step for marketing. While a useful appraisal method, a SWOT analysis does not, however, have the strength to be the only guide to product development. It contributes to projecting an image for the place, yet it is easy for chosen responses to be selective, at times ignoring the dynamics of the urban environment and the community.

Unlike a fabricated product, a town or city is a composite and complex resource, yet as a destination product, a place is marketed through a series of selected images: the canals of Amsterdam or the spires of Oxford for example. Marketing relies heavily on an image that will sell a product to a target market. Often only a single image or a few words are employed to depict an urban environment to conjure up a collective image, which is likely to be determined at national level. Furthermore, communicating the image to the chosen and desired market involves the use of language and interpretation that are going to be familiar to the recipient, portraying therefore the guest's image of culture and society, rather than the actual or the local's own identification with a place. In a desire to project a recognisable or familiar image, the product becomes globalised at the expense of local distinctiveness, the actual quality that is the attraction.

What is being sold by an agent and purchased by the visitor is the means of travel to a destination, the accommodation at the destination and the 'dream' that the destination offers. Quite often the purchase is an 'off-the-peg' package. The place enters into no direct or profitable contract with the visitor. The most common characteristic of the historic town to the visitor is the image which has been purchased. Alongside the chosen images and attributes, other factors such as climate and accessibility also contribute to the consumer's choice of purchase.

In Ireland the launch of a culture-based approach to tourism aimed at revising the 'Irish' heritage product, which had been identified as being 'tired'; its management, which was 'unprofessional'; and its interpretative planning, which was 'unimaginative', lacking originality and variety against what was acknowledged as an island of outstanding scenic beauty with a complex history. The initial phase involved a review of a distinctly Irish heritage, its marketing and promotion, including natural, built and cultural heritage (literature, music, dance, folklore) with considerations for the future. Implications for the development of cultural tourism were then identified; these included a continuous need for the conservation of heritage, information (to visitors), participation in attractions and presentation. The investment in upgrading the 'Irish heritage product' for tourism was considerable, and 50 per cent of it was directly in the heritage area. The project proved successful, within the first five years (1988 to 1993) yielding a revenue growth of 69 per cent (Browne 1994).

Increasing visitor potential

Developing the value and attractiveness of a place takes many forms. With the desire to attract more people, historic towns are being 'upgraded' with the addition of 'attractions' in the hope of keeping the destination attractive or appealing to a wider visitor base. Tourism development is likely to be part of a larger regional plan, in which development objectives overlap, integrating existing land use and development plans and considering established tourism activity.

Marketing is a tool of tourism management, closely linked to both existing and potential visitor markets; the product is either marketed to a known market or developed to attract a larger market. For example, the distance to a place and ease of access play an important part in the visitor perception of a destination. Marketing objectives, in conjunction with development planning objectives, have to consider one of several options: to focus on a market sector which is likely to make the journey; to ensure the attraction is worth the journey; to carry out a cost–benefit analysis which will investigate whether investment in a transportation network could increase arrivals.

Quite often historic towns are a link attraction to another leisure or travel activity, links which must nevertheless be carefully considered. Where historic towns become an added attraction and a day trip, as Toledo has become from Madrid for example, or Canterbury from London, the benefit is to the main destination, with limited return to the smaller historic town. In such cases a stronger local marketing strategy to attract longer-staying visitors becomes significant. Alternatively, a small town is marketed with a nearby attraction or surrounding landscape, or it becomes part of a regional attraction, a typical hill town of a scenic region for example. New concepts of regional promotion or link promotion (Medlik 1995) should be explored for marketing destinations which may not be successfully competing on their own. A small historic town in Central Europe may not warrant a lengthy car journey, but as part of a tour of several historic castles in the region it has the potential to be marketed as an ideal place for an overnight stay.

Linked destinations can be developed into the more substantial attraction of a heritage trail, by including other attractions such as areas of natural and scenic beauty, rural interest or archaeology. Travel between linked destinations becomes part of the attraction and can include walking, horseback riding, cycling, motoring or using a canal boat. Like the caravanserai on the ancient caravan routes, each a day's camel journey apart, the destinations must be conveniently located for the proposed activity. However, unlike the caravan routes, a trail is not fulfilling a purpose if it simply becomes a combination of attractions with a route between them; if it is carefully planned, the route will also provide an enjoyable experience with adequate and desirable facilities for the visitor, using existing resources where possible and considering environmental impacts, especially any in rural areas which become part of a trail.

A town or city is likely to be marketed concurrently to different purchasers through the use of different images, to attract more business or to increase public support for the environment. In a competitive environment, image marketing has become a professional pursuit, as European towns adopt logos and slogans, as in the United States city governments set aside large budgets for city marketing and as developing countries turn to international advertising agencies to produce their promotion material. The services and facilities offered at a place complement a visual image and some of these may be referred to in the advertising image, such as a view onto the historic Grand Place in Brussels with a smartly laid restaurant table in the foreground.

Developing a visitor strategy

A tourist is 'a temporarily leisured person who voluntarily visits a place away from home for the purpose of experiencing a change' (Smith 1978: 55). The word 'tourist' often implies a stereotype, mainly because these individuals gain a collective identity while travelling in a group, and a number of studies have provided classifications of tourist types (see also Smith 1978; Murphy 1985).[1] Part of the travelling experience involves undertaking activities that are not part of daily life at home. 'The average tourist is a collector of places, and his appetite increases as his collection grows' (MacCannell 1976: 13).

To the 'collector', historic towns represent a cultural product and are more attractive to those who are intellectually stimulated in their travels. The role of the marketing professional is to establish means for communicating the product to the potential market, the first step of which is the identification of a desirable target market. Current research shows that tourists who are more likely to visit historic towns are predominantly educated and come from managerial and professional classes, and that they are on average an older group of visitor with a developed interest in history (Ashworth and Larkham 1994) – 'middle-class' visitors, combining a level of affluence for overseas travel or for additional holidays, which often include visits to historic towns.

Tourism promoters invariably claim a desire to attract 'quality' tourism, often thought to be affluent, high-spending 'five star' tourists. A Turkish Minister for Tourism once famously announced that Turkey no longer wished to receive the 'cheap' backpacker class of tourist – a narrow approach, especially as the much-desired five-star tourists expect and demand five-star service, which can become a drain on scarce resources and can increase imports. Furthermore, they are the first to be able to afford the next 'unspoilt' and fashionable destination. For a limited period of economic gain a destination can become a short-term and capital-intensive market. A more modest group of visitors with fewer demands for imports may prove to be the more valuable when it comes to a balance of income and outgoings from a local economy. Likewise, small and independent groups staying for longer are likely to be more beneficial to historic towns and better patrons of local establishments than larger organised groups on shorter stays (Orbaşlı 1994).

Simulating future scenarios for five, ten or even fifty years encourages development control, thereby avoiding reactive overdevelopment to boom-time tourism, while forecasting visitor numbers and building up visitor profiles assist in the development of environmental impact scenarios. A visitor and marketing strategy also has to evaluate carrying capacity, understanding and regulating ideals for economic and social gain without environmental loss. However, for lack of an established system or method and given the complexity presented by the urban situation, environmental impacts of tourism and carrying capacity often go unmeasured. Visitor impact is more closely related to the type of visitor than it is to numbers; in equal numbers a group of elderly tourists seeking culture or a group of excitable youths will have very different impacts on a place. It is also beneficial in an expanding market to recognise the management need in advance.

Visitors impose pressure on fragile environments, with some of the greatest pressures resulting from the high-peak short-stay visitors common to historic towns. Nevertheless, central governments, with little experience of the tourist industry, are seen to be keen to attract as many tourists as possible. The control of tourist numbers and the marketing of a place may cause conflict between local needs and national policy. In recent years, particularly among countries that have experienced tourist congestion, *quality*, not quantity, tourism is becoming a chosen and necessary marketing strategy, particularly where planning is destination led. In the Netherlands, for example, towns are not only being given more autonomy and responsibility for marketing and promotion, but growing collaboration between local tourist boards and local authorities is involving local tourist boards in urban (product) development.

Visitor management also constitutes an integral component of tourism management and planning. Guidance formulated by the English Historic Towns Forum (1994) for a visitor management strategy is a useful guide and can be summarised as follows:

- research into visitors who are visiting the location (time spent, movement and spending patterns); study of flow patterns and an evaluation of preference for spaces, most of which can be charted by computer;
- the identification of objectives;
- consultation and development, local participation and identification of funding partners;
- the development of an action plan;
- implementation (EHTF suggests a three-year programme);
- an annual strategy review looking at benefits for residents and visitors and a post-impact evaluation to monitor success.

Marketing must also consider the pace and length of visits, from a day trip seeing the major sites to a long weekend taking in the museums and some shopping, or a longer stay of four days to a week enjoying an historic town at leisure, sitting in cafes watching life go by, spreading visits to major attractions over the visit with opportunities of discovering some less well-known attractions. The English Tourist Board in 1972 had calculated that a visitor staying overnight spent three times as much money as a day visitor did. In order to accommodate and nurture longer-staying visitors, the destination must be able to provide sufficient leisure facilities and cultural attractions, coupled with a good service base, to ensure visitor satisfaction. While the rushed lifestyle of a working visitor who is taking a second holiday only allows for a weekend break, an ageing population may become a good target market for longer stays.

Planning for the future

Coping with sudden growth

The growth of tourism can be rapid and sudden, and in the absence of planning its impacts become unexpected and greater. Urban and rural destinations the world over are being 'surprised' by a sudden influx of tourism which has been caused by changes in a political situation or a change in fashion. The Gambia, for example, experienced a 63.6 per cent increase in visitor numbers between 1981 and 1985 (Erlet 1991: 9). Czechoslovakia had just emerged from a socialist regime when in

1990 visitor numbers reached five times the number in 1989. Infrastructure was insufficient, accommodation facilities were too few and traffic and overcrowding soon became a problem, primarily because the authorities had not had a chance to plan for tourism (D. Hall 1990). Similarly, in Poland tourist numbers increased from 18 million in 1990 to 74 million in 1994. In referring to Krakow, a former minister for tourism pointed out that 'unfortunately, the historic old town is not yet prepared for such wide tourism growth' (Paszucha 1995: 44). While western visitors flock to newly discovered destinations in an attempt to capture the 'unspoilt' and benefit from cheap prices, their hosts are faced with new western service demands, and expectations of higher standards as well as suddenly having to cope with increased environmental pressures. The smaller the place, the greater are the pressures that are felt, as is the case in small island communities for example. Chelidoni (1997) relates the pressures on the Greek island of Kos of 20,000 inhabitants where annual visitor arrivals reach 900,000; she notes that when there was no planning administration in place, the tourist boom significantly altered the urban structure of the capital Kos, where the population could increase by 200 per cent at peak time.

At the end of the war from which Croatia emerged as a separate and independent state, the opportunity for redefining and planning for tourism presented itself. This was particularly the case in the popular coastal areas, which in the former image of Yugoslavian tourism had come to be associated with 'cheap' state-run hotels and nudist beaches, frequented by 'no-frills' packages. The new state of Croatia had the benefit of a new name which it could use to promote a new image emphasising the qualities of historic towns like Split and Dubrovnik on the Dalmatian coast, the diversity of cultural activity and the quality of the wine. In the immediate post-war period plans were under way for a more sensitive approach, including the establishment and location of new resorts, as most of the former establishments had been damaged during the war. But the dependence on foreign investment to rebuild tourist services means that some of the opportunities for sustainable development have been lost.

Forward planning plays a vital role in the future and long-term success of a place and involves being prepared for the right market. In the complexity of decision makers and the global politics of tourism, it is essential to set sustainable objectives and, moreover, to adhere to them, while controlling development at local level is paramount.

Environmental consciousness and sustainable tourism

Environmental issues have become a public concern and they appear high on the recent political agendas of many developed countries. With growing pressure and concern about the environment, agents and operators are trying to look 'green' and environmentally friendly in their images in response to customer demands for a high-quality environment and for so-called 'eco' products. What has come to be known as green or eco-tourism is more likely to be a marketing strategy adopted by its agents, and alternative tourism often implies an 'unspoilt' destination, where any visitor may be more harmful than useful to the environment. However, the underlying dichotomy is that many small and local developments which are more likely to be environmentally conscious continue to compete with the wealthy and influential operators from the West who have budgets and marketing managers to promote 'environmentally friendly' images. Similarly, responsible tourism aims at small-scale and incremental development of tourism. However,

> its basic ineffectiveness at addressing the problems means that it is in danger of being nicely co-opted by both the tourist and the tourism industry alike in an attempt to salve quality, consciences and promote seemingly more conscientious marketing.
>
> (Erlet 1991: 18)

In response to consumer demand in the 1990s, tourism, like a number of other industries, started to develop a 'green' and 'alternative' side. 'Alternative tourism emphasises avoidance of environmental damage, scaling down, the issue of who benefits, and cultural sensitivity' (de Kadt 1990: Introduction). The understanding of alternative tourism has been used in a variety of different situations, including a rejection of 'normal', 'mass' or 'mainstream' tourism. On the local front, alternative tourism is concerned with local, small-scale developments with community involvement, and 'cultural sustainability' (de Kadt 1990: 5). However, the meaning of 'alternative' can also be debatable and what appears to be alternative to one group may not be to another. But this new consciousness can be embraced and historic towns have many opportunities to offer 'alternative' experiences, such as the use of an historic building for visitor accommodation, without having to provide all the expected modern amenities which are damaging to the historic fabric, such as air conditioning, indoor swimming pools and large car parks.

Sustainable development is concerned with maintaining balanced economic growth and conserving natural resources. According to the World Commission on Environment and Development publication *Our Common Future* (1987: 1), 'The essential prerequisite of sustainable development is to meet the needs of the present without compromising the ability of future generations to meet their own needs.' Tourism is a complex industry, many aspects of which are immeasurable, including its implications for the environment and its social impacts on the host society. It has also been argued that sustainable tourism is a 'myth' and that a choice has to be made between tourism and the environment. Setting targets for sustainable development may not therefore always be completely effective in achieving results, especially as there will be a number of other influential factors, and reasons for change are not all tourism dependent. Coastal pollution for example has many contributors, not simply tourists or tourist developments at a resort.

For sustainable goals to be achieved in historic towns, not only does the importance of local-level decision making for the product image and product development have to be recognised, but management has to move from being reactive to being proactive, incorporating action planning and the flexibility to cope with change and fluctuations in the market.

Preparing a tourism development plan

The importance of planning for tourism development is obvious, yet it is often overlooked or reduced to too tight a time frame. A tourism development plan needs to be viewed as a complex concept and not simply as a blueprint or bound report.

Fig. 5.5 Will Dubrovnik be able to develop a new image as a culturally attractive centre or allow developers to turn it into a 'historic' day-trip destination for cheap resort holidays?

(a) a picture postcard

(b) or a place

A successful masterplan is an operational framework of development and implementation objectives, with established links to the urban mechanism from policy and physical planning to design, city centre management and marketing. Planning is an essential part of what can be thought of as tourism preparedness. The stages of a commonly agreed framework for tourism development planning as adapted from Laws (1995), Page (1995) and Boniface (1995) and physical planning procedure suggested for historic towns (Feilden and Jokilehto 1998) are summarised in the following table.

Preparatory stages

- identification of the current situation: research, including evaluation of the site, community, economic and political background; surveys, data collection and analysis of data;
- forecasting growth, development patterns and future events;
- setting tourism and development objectives.

Planning

Effective long-term planning, based on sound methodological approaches:

- coordination of marketing and product development;
- consultation and community involvement (as essential);
- identifying investment incentives (public and private involvement and partnerships);
- assessing feasibility and desirability of options.

Implementation

- maintaining and assessing quality;
- continuous monitoring and periodic review.

Research, planning and implementation cannot be separated, and must be seen as a continuum and a continuous cycle. An urban development plan will only touch on small and specific aspects of a town, but with the wider objectives of improving the whole. Planning for urban tourism takes place in the previously outlined dichotomy of physical planning and market planning. Conflicts and contradictions arising in these two disciplinary spheres need to be overcome through a more collaborative and strategic approach to development planning.

Strategic thinking and planning for historic towns can be thought of as a physical planner's masterplan, showing the vision and the overall policy with a specific area designed within them. Even the most defined management plan is the result of an evolutionary process, where inputs are debated with the various players as an ongoing process which remains evolutionary. The tourism development plan is a framework or focus for developing a masterplan, guided also by a vision.

Planning for tourism incorporates many different concerns and it is also an evolutionary process. For an approach to be both practical and visionary, the ideal plan incorporates a twenty-five- to thirty-year vision and objective, a five-year forward-look plan and annual development plans concerned with management issues; notably

- action planning to respond to immediate needs and demands;
- established plans to consider the positive development of a place;
- a long-term visionary view and strategic objectives.

Re-evaluating planning parameters

The previous chapter highlighted the importance of *local*-level decision making, the need for *partnership* and the involvement of the *community* as an active partner. Action planning is an alternative to the traditional linear approach to planning, as it combines thinking (planning) and doing into one simultaneous activity. Therefore, it has to be locally based and it is more likely to involve participants from all interest groups. It is an opportunity-driven approach with an emphasis on identifying and prioritising immediate problems; but alongside the achievable action there is also a need for strategic intervention and long-term planning. Before a more proactive planning approach can be introduced, the obstacles of separate disciplinary groups in operation and the time frame which governs most decisions also need to be revisited.

Time, described as the fourth dimension of design, buildings and cities, is itself a multi-faceted concept. The concept and use of time in urban life are rapidly changing. Places are moving closer together in time as a result of transportation and communication technologies and the world is becoming a twenty-four-hour place. Time and location, for example, have both become irrelevant to a US computer programming company downloading at the end of the working day to a counterpart operation in India, which continues the work through the US night and Indian day before downloading back to the US. At the same time, better lighting, technological advances and changing work practices create the twenty-four-hour city of work, leisure and entertainment.

In planning, five years is a very short period, yet it is a commonly selected target in the preparation of both physical and development plans. A differential is apparent between the five-year scale of development planning and the hypothetically 'infinite' time attached to sustainability. A typical five-year development plan cannot effectively accommodate long-term sustainable planning, but if it is set out within a strategic framework it can contribute to sustainable objectives. Nevertheless, current time constraints on planning are closely linked to budgetary targets and pre-defined completion dates. Particularly in the case of international or short-term regeneration funding, a place can be subjected to overdevelopment in the short term, partly to provide tangible or visible results to the funder, but leaving behind a growth momentum and development which cannot be sustained in the long term.

Each discipline involved in the urban environment works to different time objectives; the urgency of a town centre management solution is not comparable to a long-term regional development issue, for example. Moreover, many of these plans continue to operate independently of the others. It is not uncommon for a five-year local development, conservation or tourism plan for a city centre to ignore a twenty-five-year transportation plan at national level. The environment benefits from both long- and short-term planning; strategies must be developed for the long term, but framed by interim development targets. The need for communication, coordination and collaboration has never been greater.

Too often decision making is embedded in a vertical hierarchical framework limiting opportunities for communication. The absence of established communication structures between government departments and professional disciplines and most importantly between the community and appointed decision makers is a hindrance to sustainable development. It is essential that direct lines of contact are established between the person making decisions on the ground and the highest decision-making level (Walls 1995). Although at a 1973 Council of Europe conference held in Copenhagen the importance of the exchange of information between tourism and conservation bodies was highlighted, the two disciplines are still far from actively communicating. Communication has to take place at all levels and between all levels; between the people and the managers, between visitors and the community, between members of a partnership, between regional and local authorities, between neighbouring towns and villages. Action planning for example depends directly on communication among all the parties involved. Formal structures need to be established and informal opportunities created for better communication. Active and influential partnerships and networks are effective platforms for communication and more interactive approaches.

Addressing a 1995 ICOMOS Conference, Sir Angus Stirling, director of the English National Trust, pointed out that 'Experience shows that little can be achieved without partnership' and called for 'better and widespread exchange of information and good practice, and results of experimentation' (Stirling 1995: 16). The key approach to planning must involve partnership, representing all interests, and local-level control. Partnership has to be three way: public, private and community (UNESCO 1998), avoiding conflict through cross-disciplinary decision-making structures.

The complexity of urban decision making, identified in the previous chapter, necessitates partnership, especially where the continuation of existing planning techniques and procedures is no longer sufficient for sustainable development objectives to be realised. Partnerships already exist in many local situations through public–private ventures or in networks set up among similar organisations. Many heritage organisations, small by nature, depend extensively on networking and partnerships to survive and to remain up to date. Historic towns today are able to benefit from a number of network organisations, including the English Historic Town Forum, or the Europe-wide Walled Towns Friendship Circle, and internationally the ICOMOS Historic Towns and Villages Committee (CIVVIH) or the World Heritage Cities Organisation based in Quebec. What is more significant is the recognition of culture as a catalyst for development and nurturing cultural partnerships for environmental development. Fleming (1996) for example suggests museums and cities should form cultural partnerships. A partnership becomes an established authority for sharing vital information, including monitoring numbers and research on visitor profiles.

Symbolising the start of the Industrial Revolution, Ironbridge Gorge in England is now a World Heritage Site. The Gorge is a major visitor attraction with numerous museums, but it is also a place to live. The management of this World Heritage Site involves a multitude of players including the Ironbridge Gorge Museum Trust, Telford and Wrekin Council, the Ironbridge Institute (University of Birmingham), Telford Development Corporation, English Heritage and the Severn Gorge Countryside Trust; these form a partnership which also includes close liaisons with local groups and they thus seek a joint vision on issues as diverse as cultural heritage, the natural environment and concerns for the local economy. Although it is a World Heritage Site, Ironbridge is a real place where people live, and conflicts inevitably arise in the development of tourism whereby economic regeneration has to concern the whole Gorge and not just the museum sites and tourist attractions. Kavanagh (1995) describes a working partnership between museum and an inner-city community in developing the Museum of Science and Industry in the Castlefield area of Manchester in a regeneration programme where partners alongside the local authority included the Department of the Environment and the English Tourist Board. In Europe local governments have started to work much more closely with the private sector and other agencies, and a growth in regional collaboration supported by the European Union is generating new initiatives for historic towns and tourism development through partnerships.

Partnership represents a framework for communication but it must also hold responsibility for realisation. Partnership should be seen as a long-term collaborative process for planning and managing tourism, sharing ownership of both policy and action. Partnerships will involve a mixture of partners; what is important is that each partner is significant to the development and that all interests are being represented, particularly those of the community. Partnership needs strong leadership, designated decision making and the power to take action.

However, the typical planning approach remains strictly linear, identifying events and procedures with a beginning, a middle and an end. Both a looser and a tighter decision-making environment is being sought: a continuous procedure of frequent review yet a loose framework to inspire creative thinking. Monitoring, evaluation and self-evaluation are all quality control mechanisms. Planners must be able to look into and plan for the future and strategic planning can be thought of as a circular process of development and assessment. Tourism is volatile; alongside sudden changes there is a slower natural change as the market reflects new levels of affluence, changing leisure interests and destination fashions. Many of the changes in the market are rarely foreseen for planning purposes, making continuous monitoring and adaptation and a framework to respond to the market even more important. In order to establish a creative and strategic thought and decision-making process, there is the need to create a more dynamic, continuous and ongoing activity environment closely linked to implementation.

Strategic approaches and a creative vision for the future

Long-term sustainable tourism growth requires a strategic approach, combining physical and market planning, with the caveat that policy and implementation should be directed from the same source. Series of critical objectives and events create a focus represented in different disciplines and at different levels of scale and complexity, but working towards common targets and objectives. Strategic and operational decision making also depends on adequate and up-to-date information and a good analysis of that information.

The conclusions of a seminar on managing tourism in historic cities held in Krakow in 1992 identified two ways of implementing policy: either through planning control or through market intervention (financial tools, grants, tax breaks and the like). However, neither is exclusive of the other and it could be argued that they are interdependent. Larkham (1996) has demonstrated that for Britain the absence of supporting funding for conservation areas is detrimental to development and growth. A forward-thinking creative approach avoids disproportionate reactions to small changes and focuses more positively on long-term change. An historic town's greatest asset is its character; it should not be sacrificed to short-term planning.

Where multi-disciplinary teams can promote new approaches, 'decision by committee' all too often stifles development, and in partnerships too, a clear leadership role has to be established. Much may depend on identifying and supporting an individual with vision and foresight. Middleton and Hawkins (1998) highlight a dilemma in decision making over the role of the visionary, where elected members and the professionals may expect it of each other, but where neither may be outstandingly qualified for the task. In the 1960s the development of Newcastle (see Chapter 1), for example, was led by the vision of the chairman of the Planning Committee, Councillor Dan Smith, who saw Newcastle as the New Brasilia (*Architects' Journal* 1980: 52). Creative vision is about identifying opportunities and making them work. The key is to be able to provide a dynamic environment in which creative thinkers can prosper and operate.

Tourism is an opportunity for urban and social development, as well as for local empowerment. But harnessing the opportunity and the global energy which marketing creates requires creative vision and often new ways of looking at or approaching old problems. A vision can also be seen as an end product, from which a more formal approach to mission statements, strategic objectives and development strategies is derived.

Strategic planning requires a global understanding both of the industry and of development, but it must seek local solutions to achieve satisfaction through good-quality people and product interaction (Murphy 1997). It must promote a flexible response to change and it must react effectively to new occurrences; it must be creative and remain dynamic. Within the strategic framework, objectives must remain open to continuous review and development. In developing a tourism growth framework, the following questions should be continuously addressed:

- how does the plan improve the environment?
- how is local distinctiveness promoted?

Summary and conclusion

In the past quarter of a century, not only has tourism grown as a world industry, but historic towns and their conservation have become very closely related to it. Planning for the sustainable development of tourism in historic towns has never been more important, but the complexity of the urban decision-making mechanism, the bureaucracy of the planning system and the short-term goals of finance continue to hinder forward-looking decisive planning and the active implementation of core objectives. Policy planning divorced from implementation becomes ineffective and counter-productive. Planning for sustainable development must begin through an understanding of urban form, heritage value, socio-economic aspirations and the market. Dower (1974: 963) emphasises the need for historic towns 'to plan tourist development with due regard to the character and capacity of the locality and the interests of its inhabitants'.

Community, the vital 'life' and character element of historic towns continues to be ignored in the decision-making and planning processes other than through token gesture. The role of development for community has to be rethought, for a high-quality environment to live in can then be sustained as a high-quality environment to visit. It is paramount that the investment of the local community and the development of facilities should be ensured, with benefits reinvested in the community interest, while the local economy is sufficiently diversified not to be tourism led. The following case study of Quedlinburg, in Germany, discusses the approaches to tourism planning for this World Heritage Site.

Heritage is a diminishing resource, and unless tourism is planned for and effectively managed in historic towns, the resource will be rapidly consumed. Planning for tourism in historic towns has to:

- react effectively to immediate needs;
- be made more thought provoking, collaborative and continuous for sustainable and balanced development;
- become strategic and visionary for the future.

A more innovative and strategic approach to planning is necessary:

- incorporating global, non-linear and visionary planning;
- breaking down established time barriers;
- bringing together disciplines, organisations and individuals through partnerships;
- incorporating action planning responding to a place's immediate needs;
- incorporating continuous assessment and quality control ensuring that action is a response to community, user and client needs.

The final chapter examines the benefits that can be achieved from tourism in historic towns and how tourism can best be managed in the historic environment.

Notes

1 Murphy (1985) favours two groups, explorers and charter tourists, whereas Smith (1978) enters a more critical discussion on interaction, defining tourists in seven groups ranging from the explorer to the charter tourist.

Case study
World Heritage Site, Quedlinburg, Germany

With little other industry, the medieval town of Quedlinburg in central Germany depends on tourism as a major economic growth area. The authenticity of the architecture is in itself an attraction, but Quedlinburg is fortunate that the pressures of tourism have not as yet been felt and that there is an opportunity to plan for tourism development.

The place

Formerly part of the German Democratic Republic, Quedlinburg is a small and well-preserved medieval walled town. It has played a significant role in German history from the tenth century, and as the imperial seat of Henry I, Otto I and Otto II it was an important centre of the Holy Roman Empire. In the eleventh and twelfth centuries Quedlinburg developed into a busy market town, for which it was well known into the eighteenth century. Like York, Quedlinburg lost its importance as an ecclesiastical centre with the Reformation in the sixteenth century, but the church of St Servatius still stands proud on the Schloßberg, the old citadel, around which the old town is clustered. In another parallel with York, the arrival of the railway in 1885 brought industry to Quedlinburg. Much of the present urban pattern of the old town was in place by 1200, and the 'new' town, with its straighter, more grid-like street pattern, developed shortly afterwards. Today it remains a small settlement of 26,000 inhabitants.

In 1994 Quedlinburg was inscribed in the World Heritage List, and continues to be the largest single conservation area in the Federal Republic of Germany (Stadt Quedlinburg 1998: 5). The attraction and distinction of the town is the half-timber architecture surviving from the Middle Ages through to the Baroque period, and including the nineteenth-century Jugendstil style. Most buildings are timber framed, of skilled craftsmanship, two to three storeys high, with steep sloping roofs. Quedlinburg was fortunately spared severe bomb damage during the Second World War and escaped heavy-handed planning in the 1960s. Its near-intact survival to date has also been attributed to poverty, which remains an issue, with high unemployment today.

Fig. 1 The old market square is developing as a focus for visitor activity in the town, and is also the location of a lively weekly market.

The town with its steep roofs and steeples around the dramatic height of the Schloßberg is defined by the surrounding Harz landscape – a setting which contributes to the World Heritage status, and one which must be preserved. The secluded agricultural land of the immediate region and its wealth of wild flowers have not only played an important role in the town's history, but continue to attract bio-technology and seed research establishments as employers today. The fall of the Berlin Wall in 1989, followed by German unification, has been a significant turning point for Quedlinburg, including the economic changes brought about by a decline in industry and the closing of mines, but also by the opening up of tourism markets and the launch of comprehensive rehabilitation programmes. The need for new industries and economic contributors, however, is paramount for the future survival of the historic town.

Conservation

In the 1960s, like many other towns Quedlinburg was the subject of deliberations and plans for urban renewal which included the replacement of its historic fabric with 'modern' development. With the exception of the Neuendorf area, to the north of the old town centre, where new developments disregarded the urban structure, the town was recognised for its national and regional importance and duly protected. Although consciousness had been raised, conservation in this period remained severely underfunded. While some conservation initiatives were launched, at a much greater pace properties were becoming dilapidated and dangerous to live in, with almost all properties in need of modernising, including the provision of indoor bathrooms. By 1990 immediate action had become vital for the future survival of the town.

In the post-unification period, the city government has been in a better position to assist property owners with grant aid for up to 50 per cent of construction work on conservation projects, but this too is becoming increasingly limited. The city council also provides guidance to owners on building techniques and intervention. In the period 1990 to 1998, over 1,000 buildings were secured, partly repaired or fully modernised (Stadt Quedlinburg 1998). The financial constraints continue, however, and following years of neglect, the work is against the clock. The repair programme cannot be phased for too long and limited resources are also being stretched for emergency maintenance and securing buildings, an investment with no direct return. While the larger properties depend on substantial outside investment, the family-occupied smaller houses are being restored by their owners, some over many years as a labour of love.

The approach to building conservation today is that each is part of a whole, inside and out, and that properties cannot be separated into facades and backs (Schauer 1990), thus avoiding a facadist appearance to the town. Wherever possible, original material, seen as evidence of history and building technique, is being retained. Inevitably some buildings have had to be demolished, particularly when they constitute a threat to others adjoining them; the salvaged components, however, are reused in other conservation projects. At the same time, considerable townscape improvements have been taking place, as streets and pavements are repaired or renewed, lighting overhauled and new street furniture introduced. New buildings are being added to the townscape, either on empty plots or to replace properties that have been lost, and it is recognised that there has to be change for the place to remain desirable as a place to live (Schauer 1990).

The conservation aims for Quedlinburg are listed as:

- retaining the urban structure and pattern;
- preserving and conserving buildings;
- establishing and enhancing residential uses;
- enhancing the commercial life of the old town;
- promoting tourism (Stadt Quedlinburg 1998: 7).

Fig. 2 For many visitors, the first view of Quedlinburg is from the Schloßberg. The local authority advocates the retention of the characteristic steep roofscape.

Fig. 3 The wealth of timber framed buildings makes Quedlinburg an immediate attraction for visitors, but further attractions have to be developed to ensure a longer stay.

A tourist town?

The attraction of Quedlinburg to tourism is undeniable, and even under the German Democratic Republic tourism was being encouraged; 36,000 visitors were reported for 1987, including Americans and Japanese, although external publicity during this period was fairly limited. The first flow of visitors after the opening of the border was west Germans visiting friends and family, and internal tourism continues to be significant. The inscription in the World Heritage List has increased interest in the town, as has the return of the Domschatz treasure. At the end of the 1990s most tourists continue to be individual and independent groups on cultural trips. A remarkable number stay two or more nights, or are on return visits. But there are also the bus tourists on day trips. More recently a new hotel has been built to cater for larger groups, and conference facilities have been introduced.

In a rare example, city planners and the tourist office are working together to develop the visitor product and promote the town. There is also a conscious resistance against becoming a model town. 'Everything here is original, nothing has been mocked up as a tourist attraction' (Radecke 1995: 7). The town's people 'do not wish to be a museum' was a concern expressed in the 1960s (Bleicke 1995) and repeated in 1998 (Stadt Quedlinburg 1998: 7). The feeling is that Quedlinburg is not and should not become a model town; it is real, it has a centre, a life and a hinterland and must therefore be preserved for what it represents today. Residential use in the old town is being encouraged with a further commitment to support locally run shops in the centre, including the discouragement of out-of-town retail outlets.

The aim is to increase the attractiveness of the place for visitors and expand the market. To date a number of initiatives have been launched, including for example:

Fig. 4 There remains a considerable amount of work ahead in safeguarding the medieval architecture of Quedlinburg.

- increasing cultural activity in the town, through concert programmes in a redundant church, and a resident theatre company;
- a proactive museums programme using the conservation of buildings and techniques as an attraction, enabling visitors to be part of the process through workshops and demonstrations;
- an annual festival started in 1998 on a medieval theme (to mark Kaiserfrühling), including animation, street theatre and entertainment, medieval plays and crafts;
- the revival of craft trades, such as weaving, through craft and pottery workshops set up in a restored building;
- a medieval theme for the annual Christmas market;
- the expansion of guided tours to include evening tours and to extend some tours to include parts of the town, such as Münzenberg, that tourists do not commonly visit.

Tourism is very important to Quedlinburg and many feel it is the only solution to the current depressed economic situation, in a town which the authorities feel has to 'to live with and for tourism'. However, Quedlinburg has not as yet been overwhelmed by tourism or felt the pressures caused by large numbers, and it can still feel 'quite quiet' in the centre. But unlike the immediate visitor influx experienced by Prague and other East European towns in the early 1990s, Quedlinburg has the unique opportunity to plan for sustainable tourism.

Issues and options

Despite the 'short-term' initiatives being taken for tourism development, Quedlinburg is also faced with the 'long-term' planning of tourism and economic development, and, furthermore, the preparedness for the management of future tourism. The development direction and planning process must respond to an understanding of the place and its qualities.

Understanding the place

The qualities of Quedlinburg that make people want to visit it and live in it are:

- authenticity of place and authenticity of fabric, not a place that is specifically 'presented';
- genuine character and natural charm;
- a desirable landscape setting;
- a community attached to the place;
- a creative environment including local artists and craftspeople.

All of this must be recognised, respected and continued through the tourism development process, which is above all an understanding of the town as an historic process itself with a living community. There are underlying tensions in Quedlinburg, between poverty and riches, and, within society, an east–west conflict. Delicate balances have to be achieved on the question of who is steering the new tourist economy and how a process can be set in train that is inclusive rather than exclusive of the local community.

Developing tourism

The economic realities of Quedlinburg dictate that conservation in the town is only going to be possible through external investment, which is being attracted through tourism opportunities. But the success of the preservation of the historic town and the development of tourism depend on carefully considered economic decisions, which cover:

- developing the visitor appeal of the town;
- developing tourism in the region, using landscape and nearby attractions;
- diversifying the local economy in order that it is not totally dependent on tourism, but including initiatives that also benefit tourism.

Planning for future tourism

Planning for sustainable tourism in Quedlinburg has a wide range of options and opportunities to consider, including:

The market:
- determining the visitor profile and the ideal market and defining ways of targeting this group;
- where necessary discouraging less lucrative groups (tour buses stopping for two hours for example);
- exploring long-stay options, and the specialist markets the town and region can cater for, such as craft training or painting classes, etc., ensuring wherever possible that the skill base is both locally generated and exportable;
- considering the accommodation needs of the target groups.

Urban growth and change:
- considering future retail and accommodation needs, how they will be provided and where they will be located;

- establishing a management plan;
- working with an informed planning mechanism to respond to future change.

Community:
- promoting active involvement locally, ensuring residents are part of the planning process and starting to benefit from tourism;
- creating opportunities, training and jobs locally (including in small enterprises and tourism);
- building on the cultural and educational needs of the visitor and the community;
- supporting local initiatives, such as the better use of local accommodation for bed and breakfast purposes.

A clear long-term vision for the place must always be retained.

6 Heritage management in historic towns

Introduction

Tourism is often a source of much-needed foreign income; tourism is a consumer of environments and human communities; tourism damages social structures. Clichés, maybe, but proved in many cases to be true. The ultimate truism is yet another cliché, namely that 'tourism is here to stay' and human mobility is increasing. One of the first trends observed in countries gaining greater economic and political freedom is the desire of the people to travel. 'To some, tourism represents an opportunity – a means of capitalising on the legacy of history – to others, perhaps it may be something of a threat unless it can be managed safely' (Stuart 1989: 1). For the urban environment tourism will continue to present the potential of a clean industry and a valuable source of income and employment. The development objective, therefore, must be to harness the source, while safeguarding the future of the natural resource, the historic town and its community. The leisure and cultural tourism industries are attracted to historic towns as a destination; and historic town authorities look to tourism as a new, clean and profitable industry. In comparison to 'smokestack' industry, tourism is deemed to be 'clean' with a potential to enhance quality of life, and reduce pollution and environmental destruction. With careful planning and management, tourism can play an important role in an environmentally sound future for historic towns.

The historic town asset is a set of values based on building stock, historic or other associations and *life*. Minimising impacts on the 'asset' base and maximising gains from tourism depend to a large extent on the organisation of tourism and tourist attractions in historic towns, and on the management of the interface between visitors and the environment. Urban management is connected to strategic planning which is connected to a good understanding of urban morphology, spatial and social relations and which can often be based on sensitive and opportunist urban design solutions. There is a role for tourism not only in the preservation of urban heritage but also in the continuation of urban culture and in promoting cross-cultural understanding. The value of tourism for urban conservation is both financial and as an impetus for awakening interest and attracting support. Tourism, managed with clear objectives, is a source of finance, both in the promotion of historic areas and in encouraging and enabling conservation work. Conservation has been described as 'the reanimation of the old in the context of change' (Walls 1995). *Continuity* is the key to conservation and both the built environment and urban life within it must be permitted to develop and change.

> The continued existence of the historical character of townscapes is a universal long-term social requirement of great importance that should have its proper place in the balance of claims on planning quite apart from the incidental economic 'tourist' value attaching to any particular townscape.
>
> (Conzen 1981: 59)

A visit to an historic town cannot be viewed as a visit to a museum or a 'time-past' re-creation.

The pressures of tourism on historic towns are twofold: the impact on the historic fabric and its associated, comparatively fragile, environment, and pressures on the 'living' urban environment. In the conservation/development process, not only do built and natural environments need to be safeguarded, but so do the communities which inhabit them. The historic town presents a great complexity of objectives, and underlying tensions, where a delicate balance has to be sought between competing priorities, including between inside and outside, insider and outsider. Heritage management, more frequently associated with historic monuments, takes on a notably different aspect in the urban situation, but the primary objective, of enabling continuing appreciation of heritage and its safeguarding and continuity for future generations, however, remains the same. This final chapter addresses the following questions:

- How can tourism be a benefit to the built heritage?
- How can the pressures of tourism be better managed?
- How can the 'special' quality of a place be maintained?

Sharing the urban resource

Tourism and building conservation

In the isolated evaluation of historic towns as tourist destinations, the mainstay of the historic town product can be identified as the physical stock of historic buildings, a collective townscape value of urban morphology and urban space alongside urban life and human activity. All of these assets, which create significance and meaning for a place, face the danger of being permanently lost or ruined if tourism is not managed sensitively.

The damage from visitors to historic buildings, streets and squares is recognised as the townscape is spoilt by overcrowding and as it is worn down by numbers and traffic. Even more irreversible damage is caused to the historic fabric through hasty restoration schemes and the capitalisation of heritage for quick profits. Today even physical erosion to townscape by tourist numbers is being recorded and monitored. Residents move out of tourist-historic areas because they are no longer desirable or affordable places to live; as their privacy and cultural framework are invaded they become irritated by tourists, noise and commercial activity. In the more conservative and traditional towns of the East, tourism may become a direct threat to the privacy attached to urban spaces in the morphological hierarchy. Historic town conservation is faced with many conflicting claims, including those of culture (identity) and tourism (development). Associated conflicts include:

- a clash of policies regarding new development and conservation;
- aspirations for modernisation as opposed to Western expectations for maintaining the 'old';
- meeting the needs of a tourist culture and those of the local culture;
- maintaining the quality of urban environment in the face of the quantity of tourists.

One of the direct benefits of tourism to building conservation is the reuse of buildings for tourist functions, which will:

- ensure that a historic building is restored;
- provide a living function for an historic building;
- decrease the number of empty properties, providing a more desirable environment by reducing the crime and violence associated with empty city centres and creating safer and more desirable places to live;
- avoid the environmental impacts of the same function being located in a new building;
- create environments which will help historic towns retain the qualities that make them attractive.

Heritage management

Nevertheless, the benefits of tourism for conservation are negligible if they are outweighed by the pressures and subsequent destruction caused by tourism. The interface between 'host' residents and 'visitor' tourists can so easily become one of tension and conflict, caused by social differences, attitudes and (limits of) tolerance. Management is 'a process businesses undertake to achieve organisational performance' (Ivanceich *et al.* 1991 quoted in Murphy 1997: 3). In the case of the urban environment it involves both an internal and an external environment, and a dynamic situation (Boniface 1995). Management of urban tourism becomes a simultaneous response to the needs of the visitor, the heritage and the heritage presenter; it is a combination of proactive design and planning measures which will reduce the pressure on resources and encourage a better appreciation of the environment for all concerned.

The search is for a more effective style of management. Boniface (1995) points out that either the traditional style of management has to be better implemented or a different style of management sought, and in the interest of cultural heritage 'we cannot afford *not* to manage tourism better' (Boniface 1995: 114, her italics). Good management will increase efficiency, but as V.T.C. Middleton (1994) warns, many management principles are common sense but always complex to implement. Efficiency of management in the urban environment is further hampered by the complex and contradictory relationships among key players in the decision-making process.

Heritage management is the management of visitors in an historic place in the interest of the historic fabric and the enhancement of visitor appreciation and experience: 'Establishing, operating and managing organisations to handle visits and manage *public access*' (V.T.C. Middleton 1994: 3, his italics). Although management is advocated for heritage, neither the market nor the product is clearly defined. Under greater financial autonomy and less subsidy, heritage organisations are learning to run businesses; they are becoming more streamlined and professional in their approach to management and marketing, taking on board financial forecasting and visitor evaluation. Heritage management is most effective in the controlled museum environment, and tourism management is most easily achieved in the enclosed resort, because each constitutes an entity of defined ownership and management, in contrast to the urban environment.

Heritage management has become an integral component of the heritage industry. 'Good heritage management with a major focus on heritage interpretation and presentation ensures that one complements the other' (Millar 1995: 115). Heritage in the historic town is embedded in a living and dynamic urban environment where many of the services provided are there for the purpose of supporting a community. Visitor management, particularly in the urban situation, is often reactive rather than proactive, responding once a threshold has been reached and the effects of numbers are being felt (Middleton and Hawkins 1998). Another layer or dimension of an existing management strategy for an urban town centre or heritage, or for visitor management, constitutes a wider set of urban design, planning and management solutions, including presentation and interpretation.

The museum entry fee, for example, is a simple yet active management tool. The price is 'pitched' to encourage the 'right' number of entrants, but to avoid overcrowding. Timed and ticketed entry, a favoured method for estate managers and museum directors, is an unlikely solution for historic towns as it defies the complex use patterns of the urban environment. The visitor management methods associated with museums, stately houses and palaces may not be directly applicable to historic towns but there are lessons that can be learnt. Many city authorities will agree that once visitors have arrived, it is not that simple to turn them away, even if urban carrying capacities are being reached. Charging tourists to enter a fragile environment, however, cannot be wholly discounted as it may constitute the only direct income from tourism that is deducted locally and it may be a vital source of finance for the maintenance and repair of historic buildings.

Foreign visitors to the town of Bhaktapur in Nepal are charged an entry fee, for example. This well-preserved brick and timber town is larger than Mdina, with visitor interest focused on a number of connected public squares, one with an active pottery workshop. As a result, the quieter residential streets seem little interrupted and the income from the modest entry tax is said to benefit the restoration of the major temples of Bhaktapur, though not residential repairs. In another example, from Vietnam, the income from visitor entry fees in the town of Hoi An directly supports grants for home owners to restore their properties. In Budapest, on the other hand, plans to introduce a tourist tax created a number of questions and debates on the allocation of the funds which were raised. Alternatively, airport or entry taxes can be introduced and used as a form of environmental tax paying for visitor pressures on the built and natural environments. Although governments

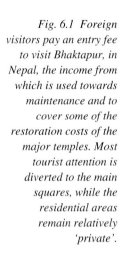

Fig. 6.1 Foreign visitors pay an entry fee to visit Bhaktapur, in Nepal, the income from which is used towards maintenance and to cover some of the restoration costs of the major temples. Most tourist attention is diverted to the main squares, while the residential areas remain relatively 'private'.

competing to attract tourism abstain from adding extras, such taxes are likely to deter only the cheaper end of the market.

Visitor management

Visitor management is not only a matter of traffic or pedestrian flow management, but involves imaginative solutions to enhance the visitor experience, maintain a favourable reputation for the destination, and ensure a high-quality environment for residents to live and work in, and visitors to enjoy. While large cities are robust and can withstand the fluctuations of the tourist industry, smaller historic towns are more likely to feel the pressures created by large numbers of visitors over concentrated periods. The dispersion and management of visitors can be achieved to a great extent through careful planning and sensitive urban design, with the support of the tourism promoter or manager.

Physical restriction is a last resort response to overcrowding, and it has on occasion been applied in Venice and considered in Prague. It is unlikely that tourist numbers to 'honeypot' or must-see attractions can be seriously reduced, though some popular historic towns are now choosing not to market themselves, in order to reduce numbers and to focus only on specific markets. A small and select number of islands (Bermuda), regions and countries (Bhutan) do put limits on the number of foreign visitors entering each year. But many places striving for tourism growth are unable to exercise strict controls, even though in the long term restrictions pay off, as the destination remains relatively unspoilt and continues to be perceived as being 'exclusive'. Even restrictive practices have strayed from originally determined quotas as foreign income, especially that collected as an entry fee, becomes attractive to national governments. Shackley (1994), reporting on the remote Himalayan kingdom of Lo (Upper Mustang), notes how over the first year of international tourism in 1992, the limit of visitor numbers was increased by the

Nepalese authorities receiving the royalties of $500 per week, from 200, to 600, and then to 1,000, consequently exceeding the limits of cultural carrying capacity in this enclosed region, but failing to generate any revenue for the local people (Shackley 1996).

It is important for national and local tourist authorities to collaborate in understanding the carrying capacity for an area in order to plan tourist development or search for alternatives. Carrying capacity is the number of people which a locality can *comfortably* accommodate without detracting from its environmental qualities, the capacity to absorb *before* any negative implications are felt. There is no defined formula for the calculation of carrying capacity in a living urban environment, and maintaining set targets is even more difficult (Page 1995), especially as carrying capacity is not denoted simply as a number, but is a variable of season, space, and cultural and natural elements (Medlik 1995). For tourist towns the major consideration is often concentration in certain areas at certain times. While a narrow medieval street may have the physical capacity to accommodate a given number of persons, the valued image and context of a medieval quarter are lost once it is overcrowded. Acceptance of capacity, however, is all too often left to 'saturation', at which point there is overcrowding and a place starts losing its attractiveness, its deterioration in value leading to a subsequent decline.

Page (1995) relates a study by Canestrelli and Costa (1991) on Venice in which they identified the ideal number of day trippers a day to the island as 10,857, with a maximum figure of 25,000; this is a modest estimate compared to the August average of 37,500 visitors a day, with frequently recorded figures of over 60,000 a day. Only when 100,000 visitors have arrived do the police close the bridge access, as this is a point of total physical saturation. Carrying capacity extends to the number of shops, hotels and other services provided, as a balance must be retained with the size and character of the place and oversupply avoided, both of which will lead to the cheapening of the place and the quality of the environment being compromised. In Antalya the oversupply of 'authentic' Turkish guest houses and shops has led to a collapse in the market, created infrastructure problems and contributed to the ruin of the historic quarter.

Where pressures are also linked to concentration the immediate need is for an appropriate dispersion strategy. Dispersion reduces pressure on a central attraction and potentially increases tourist time spent in a locality. Chosen visitor strategies have to respond to the individual case and specific needs and be appropriate to the culture. A thorough understanding of the urban situation, morphology, space, and associated socio-economic factors is essential. Needs have to be carefully balanced, especially in response to the size and realities of the town. For the case of small and contained historic towns such as Mdina in Malta, urban centre management solutions are unlikely to make much difference.

In the city of Bath, a World Heritage Site, where the year-round bus tours already provide a good view through the first-floor windows of the Royal Crescent (Boniface 1994), a tourism management proposal to spread the load of tourists away from the centre by promoting other parts of the city was met by protests from residents in these middle-class areas not wishing to be further disturbed by tourists (Laws 1995). Several issues are highlighted by this case: not only the disturbance tourists can cause to residents who do not wish to be living in a world heritage fish bowl, but also the power of richer residents to speak up, and the balance that has to be maintained by the city authorities dependent on effective tourism management and such residents for long-term economic stability.

However, it should also be noted that some pressures are the outcome of a conflict among the historic place and contemporary lifestyles and resident demands, including parking problems and the demand for certain types of shopping facilities.

Better management of tourism in historic towns

Orientation, information and interpretation

Assuming most visitors are new to the place in which they arrive, the immediate need is for the portrayal of a positive first impression and then a means for orientation and direction. The process or method of orientation and direction from the point of arrival is all part of a visitor management and dispersion strategy as it highlights attractions and directs the experience of the visitor. There are many methods and media for interpretation in historic towns; most importantly they must not be obstructive to the place and its daily life, and to be successful they must make the visitor feel part of the place and not just a spectator.

Information and interpretation

The aim of interpretation should be to provide sufficient information to familiarise the visitor with the place and to inform. Stirling (1995: 16) advocates that a 'higher priority of education and information [be] available to the visitor as an integral part of all tourism policies'. The quality of interpretative tools and the information they provide are paramount in securing a better understanding and respect for a place. At the same time, in a competitive environment where people are becoming more widely travelled, poor-quality or sub-standard interpretation is no longer acceptable. Interpretation also serves management, as better awareness leads to respect and better care of the environment. Any information provided must not be overwhelming, nor should it distract from the inherent qualities of a place.

Key deliberations lie in how much information is fed to the visitor, the methods by which this is done and the appropriateness of the chosen method to the surroundings and urban character. Interpretation in the more static museum situation is through signboards, recorded commentary and the like. Increasingly, similar tools are being applied in the urban environment. While explanatory signs are useful for major buildings, an abundance of signage not only creates a museum-like environment but also devalues the 'not explained', while the use of headsets and similar interpretative media isolates visitors from the place. In a museum the attraction is the objects, and a museum style of interpretation, whether it be information boards or headphones, ignores the rich urban and human dimension of towns. In a town visitors have the unique opportunity to perceive, understand, live and be part of urban life. The attraction of festivals to many visitors is that they are not simply spectators but have an opportunity to be participants in what is an element of local life.

Interpretative media in town centres include signposts, display or information panels and plaques on buildings, supported by loose material such as maps, guidebooks and leaflets. Signage is a planning tool to highlight attractions and guide visitors. A signpost to a major cathedral may also point to a less well-known museum, drawing visitors' attention to it. Absence of signage, on the other hand, helps to reduce pressures at an over-subscribed location; for example the removal of roadside signs on a motorway to 'historic . . .' will lessen casual passing trade.

Information and signage have to be sensitive to the location and provide a recognisable focus for the visitor. Today, signage and other forms of urban interpretation materials have become familiar 'catalogue' items, compounding similarity in historic towns. A re-evaluation of the interpretation scheme in St Andrews in Scotland recognised the importance of both rationalising signposts and using imaginative design ideas, adapting a scheme using slim vertical panels set against buildings at key junction points.

Fig. 6.2 Attraction signposts commonly follow the same 'heritage' imagery:
(a) in York;
(b) in Covent Garden, London.

(a)   *(b)*

More innovative tools for direction and interpretation are available to the urban designer, including pedestrian arrangements or inviting vistas created down streets. A vista or a glimpse capturing monuments or major buildings with a pedestrian-friendly street leads the visitor through urban space; and a sense of discovery encourages the visitor to find more as complexity naturally unravels itself. Meaningful use of space heightens appreciation of it. A market square used as a car park is more likely to be ignored as visitors distance themselves from the car environment; whereas a pedestrianised market square becomes a highlight, a place to linger and somewhere to discover attractions, as well as a point of orientation (see also Figure 2.12 and Figure 1, Quedlinburg).

Providing the interpretation:
visitor centres, multi-media and active interpretation
A more direct approach to interpretation is a specifically created visitor centre, nowadays taking over from the more traditional tourist information office. A visitor centre, conveniently located and providing a reliable service, may become a focus and promotional opportunity. In response to competition and visitor demand and in order to remain attractive to a wider audience, much of the interpretation is turning to anecdotal multi-media frames of history which eventually bear little connection to the urban environment being visited. With a growing interest in theme parks and theming, the visitor, however, has come to expect the multi-media, the

recorded tape tour and the themed interpretation. It can be argued that the present-day multi-media visitor centre is also a tendency towards museumising the city (see Chapter 3). A city museum or visitor centre often takes on a role of historic interpretation for the historic town. Interpretation, which is a useful and enjoyable educational tool, highlights the vital distinction between history (historic event) and contemporary life. A visitor centre is also an important opportunity to provide information and direction on a wide range of leisure and cultural activities which may not be known to the visitor, and if it is carefully organised it can act as a cultural focal point for the place, not just as a visitor facility.

More active interpretation of the historic environment extends to the use of actors and street theatre, at times not dissimilar to the animation common to the theme park environment. Seen purely as a tourist attraction, little of this has any relevance to everyday life. The use of town criers in several English historic towns, for example, is seen as a tourist gimmick by tourists and locals alike. The need for animation, clearly a theatre, to an urban environment which is becoming a stage set must be carefully considered in the interpretation it is providing and the image it is portraying to the visitor. On the other hand, the use of more traditional dramatic animation organised by local groups in celebration of a certain day or event, rather than the start of the tourist season, could be more 'real' to the life of the city. For example, the wagon plays associated with the four-yearly cycle of Mystery plays in York are primarily the celebration of a local event put on by a large cast of local amateur actors (Figure 6.3). In the West the differentiation of past and present, the everyday and the 'acted', is established, whereas animation in cultures less familiar to the visitor often leads to misunderstandings; even restaurant waiters or hotel staff in 'traditional' dress which is no longer common are easily taken, wrongly, by the visitor as being in their everyday attire.

Fig. 6.3 The medieval wagon plays are organised and performed by local amateur groups in York during the four-yearly cycle of Mystery plays.

Heritage trails

A heritage trail or walk can be seen as an opportunity to present a better, and also a chosen, view of a place to visitors, to increase visitor circulation, to allow visitors to discover and appreciate other aspects of the town and to ensure attractions in less central locations are also visited. Heritage trails contribute to visitor management, reducing pressures on central popular areas and extending time spent in a town. Some examples of well-known trails include the Sherlock Holmes Trail around London's Baker Street and the Freedom Trail through Boston's North End, marked with a red line. Possibly because of the scale of Boston and the robustness of the area, the trail does not become an intrusion and even the bold red line does not appear obtrusive. The use of a city wall as a pedestrian route is also a way of providing visitors with an alternative view of a place. An alternative to an established trail is to provide regular guided walks, which if well managed provide visitors with a much more in-depth understanding of a place, without the trouble of having to read about it.

Designed predominantly for the Western market, the heritage trail and in some cases visitors walking around with headsets will be seemingly out of place in other cultural environments. First the chosen route has to be carefully considered and should not interfere with local life if this is going to prove unwelcome. A European suggestion for the small Jordanian town of Salt includes a proposal for 'town trails' and a 'heritage centre' (RSS 1991), both of which are awkward impositions onto a small traditional town. Foreign men wearing shorts peering into courtyards are

Fig. 6.4 The city walls of York have become an additional attraction as a pleasant walk and an ideal way of seeing the old city.

unlikely to be welcome in the strictly 'private' residential areas of an Islamic town. Even the identification of a row of cottages on a heritage-trail map may cause resident irritation from tourists peering through their windows.

Interpretation is a delicate balance among providing sufficient guidance, not oversimplifying the experience and allowing the visitor to be free to discover the complexity of an urban environment. Often there is scope to be more imaginative than simply depending on signposting and designated trails, ensuring that the visitor feels there is more to discover while not being overwhelmed by the place.

Planning and managing urban use

The oversupply of service soon makes the product cheaper, whether it is too many hotels competing for the package deals or too many cafes in a square. St Mark's Square, Venice, however, will never have enough cafes charging exorbitant amounts for small cups of espresso. The amount, location and distribution of services can play an important part in managing visitors and tourism in historic towns. Planning authorities are able to regulate the location and distribution of some establishments through licensing agreements, while safeguarding residential areas or religious uses.

Multi-functional use in city centres is universally becoming recognised as desirable (see Jane Jacobs 1962 among others), and many West European and North American cities are attempting to revitalise their dormant 'modern' city centres. This desired and recently re-established multi-functionality is the predominant and existing pattern of historic centres encompassing commercial, administrative, residential, light industrial, entertainment and leisure uses. Most of these functions closely overlap as part of the unique quality of an historic town. This interrelation, however, is not coincidental, but the outcome of established relationships among production, retail and daily life. Use designation to empty plots and changes of use by planning authorities play an important role in delivering and maintaining a quality of life for all concerned, including the nature and distribution of new uses connected to tourism.

Ultimately the location of services and facilities directs flow patterns. Removing some services from a bottleneck or popular attraction reduces pressure, whereas relocating them a little further away helps to distribute loads, thus making another part of the town attractive. Leaving a popular cathedral square free of facilities will ease the pressure, whereas promoting restaurants and bars along a river front or dock could start regenerating a derelict industrial area. Making an underused space, square or park more attractive with new facilities, new features or an exhibition will also distribute loads, provided that it is actively promoted. The use of squares, pedestrian intersections and parks in Barcelona creates some very attractive environments in the urban fabric, appealing to visitors as a sense of discovery and an opportunity to mingle with locals. In the colder climate of Berlin, on the other hand, the utilisation of railway arches for antique or book shops and cafes has helped create attractive and lively environments.

In response to tourist pressures, land use planning and use allocation, as part of tourism planning, must closely relate to existing local plan objectives for land use and take into consideration physical pressure points. Careful and situation-dependent decisions have to be made and balances sought. For example,

*Fig. 6.5 Cordoba:
(a) A few streets
away from the 'tourist
centre'...
(b) calm is regained.*

(a)

(b)

concentrating tourist functions into central locations allows for quieter residential areas, which can be used for tourist accommodation, whereas dispersing tourist developments can spread the benefits of tourism to a larger part of the town as well as easing pressure points. The opening times of cultural and leisure attractions and retail activity are a determinant of usage in urban spaces and loads at a given time, and can contribute to making an historic town or area attractive over a longer time period. The cultural attraction of the Pompidou Centre in Paris has created a social and leisure focus for the surrounding area.

It may be that certain areas of a town become designated as 'tourist' areas. While in the case of a large metropolis such as London, Leicester Square and Piccadilly Circus can be dismissed and avoided by Londoners as tourist centres, this is not possible in smaller towns, where resentment is felt if a previously enjoyed centre becomes overwhelmed by tourist activity, especially if locals are deterred from favourite haunts for economic reasons and 'tourist pricing'. The absence of locals in central areas is an indication that a capital of 'urban life' is being rapidly consumed, remembering also that the visitor covets the place where the locals eat or hang out.

Commerce

In the latter part of the twentieth century the western world has become a consumer society and shopping a leisure activity. A tourist attraction undoubtedly encourages commerce and today cultural attractions not only are overwhelmed by commercial activity, but also are in competition with retail. The control and distribution of commercial activity are an invaluable means for controlling and guiding tourists to certain locations where their needs can be best addressed, and even an under-valued tourist attraction can be made more attractive with an increase in shopping facilities. In the commercial districts of eastern towns, retaining the urban fabric supports the existing informal tradition and with it the growth and change of crafts within their own environment. While a display of local crafts in themed craft villages helps preserve maybe long-forgotten skills, the nurturing of the actual craft and commercial environment allows for the natural development of the craft tradition.

However, the importance of heritage value over commercial and economic gain must be recognised and commercial activity remain appropriate and sensitive to the qualities of an historic area. Concentrating tourist commercial areas means that they can then be supported by other amenities and hospitality services, such as cafes and restaurants. Dispersion of commercial activity, on the other hand, spreads the load and pressure from a single locality and may help to create a new focus, such as the waterfront developments in Barcelona in the late 1980s. Tourism-related commerce has to be balanced against local need and appropriateness to the place. Local and established trade is part of continuity in the urban environment, and a tourist trade 'take-over' creates tourist ghettos, at the expense of community and character.

Local culture or climate influences activity in a commercial area. In Northern Europe most shops close between five and six o'clock in the evening and in the absence of residential uses a central area can quickly become isolated and empty. In the Mediterranean region, on the other hand, climate and social lifestyle dictate that shops close at midday, to reopen in the cooler early evening hours and close late, depending on demand. Thus the commercial district is occupied for a longer part of the day and many cafes and restaurants are integrated as shopping spills into evening activities which keep the area 'alive'. Entertainment and noise,

Fig. 6.6 Tourist commerce need not overwhelm historic towns; there are many sensitive ways in which commerce is incorporated into historic fabric, such as these examples from: (a) Mdina in Malta (b) Erfurt in Germany.

(a)

(b)

however, can deter residential use, threatening accepted levels of calm and privacy. In the Plaka district of Athens, residents started leaving the area when noise levels from entertainment establishments became intolerable.

In Islamic towns both morphological and social conflicts arise between tourist commercialism and 'private' residential quarters. First, the neighbourhood unit is not physically formed to accommodate such activity, as it is typically a tight network of streets and cul-de-sacs with few public open spaces. Second, in residential quarters the ground level is used for access, and it is enclosed by high walls so as to ensure privacy in houses, with openings only on the upper levels. Penetration of commercial activity at the ground level not only damages the physical fabric but alters the character of the townscape. Moreover, it is a deliberate intrusion into the cultural and social privacy carefully secured through urban patterns and architecture. Today, residential quarters in many of Turkey's coastal historic towns have been transformed into a thoroughfare of retail activity, rendering the values they represent worthless.

Retaining an existing private–public segregation could benefit both residents and visitors. The hustle and bustle in the crowded markets, contrasting with the calm and quiet of 'private' residential areas, feed tourist expectations and they are more attractive than a continuous tourist retail extravaganza, which tourists eventually avoid. In Antalya, for example, tourists are now seen to walk around rather than through the old town, and the retail take-over in Kuşadası has been such that few visitors today would even know it is an historic quarter. To a certain extent

Fig. 6.7 (a) (right) Every piece of spare space is used for commercial activity in Antalya. (b) (overleaf) High ground-floor walls and small openings indicate 'privacy' in residential neighbourhoods, Bergama, Turkey.

(a)

(b)

the physical urban language communicates a place and its use to the visitor; whereas a tourist shop legitimates the visitor's presence, uninviting high walls and a maze of streets often prove a deterrent, and experience shows that very few visitors will delve too deeply, ensuring the continuity of a certain level of privacy (Figure 6.5b).

Enhancing the cultural experience
The typical visitor to historic towns is intellectually stimulated and culture seeking. Adding to the cultural attraction of a place through appropriate and sensitive 'events' can be a better investment than introducing new, including multi-media, attractions. Historic locations such as cathedrals, castles, palaces and open-air theatres are ideal settings for cultural activities, as such activities and events increase their use and attract attention to their historic qualities. Classical music concerts in the open courtyard of the Rector's Palace in Dubrovnik or the use of Greek amphitheatres for open-air theatre and concerts in Greece and Turkey are typical examples. Night-time use adds a cultural depth which contrasts with the daytime activity of a place, enticing visitors to spend the night. Nevertheless, the chosen cultural activity must be appropriate to the setting and a balance needs to be sought between enhancing and using a building through cultural activity and the potential damage caused by overuse, for example thousands of spectators in an ancient theatre. Vibrations from rock concerts at the ancient theatre of Ephesus have damaged the historic fabric, as have the pressures of modern equipment and

heavy service vehicles driving into historic town centres or over archaeological material in order to service events.

The reuse of redundant buildings in town centres not only provides visitors with the opportunity to stay in 'different' and 'authentic' buildings associated with the historic environment but also keeps them closer to the commercial centre and the facilities it offers, increasing the potential for direct economic benefit to the town. Tourism projects must also be balanced with city-wide policies for land use and transportation. Car parking facilities do, however, play a role in determining the choice of accommodation.

Traffic and transportation management

Traffic congestion, parking and access difficulties have been identified as major challenges to historic towns, and at times a threat to the integrity and attraction of the historic environment. Transport and traffic planning and management in historic towns involve the use of transportation to reach the destination and associated parking; they also cover all forms of transportation within a locality from cars and public transportation systems to cycle routes or waterways transport. The point and mode of arrival are very significant and a key to the planning of orientation and interpretation facilities. The location of a railway station in relation to an historic centre, for example, can play a significant role in tourism development.

Traffic calming and regulation in cities, including pedestrianisation schemes, are modest attempts only, and are effective only if they are tied into wider regional or nationwide policies on transportation, car use and public transport.

The car

In the post-war period leading urban thinking, including CIAM (International Congress of Modern Architecture), identified the car as the new symbol of urban living, making vehicular transport a dominant power in urban planning, and thus

Fig. 6.8 The planned removal of cars from this square in Quedlinburg will increase appreciation of the environment and open it up to better public use.

the development of public transportation including trams or light rail systems was not sufficiently encouraged. By the time the Buchanan Report *Traffic in Towns* (1963) challenged these attitudes, the car had become established as the major form of transportation in the western developed world, with the rest of the world aspiring to the same. The private car has become such a global aspiration that despite overcrowded roads, parking problems and growing environmental concerns, it is a legacy difficult to eradicate. The simultaneous decline of public transportation systems in favour of the car further militates against environmentalist efforts to reduce car usage.

In England it has been estimated that 70 per cent of tourists arrive in historic towns by car (English Historic Towns Forum 1994). Accommodating vehicular traffic is a major concern for many historic town authorities, and one which will be closely linked to a national transportation policy. Finding parking solutions particularly has become a serious concern, as the problems of welcoming and orientation are compounded when a visitor's first view of a place is a car park, a sea of cars. An approach heralded in a number of historic towns in Western Europe, including English ones, is 'Park and Ride', whereby an out-of-town car park is provided for visitors coming into the town, with a frequent and free bus service into the centre. In York, for example, the scheme has proved very successful, but nevertheless it continues to favour the car driver. The local bus service which non-car owners remain dependent on compares badly with the frequency and apparent efficiency of a Park and Ride service. A similar and successful scheme has been in operation in Bologna since the 1980s.

For the tourist-historic town the second largest pressure is the arrival of tourist buses into the urban centre. Associated with mass tourism, they are often too large and disruptive to narrow traditional streets and a visual eyesore in their numbers. Calculated per person the bus group may be more environmentally friendly, but questions arise as to how near an attraction these buses should come, with the

Fig. 6.9 Tourist buses are both an intrusion and dangerous to the fabric of historic towns.

associated and obtrusive parking. As few as three large, high buses within an historic environment can be visually obstructive. Further environmental concerns are raised as buses line up in front of a 'short-stay' attraction with their engines running. Bus tourists also represent the short-stay and regulated day visitors. Some solutions include strict regulation and the introduction of permits or dedicated parking locations with transfer to the centre on lighter local transportation systems.

Planning transportation systems

A transport planning approach needs to be coordinated and responsive to local needs. 'Transportation should be planned for the citizens. Tourists need different facilities' (Feilden 1990: 16). Not only should the point of arrival link into the transportation network, but various transportation forms should link into one another, with a tram or bus stop positioned by a riverside pier for example. To be successful, pedestrianised zones also need to tie into transportation systems. Good external links such as location on a major railway network will help reduce the pressures of cars and parking; but it has to be supported by a good local network to be successful. The high-speed railway arrival in York is very efficient, but other transportation links to the region are so unreliable and uncoordinated that visitors to the region continue to arrive by car.

Another concern is the poor environmental quality in towns which is caused by heavy traffic and congestion. In response some cities are opting for road pricing schemes or increasing road taxes. Practical measures for mass transportation schemes include tramways, underground rail systems, bus networks and the better use of waterways. Transportation has to be cheap to be attractive and must primarily serve the local need; having achieved this critical mass it will go on to serve the visitor. Transportation networks require large capital investments, and future needs have to be clearly considered, to cover for example changing work practices or a growing ageing population. The appropriateness of a mass transport system into an historic environment also has to be considered. The detriment of building an underground system in an historic area or the appropriate size of buses for narrow streets, for example, has to be considered, but a tramway does not have to imitate an historic model either.

Tourism may be a catalyst in the development of light rail systems and trams, in some instances for their authentic value. The reinstatement of trams or light rail systems has provided not only a good tourist attraction but also a convenient means of transportation for residents and visitors. One example is along Istiklal Street in Istanbul's popular Beyoğlu district, which is an important through route but also a popular shopping area, where the tram provides a means of transportation but allows the remainder of the street to be a pedestrian zone.

City tours may provide a good view of attractions, but an inappropriate choice of vehicle can be disruptive. The open-top double-decker bus tours, popular and successful in Edinburgh and London, where they are perceived as a continuation of the bus network, are choking the city centre of York. Residents protesting against the number of buses, belonging to rival companies, realised they could not be restricted, because they are private enterprises competing in a 'free market', and the bus companies have little interest in residents, who are not potential customers.

Fig. 6.10 The reintroduced trams in Istanbul's popular Beyoğlu district.

It may pay, however, for the West to look at some of the more environmentally friendly urban transport systems of the developing world, including the better use of cycles and cycle rickshaws, of which an experimental business was launched in Oxford in England. Car travel cannot be completely eliminated and transportation policy has to plan to accommodate, but not be dominated by, the car. An integrated traffic approach also advocated by the English Historic Towns Forum is to consider all options, including pedestrian needs and cycling. An increase in city centre living increases the importance of providing sufficient car parking and access for residents and thereafter a transportation system which will be good enough to actively discourage car usage.

Fig. 6.11 This small 'train' may appear like a gimmick, but it is a low-impact way of conducting tours around Quedlinburg.

Pedestrianisation to manage traffic

Since the early 1970s, in Europe many successful schemes stopping through traffic and introducing pedestrianisation have benefited both shoppers and shop-keepers; these schemes allow vehicular access in early morning and evening hours. With the commercialisation of historic centres, restricting traffic and parking provides safer pedestrian areas. The story has been told of many places where shopkeepers and local businesses have protested against pedestrianisation and have later come to value it immensely as an excellent boost to their businesses.

Such schemes suffer the disadvantages of restricted access for residential use in the centre and the concentration of parking problems on the immediate periphery of the pedestrianised zone. Completely pedestrianising central areas as a blanket policy may also isolate surrounding areas from the benefits of tourism and commerce. Furthermore, pedestrianisation may also be limiting to other forms of popular transport such as bicycles or rickshaws, common to many Asian cities. Selective and imaginative pedestrianisation can add more interest to a location. In Edinburgh the Royal Mile, which runs through the Old Town, was not fully pedestrianised, but the widening of pavements increased activity and was further supported by traffic regulation discouraging through traffic. This created a lively pedestrian area which encourages visitors to explore the Old Town and wander in the maze of small streets that surround the main thoroughfare. The creation of a central pedestrian alley in the Spanish *rambla*, for example, creates a new attraction of city life between two negotiable streams of traffic. The interface and links between pedestrian and traffic zones have to be carefully designed and have to be recognised as being as important as the pedestrian zone.

With good access to central locations, visitors are encouraged to lodge centrally, thereby benefiting the local economy. The restriction of traffic and parking does, however, often result in peripheral accommodation being developed and becoming

Fig. 6.12 The Ramblas in Barcelona, both a pedestrian zone and a place for urban activity.

the monopoly of the larger operators. Consequently, evening and night-time activity in the centre is reduced, particularly when a centre is no longer at a walkable distance from the accommodation; this renders the centre dangerous at times. In a typical inside–outside dichotomy, an out-of-town hotel may be owned by a multinational chain whereas a small cafe or restaurant in the centre is locally owned. However, an example from Lyon is worth considering, where the large-chain hotels were not interested in investing in the old town because it lacked vehicular access and views. One of the most popular hotels in Lyon, however, is an independent initiative converted from four buildings which were restored around a covered courtyard (Repellin 1990).

Pedestrianisation for pedestrian enjoyment

The aim of reducing traffic in town centres is to improve environmental quality for users. Pedestrianisation schemes must be treated with great care, and planned and designed for the sought-after quality. Pedestrian networks must above all be attractive to pedestrians, allowing for the discovery and appreciation of the environment, as well as being inviting. Arcades for example encourage penetration into the built environment and make pedestrian movement more dynamic.

The choice and use of surface materials are also important; whereas concrete paving blocks are common to new towns, cobblestones are favoured in historic towns. Figure 2.2 illustrates the love of cobbled streets which is shared by visitors and the marketing profession alike. Cobblestones provide an acceptable texture and colour to the paving of roads in an historic town but many neatly laid contemporary cobbled streets bear little resemblance to their historic forebears. And even cobbled streets have been contested at times. In the old town of Lyon they were asphalted over when stiletto heels were fashionable, and only reinstated once heel fashions became more accommodating (Repellin 1990). But other

Fig. 6.13 The choice of paving in old towns should compliment the local architectural idiom.
(a) Red-brick paving in Bhaktapur, Nepal.
(b) Original paving in Quedlinburg, Germany.
(c) Newly laid cobblestones and public art in a small square in Maastricht, The Netherlands.

(a)

(b)

(c)

considerations also arise, as disabled users and the elderly need surfaces that are easy to negotiate. Most importantly, the use of natural materials not only continues a tradition but best enhances the character of a place – materials such as the red-brick paving used in the historic towns of the Kathmandu valley (Figure 6.13a), or the cobbles from the local river bed in Quedlinburg (Figure 6.13b).

Street furniture is an important part of the pedestrianised environment. For many early schemes local authorities frequently purchased the standard flower-pots and benches from the paving providers. Questioned even in the modern shopping districts of Germany's industrial Ruhr area, they are inappropriate and often unsympathetic to historic town environments. So are the now widely available catalogue-purchased 'heritage' lampposts and benches. Street furniture and lighting must be seen as an integral part of townscape design, not re-creating an 'authentic' that may never have existed, but designing for contemporary urban life. As users are unlikely to want to 'experience' open sewers or the absence of telephone booths, they should not have to be subjected to mass-produced imitation gas lamps.

The role of design

Managing an historic town centre and visitors within it may be dependent on national, regional and particularly local policy, but some of the most effective solutions will be innovation and design led. Authorities have to recognise the importance of design and creative initiative. Design provides imaginative solutions, the subtle language of direction, aesthetic, townscape value, and reflection of quality as well as being an effective management tool. Among the many conflicts that have been identified in the historic town environment, there is the physical tension between the old morphology and the new. The junction or interface of the two, sometimes a physical barrier such as a city wall and in other cases the boundaries of a conservation area, is an important point for consideration, and through good design a dialogue is established and an interface better managed. The design role covers many aspects of an historic town, including:

- urban design;
- design of pedestrian areas, materials and interfaces;
- appropriate car parks;
- transportation and related facilities;
- visitor facilities, information booths, kiosks and the like;
- street furniture;
- heritage trails;
- signage.

(a) *(b)*

Fig. 6.14 Rather than catalogue 'heritage' items, lighting, like other street furniture, should be appropriate to the place and setting: (a) In front of York Minster; (b) On the Paseo de Gracia in Barcelona.

Fig. 6.15 Visitor facilities like these public toilets in York do not have to use an 'historical' stylistic language.

The innovative role of the designer must not be overlooked; it should be encouraged wherever possible. Design is not an add-on commission, but an important part of the planning, development and renewal process. Good design (and good detailing) complements rather than imitates or overpowers; it does not have to be obvious but it must enhance, as poor design only devalues a place. Designers must start by understanding the old town, its values and dynamism; and they must also remember that design is for the benefit and enjoyment of all, particularly the people who call a town their own.

Enhancing the place

Visiting an historic town is not about going to a museum or a journey into the past to see how people used to live; it is a pleasurable experience of leisure and cultural activity in a place where people still live.

The people value

It is an established fact that historic towns are attractive to visitors not only for their physical qualities but also for the 'life' within them. Why is it then that tourism so often deters people from 'living' in historic quarters?

An historic centre must remain sufficiently attractive, convenient and safe for the people to want to live there; if it is a good place for the residents, then it will also be a good place for the visitor to enjoy. It is often forgotten that the things 'real' people do are attractive to visitors. Fruit and vegetable markets, for example, are often more interesting to tourists than stalls selling tourist paraphernalia. Tourists do not want to go to places full of people like themselves, but to where the locals go, eat, live, etc. It is also a truth, however, that locals avoid establishments they perceive to be for tourists.

The people of a place not only belong there, but are part of a natural and irreplaceable resource. Developers need to look at ongoing activity before devising

Fig. 6.16 Flea markets, such as this one in Madrid, attract visitors and locals alike.

Fig. 6.17 Markets where locals shop are just as interesting for visitors (Dubrovnik, Croatia).

exhaustive plans for tourism development through added attractions. For a place to 'work', development objectives have to respond to the people; any development, from better transportation networks to increased cultural activity, must first be relevant to the resident community. Revitalising a former mining town with culture that is 'out of touch' with the people is not serving the aim of rehabilitation and can only be short lived.

Keeping a creative spirit alive
The enjoyment of architecture will always be a minority pleasure, but the spirit of place has more general appeal (P. Harrison 1990). Old towns often generate and

harbour a creative spirit, an artistic community which is quickly displaced through gentrification and the take-over of the tourism industry. In most West European towns this is long forgotten as fashionable and expensive art galleries occupy the smart streets of 'conserved' old towns, and commercial 'artists' line themselves up in cathedral squares. A contrast is afforded by the urban spirit captured in bombed-out Dubrovnik, a newly emerging Tallinn in the early 1990s or Quedlinburg after the fall of the Berlin Wall.

Art creates a dialogue between people and place and is also a means of communicating the values of a place to others. It is an extremely delicate balance to retain this dynamic spirit as places become gentrified and the artistic community is squeezed out. The value of art to a place is when it has been nurtured in the area and not when it has been implanted. Crafts also play an important part in a community's life, but they often become falsely interpreted for the tourism trade, becoming cheaper rather than richer, mass produced rather than exclusive.

The fact that tourism encourages the continuation of a craft tradition is in most cases a myth, as mass tourism favours the cheaper end of the market. However, some crafts may benefit from tourism, evolving in response to demand. The craft tradition in any community is a reflection of contemporary lives; it is true that many traditional crafts and craft skills are rapidly being lost, but this too is a reflection of contemporary lifestyles. Many craft trades that thrived at the beginning of the twentieth century have been superseded through modern agricultural practice, transportation and mass production. Crafts are in continuous evolution in response to daily living and locally available materials, and must be permitted to develop and at times die. Historic buildings also reflect the crafts tradition, and the value of craft that has gone into each building represents human value (Repellin 1990). A living and dynamic environment, giving vent to its own creative spirit, through links of art and architecture, includes good new buildings but much else as well.

Fig. 6.18 Art in the urban environment can be spontaneous. An installation in Erfurt, Germany, soon after the Wall came down.

Environmental value

'Eco-tourism' is an unlikely label to be attached by travel agents to the historic town short break, but much of the use and activity in an historic town can be environmentally considerate. The reuse of an area, the reuse of existing buildings, the lower energy demands of existing buildings or the pedestrian scale which encourages walking are just some aspects. More direct measures such as the reduction or restriction of vehicular traffic contribute to environmental quality in historic towns. The old towns of the East are even better examples of energy efficiency. Many of them operate with pedestrian or cycle-based transportation, production to consumption takes place within the same area, and many are also centres of recycling, through the reuse of waste materials as part of the indigenous industries.

In an era of growing environmental consciousness, the value of the old town cannot be overestimated. Before a tourist cycle of economy is imposed on old towns, some of the depth and importance of their industry and activity should be reassessed. In this respect the West has much to learn from the East, where resource preservation and environmental concern are still imperative to the economy. The inner courtyard smithy or the greasy mechanic's workshop may be the first to go when a clean tourist image is being created, but they are a vital link in urban survival and the 'life' of an historic town.

Adding value

However popular historic towns become, at times there is the need to enhance the so-called 'product' by adding value, not simply because it is a product but also because the town is a place where people live. The added value that makes a locality different from and better than others may no longer lie only in its historic qualities, but may also be sought in the active elements of the town or modern-day additions. This may occur by increasing the cultural attraction through music events or theatre as in Quedlinburg, for example, or through staging a special event. Glasgow in its historic associations is most likely to be known as a dirty industrial city, but it has successfully employed added value to great effect. The first of these activities was the Burrell Collection, which opened in 1983. The Glasgow Garden Festival was organised in 1988; and in 1990 Glasgow became Cultural Capital of Europe, with a year-long celebration of cultural activity; most recently, in 1999, it was City of Architecture & Design. In each case culture was used as a tool for urban renewal, improving the city and turning it into an attractive place to visit; while each event was seized as a marketing opportunity, and in the portrayal of the Glasgow identity.

Using events such as festivals or expositions to concentrate on a place creates new meaning, and a focus. Festivals, like added culture, have to be locally generated and relevant. The popularity, depth and interest in an event, be it religious fiesta or literary festival, are based on local will and involvement. Events in historic towns need not be historic or 'traditional', nor need they be forced to be repeated annually. At times the one-off is more successful in focusing local interest and outsider attention on a place. While a 'tired' event devalues a place, an innovative one draws attention to it and creates a new value of place for the residents (see Figure 4.5).

Maintaining value

The 1995 ICOMOS Conference on Historic Cities and Sustainable Tourism stressed particularly in conclusion the importance of quality and the high-quality product. Quality is best achieved and value best maintained by ensuring that the input comes from local sources. Local residents, businesses or artists are the best resource an historic town has and yet they are often the first casualties of market forces. The basis of quality is not necessarily a subscribed formula, such as the prerequisites for stars in hotels, but it depends on an understanding of the 'self value' of a place, its own uniqueness. Small businesses are more likely to reflect unique features and characteristics of the place and of the local culture. All too often businesses become based on 'imported' products and imported cultures. The visitor–host encounter takes place mainly through local businesses. Furthermore, they collectively dominate the environment and its quality as perceived by the visitor (Middleton and Hawkins 1998).

The local is deterred from the tourist restaurant either because it is too expensive or simply because it is a tourist restaurant, while the visitor goes in search of where the locals eat out: a common story and one in which there are a number of lessons. The host–guest relationship is unlikely to be completely smooth with everyone meeting and chatting in the central square, but it is a relationship that can be eased and that can even prosper. More local control of the product and, as importantly, its marketing will increase the feeling of ownership, and lead to a more direct give and take relationship with the visitor. Each place would like to welcome the ideal visitors, arriving in a small family group by train, staying in a local bed and breakfast for a few nights and spending liberally at local establishments and shops. However, Venice will be plagued by the East European bus tourists for some time to come yet and it is more important to manage and develop the existing tourist base than dream of what may sometimes be impossible.

Summary and conclusions

This final chapter has addressed the management of visitors in historic towns. In planning terms it is about making and keeping a place attractive. The best ingredient in each case is the unique character and distinctiveness, which must be enhanced and not compromised with off-the-shelf management solutions. A sun-drenched Italian piazza cannot be re-created in England, and many aspects and qualities of Bath would look out of place once removed from an English landscape setting. City authorities have to work towards enhancing the values of the place and the lived-in environment through the resource best available to them, the local community.

Urban management in the historic environment involves a thorough understanding of the place and the aspirations of the people who live in it. There are many conflicts in historic towns, between old and new, preservation and development, insiders and outsiders, locals and visitors. Collaborative decision making at the local level is about balancing need. Much tension can be avoided and pressures of tourism lessened through informed management decisions supported by good design solutions for the lived-in environment.

In conclusion

Montgomery (1998: 95), writing on the design of new cities, lists urban qualities that are appreciated by users:

- a sense of place;
- activity within and permeability of urban form;
- a mixture of building type and age;
- an involvement in the activity of change;
- an encouragement of diversity, mixed land ownership, and small and large businesses;
- social interaction in the public realm;
- a place that has identity, image and meaning;
- the adaptability of the urban environment and its buildings for longer than their intended life expectancy of function;
- human scale.

They are very much the qualities inherent and valued in historic towns. In the way they are intended for contemporary developments, the above guidelines should also be informing growth and change in historic towns. In times of rapid change historic towns and centres are a reference of stability through familiarity and recognition; but they are also dependent on 'keeping up' with change to remain valid and active.

Globally, change is taking place in many forms, some of it at unprecedented speed, such as is the case with information technology. Accessibility and location values are changing, and urban economies are moving from industry and production to service and consumption. The public and private sectors are no longer separate entities. Work, private and leisure time, and thus environments, are becoming linked in the new complexity of human life and activity. There is more conflict and confusion in the way that contemporary society is developing. Leisure activity is increasing, as is travel, but at the same time the pressure of work is increasing, at a time when work patterns are also changing. There is a growing merger of leisure and work in human life through flexible working schedules, but with fewer opportunities for long periods off. Travel and place take on a new dimension, as people have less time to travel but can be in 'another' place while still working. Historic towns provide a pleasant setting, environmental qualities and the added benefit of cultural products, making them attractive as living/working environments. In all spheres good quality is being sought: environment, place, space and leisure.

Tourism is a growth industry and will continue to develop in the historic town and culture markets. Technology is more likely to encourage than diminish travel and cultural pursuits as people continue to seek the 'real' thing. However, too many historic towns have succumbed to becoming 'products' with standard features, as local distinctiveness has given way to predictable environments. Local distinctiveness is not 'a typical Suffolk village'; it is the dynamism of the moment, the ever-changing qualities that make a place a place. The historic town approach to conservation and tourism must be re-addressed. An historic town is not a visitor attraction, it is a place; as a place it *may* be attractive to visitors.

Local governments as leaders in the urban environment have to:

Understand
- Each case to be unique, presenting its own problems and strengths.
- The unique qualities of the place and what make it special.
- The urban environment as a living organism and an ecosystem.
- The place, its morphology and its spatial characteristics.
- The ways in which urban space is being used and interpreted.
- The spirit of the place.

Promote
- Focused decision making.
- Local initiative, thus avoiding dependence on global operators.
- Partnerships, representative of all interests, but with a leadership that has the power to make decisions.
- The avoidance of decision making by committee; an elected leader with the power to decide.
- Fewer situations which put the financier in the role of decision maker.
- Multi-disciplinary communication, coordination and collaboration.
- A community part in decision making.

Plan
- For the local community.
- For local and communal values of culture and heritage.
- For the right market.
- Strategically with a creative vision.
- For the long term.
- For future developments, through adequate preparation, consideration and forecasting.
- Through a process of continual monitoring, self-evaluation and quality control.

Consider

- The environmental opportunities which exist in historic towns.
- Innovative and creative design solutions for the best interests of visitor management so as to maintain a high-quality environment.
- The importance of aspiring towards the highest quality.

Bibliography

ABC-Clio Inc. (1985) *World Economic Data*, California: ABC-Clio.

Abrahamsen, P. (1978) 'Citizen participation in safeguarding the architectural heritage in towns' in *3rd European Symposium of Historic Towns*, Munich: Council of Europe.

Abu-Lughod, J.L. (1980) 'Preserving the living heritage of Islamic cities' in R. Holod (ed.) *Toward an Architecture in the Spirit of Islam*, Philadelphia: The Aga Khan Awards.

Aga Khan Program for Islamic Architecture (1982) *Urban Housing: Designing in Islamic Cultures 2*, Seminar, Cambridge, Massachusetts.

Aga Khan Program for Islamic Architecture (1983) *Adaptive Reuse: Designing in Islamic Cultures 3*, Seminar, Cambridge, Massachusetts.

Aga Khan Program for Islamic Architecture (1984) *Continuity and Change: Designing in Islamic Cultures 4*, Seminar, Cambridge, Massachusetts.

Aga Khan Program for Islamic Architecture (1990) *Urban Regeneration and the Shaping of Growth*, Seminar, Cambridge, Massachusetts.

Agnew, J., Mercer, J. and Sopher, D.E. (1984) *The City in Cultural Context*, Boston: Allen & Unwin.

Aina, T.A. (ed.) (1990) 'Community based organisations', *Environment and Urbanisation* 2, 1, April.

Akçura, T. and Çapar, M. (1973) 'Imar planlarında tarihi kent dokusu ve tarihi eserlerle ilgili tutumların incelenmesi', *Mimarlık* 8: 8–10.

Aktüre, S. (1975) '17. yüzyıl başından 19. yüzyıl ortasına kadarki dönemde Anadolu Osmanlı şehrinde şehirsel yapının degişme süreci', *METU Journal* 1, 1: 101–28.

Aktüre, S. and Şenyapılı, T. (1976) 'Safranbolu'da mekansal yapının gösterdiği nitelikler ve koruma önerilerinin düşündürdükleri', *METU Journal* 2, 1: 61–96.

Akurgal, E. (1970) *Ancient Civilisations and Ruins of Turkey*, Ankara: Türk Tarih Kurumu.

Akurgal, E. (1992) 'Foça örnek bir kent olma yolunda', *Ege Mimarlık* 92/3–4: 30–1.

al-Asad, M. and Serageldin, I. (1997) 'Conservation of Old Sana'a' in I. Serageldin (ed.) *The Architecture of Empowerment: People Shelter and Livable Cities*, London: Academy Editions.

al-Radi, S. (1997) 'Restoration of Old Bukhara' in I. Serageldin (ed.) *The Architecture of Empowerment: People Shelter and Livable Cities*, London: Academy Editions.

Alzoabi, A.Y. (1992) 'The architectural heritage of Salt City, Jordan: a strategy for conservation and restoration', paper presented at 9th Inter-schools Conference on Development, Cardiff (unpublished).

Anastassova, L. (1993) 'Tourism, society and culture in Bulgaria: present situation, prospects and training needs' in *Tourism, Culture and Environment in Cities, Islands and Small States*, Workshop, Valletta: Council of Europe.

Andric, I. (1994) *Bridge over the River Drina* (translated by L.F. Edwards), Harvill, London.

Antoniou, J. (1981) *Islamic Cities and Conservation*, Switzerland: The Unesco Press.

Appleyard, D. (ed.) (1979) *The Conservation of European Cities*, Cambridge, Massachusetts: MIT Press.

Archer, B. (1973) *The Impact of Domestic Tourism*, Bangor: University of Wales Press.

Architects' Journal (1969) 'York conserved', *Architects' Journal* 149, 9: 1744–64.

Architects' Journal (1980) 'Newcastle: view of the city', *Architects' Journal* 172, 28: 50–61.

Architectural Review (1965) 'New York among the old', *Architectural Review* 138, 824: 273–6.

Arel, A. (1992) 'Eski eser tahribatı ve korumasıyla ilgili bazı gözlemler', *Ege Mimarlık* 92/2: 49–50.

Arkon, C. (1992) 'Günümüz korumacılarının sorunları', *Ege Mimarlık* 92/2: 51–6.

Art (1990) 'Mit Zähigheit ans Ziel', *Art* 9: September: 56–68.

Arts and the Islamic World, 'Traditional Architecture of Dubai', special supplement, *Arts and the Islamic World*, 27 and 28.

Ashworth, G.J. (1997) 'Struggling to control the past', *In Focus* 22: 4–5.

Ashworth, G.J. and Larkham, P.J. (eds) (1994) *Building a New Heritage: Tourism, Culture and Identity in the New Europe*, London: Routledge.

Ashworth, G.J. and Tunbridge, J.E. (1990) *The Tourist-Historic City*, London: Belhaven.

Ashworth, G.J. and Voogd, H. (1990) *Selling the City: Marketing Approaches in Public Sector Urban Planning*, London: Belhaven.

ASM (Association pour le Sauvegarde de la Medina) (1985) 'The "Hafsia", Tunis', Mimar 17.

Bairoch, P. (1988) *Cities and Economic Development: From the Dawn of History to the Present*, London: Mansell.

Balabanlılar, M. (1992) 'Akdeniz'in temmuz limanında', *Cumhuriyet*, 20 July.

Balchin, P.N. and Bull, G.H. (1987) *Regional and Urban Economics*, London: Harper & Row.

Bandarin, F. (1979) 'The Bologna experience: planning and historic renovation in a communist city' in D. Appleyard (ed.) *The Conservation of European Cities*, Cambridge, Massachusetts: MIT Press.

Beedham, B. (1991) 'Turkey: star of Islam', *The Economist*, 14 December.

Bektaş, C. (1992) *Koruma Onarım*, Istanbul: YEM Yayın.

Berksun, F. (1992) 'Koruma Yüksek Kurulu ve Koruma Kurulları üzerine bir irdeleme', *Ege Mimarlık* 92/3–4: 28–9.

Berque, J. (1980) 'An Islamic Heliopolis?' in R. Holod (ed.) *Toward an Architecture in the Spirit of Islam*, Philadelphia: The Aga Khan Awards.

Bevan, B. (1938) *History of Spanish Architecture*, London: Batsford.

Bianca, S. (1975) *Architektur und Lebensform im islamischen Stadtwesen*, Zurich: Artemis.

—— (1978) 'Fez: toward the rehabilitation of a great city' in R. Holod (ed.) *Conservation as Cultural Survival*, The Aga Khan Award for Architecture.

Bilgen, P. (1988) 'Antalya: a case for tourist influence in conservation', unpublished MA thesis, Institute of Advanced Architectural Studies, University of York, York.

Binney, M. and Hanna, M. (1978) *Preservation Pays*, London: SAVE Britain's Heritage.

Bleicke, E. (1995) *Das Leben eines Architekten in Quedlinburg*, collected papers.

Bodlender, J. and Lickorish, J.L. (1991) *Developing Tourism Destinations: Policies and Perspectives*, Harlow: Longman.

Boissevain, J. (1993) '"But we live here!": problems of cultural tourism in Malta', *Tourism, Culture and Environment in Cities, Islands and Small States*, Workshop, Valletta: Council of Europe.

—— (1994) 'Discontent in Mdina', *In Focus* 12: 12.

—— (ed.) (1996) *Coping with Tourists: European Reactions to Mass Tourism*, Oxford: Berghahn Books.

—— (1997) 'Problems with cultural tourism in Malta' in C. Fsadni and T. Selwyn (eds) *Sustainable Tourism in Mediterranean Islands and Small Cities*, Malta: Med-Campus.

Böke, H. (1990) 'Restorasyon "bilimsel bir süreç" olmak zorundadır', *Yapı* 105: 35–6.

Boniface, P. (1994) 'Theme park Britain: who benefits and who loses?' in J.M. Fladmark (ed.) *Cultural Tourism*, London: Donhead Publishing.

—— (1995) *Managing Quality Cultural Tourism*, London: Routledge.

Boniface, P. and Fowler, P.J. (1993) *Heritage and Tourism in the 'Global Village'*, London: Routledge.

Borley, L. (1994) 'Managing strategies and financial considerations: historic properties' in R. Harrison (ed.) *Manual of Heritage Management*, Oxford: Butterworth-Heinemann.

Bradford Council (1991) *Bradford*.

Breeze, D.J. (1994) 'Marketing our past' in J.M. Fladmark (ed.) *Cultural Tourism*, London: Donhead.

Browne, S. (1994) 'Heritage in Ireland's tourism recovery' in J.M. Fladmark (ed.) *Cultural Tourism*, London: Donhead.

Buchanan, C.D. (1963) *Traffic in Towns: A Study of the Long Term Problems of Traffic in Urban Areas*, London: HMSO.

Buck, V.J. (1976) *Politics and Professionalism in Municipal Planning*, Beverly Hills: Sage Publications.

Building Design (1999) News, *Building Design* 1383: 2.

Burkart, A.J. and Medlik, S. (1974) *Tourism: Past, Present and Future*, London: Heinemann.

—— (eds) (1975) *The Management of Tourism*, London: Heinemann.

Burke, G. (1971) *Towns in the Making*, London: Edward Arnold.

Butt, R. (1988) 'Auditing your heritage assets' in *Heritage and Successful Regeneration*, Strasbourg: Council of Europe.

Calvert, A.F. (1907) *Granada and the Alhambra*, London: The Bodley Head.

Canclini, N.G. (1998) 'Cultural policy options in the context of globalisation', *World Culture Report 1998: Culture Creativity and Markets*, Paris: Unesco Publishing.

Cantacuzino, S. (1975) *Architectural Conservation in Europe*, Oxford: Architectural Press.

Çeçener, B. (1992) 'Ülkemizde taşınmaz kültür ve doğa varlıkları koruma olayı ve bu konuda bazı eleştirel görüşler', *Ege Mimarlık* 92/2: 46–8.

Cessarelli, P. (1979) 'Venice: urban renewal, community power structure and social conflict' in D. Appleyard (ed.) *The Conservation of European Cities*, Cambridge, Massachusetts: MIT Press.

Chelidoni, K. (1997) 'Presentation of an intervention strategy: a case study of the island town of Kos' in C. Fsadni and T. Selwyn (eds) *Sustainable Tourism in Mediterranean Islands and Small Cities*, Malta: Med-Campus.

Cockburn, C. (1991) 'The people's environment', paper presented at International Symposium on Cultural Aspects of Urban Conservation in the Third World Countries, Istanbul (unpublished).

Cockburn, C. and Orbaşlı, A. (1997) 'Marketing historic towns; a western approach to urban conservation for tourism' in C. Fsadni and T. Selwyn (eds) *Sustainable Tourism in Mediterranean Islands and Small Cities*, Malta: Med-Campus.

Conzen, M.R.G. (1981) 'Historical townscapes in Britain: a problem in applied geography' (paper first published in 1966) in J.W.R. Whitehand (ed.) *The Urban Landscape: Historical Development and Management*, papers by M.R.G. Conzen, Institute of British Geographers Special Publication 13, London: Academic Press.

Corina, L. (1975) *Local Government Decision Making: Some Influences on Elected Members' Role Playing*, York: University of York.

Council of Europe (1966) *Leisure in Our Life*.

Council of Europe (1977) *Historic Town Centres in the Development of Present-Day Towns*, Symposium, Strasbourg: Council of Europe.

Council of Europe (1985) *European Conference of Ministers Responsible for the Architectural Heritage*, Strasbourg: Council of Europe.

Cravatte, H. (1977) 'Introduction', *Historic Town Centres in the Development of Present-Day Towns*, Strasbourg: Council of Europe.

Crookston, M. (1992) 'Issues of regeneration for low income cities', paper presented at Urban Regeneration and Urban Design for Low-Income Cities, 9th Interschools Conference on Development, Cardiff (unpublished).

Cumhuriyet (1992) 'Türkiye, turizmde birinci ligde', *Cumhuriyet*, 14 July: 12.

Cummin, D. (1972) *York 2000*, York.

Davey, K.J. (1993) *Elements of Urban Management*, Washington DC: World Bank.

Davidson, H.F.D. (1979) 'The Jordaan and Haarlem neighbourhoods in Amsterdam: planning for the future of a historic neighbourhood', in D. Appleyard (ed.) *The Conservation of European Cities*, Cambridge, Massachusetts: MIT Press.

Davies, K. (1996) 'Cleaning up the coal face and doing out the kitchen' in G. Kavanagh (ed.) *Making Histories in Museums*, Leicester: Leicester University Press.

Debelius, H. (1972) 'For better or worse tourism is keystone of economy', *The Times*, 11 May: v.

de Kadt, E. (ed.) (1980) *Tourism: Passport to Development?*, New York: Oxford University Press.

—— (1990) 'Making the alternative sustainable: lessons from development for tourism', Institute of Development Studies, Brighton: University of Sussex.

Demetriades, L. (1989) 'Case study of Nicosia', *Historic Towns and Tourism*, Strasbourg: Council of Europe.

Department of the Environment (1975) *Positive Conservation*, Yorkshire and Humberside Regional Office.

Department of the Environment (1982) *Whose Town Is It Anyway?*, Conference held to review the European Campaign for Urban Renaissance in Britain, London: HMSO.

Dietvorst, A.G.J. (1994) 'New heritage in Europe' in G.J. Ashworth and P.J. Larkham (eds) *Building a New Heritage: Tourism, Culture and Identity in the New Europe*, London: Routledge.

Dölling, R. (ed.) (1974) *The Conservation of Historic Monuments in the Federal Republic of Germany*, Landshut: Isar-Post.

Dower, M. (1965) 'Fourth wave: the challenge of leisure', *Architects' Journal* 157: 123–90.

—— (1974) 'Tourism and conservation: working together', *Architects' Journal* 166: 941–63.

Duncan, G. (1990) 'Edinburgh, today and tomorrow' in P. Harrison (ed.) *Civilising the City: Quality or Chaos in Historic Towns*, Edinburgh: Nic Allen Publishing.

Duwe, P. (1989) 'West Berlin', *Architects' Journal* 189, 4: 58–9.

ECE (Economic Commission for Europe) (1976) *Planning and Development of the Tourist Industry in the ECE Region*, New York: United Nations.

Ecevit, B. (1991) 'Turistlerden şikayet yağıyor', *Cumhuriyet*, 27 June: 3.

—— (1992) 'Büyük yatırımın cenaze töreni', *Cumhuriyet*, 13 July: 5.

Economist (1974) 'Don't give them napkins', *Economist*, 13 April: 38.

Economist (1977) 'Winners and losers', *Economist*, 3 September: 90–1.

Economist (1980) 'The huddled masses stay away', *Economist*, 19 August: 39–40.

Economist Books (1990) *The Economist Book of Vital World Statistics*, London: Economist Books.

Economist Publications (1987) *The World in Figures*, London: Economist Publications Ltd.

Ekinci, O. (1992) 'Kent planlamasında kültürel kimlik sorunu', *Ege Mimarlık* 92/2: 39–42.

—— (1993) 'Turizmi teşvik yasası ve yağmalanan Istanbul', *Istanbul* 6, July: 18–23.

Elbi, N. (1988) 'Imar planı çalışmalarının arkeolojik sit alanları açısından kentsel değişime etkisi: Bergama Ulu Cami – Talatpaşa – Kurtuluş mahalleleri koruma geliştirme planı'.

Eldem, N., Kamil, N. and Yücel, A. (1978) 'A plan for Istanbul's Sultanahmet – Ayasofya area' in R. Holod (ed.) *Conservation as Cultural Survival*, Seminar, The Aga Khan Awards.

Eldem, S.H. (1984) *Türk Evi – Osmanlı Dönemi I*, Istanbul: TAÇ Vakfı.

England, R. (1990) 'Architecture for tourism', *International Academy of Architecture Journal* 1990/2.

English Historic Towns Forum (1994) *Getting It Right: A Guide to Visitor Management in Historic Towns*, Bath: EHTF.

English Tourist Board (1972) *A Study of Tourism in York*.

English Tourist Board (1974) *Tourism and Conservation*.

Erder, C. (1986) *Our Architectural Heritage: From Consciousness to Conservation*, London: United Nations.

Eren, N. (1963) *Turkey Today and Tomorrow*, London: Pall Mall Press.

Erlet, C. (1991) 'Sustainable tourism in the Third World; problems and prospects', Discussion Paper 3, Department of Geography, University of Reading.

Esher, Lord (1968) *York: A Study in Conservation*, London: HMSO.

Ettinghausen, R. and Grabar, O. (1987) *The Art and Architecture of Islam: 650–1250*, Harmondsworth: Penguin.

European Heritage (1974–5) Issues 1–5, London: Purnell.

Evans, B.M. (1994) 'A celebration of enterprise' in J. M. Fladmark (ed.) *Cultural Tourism*, London: Donhead.

Fadel, R. and Serageldin, I. (1997) 'Renewal of the Hafsia quarter, Tunis' in I. Serageldin (ed.) *The Architecture of Empowerment: People Shelter and Livable Cities*, London: Academy Editions.

Fakhoury, L.A. (1987) 'Salt: a study in conservation', unpublished MA thesis, Institute of Advanced Architectural Studies, University of York.

Faroqhi, S. (1981) 'Urban development in Ottoman Anatolia', *METU Journal* 7, 1: 35–51.

—— (1984) *Towns and Townsmen of Ottoman Anatolia*, Cambridge: Cambridge University Press.

Faux, R. (1971) 'An eye to the future while celebrating the past', *Times*, 7 May: 14.

Feilden, Sir B. (1982) *Conservation of Historic Buildings*, London: Butterworth Scientific.

—— (1990) 'Opening address' in P. Harrison (ed.) *Civilising the City: Quality or Chaos in Historic Towns*, Edinburgh: Nic Allen Publishing.

Feilden, Sir B. and Jokilehto, J. (1998) *Management Guidelines for World Cultural Heritage Sites*, Rome: ICCROM (second edition).

Fethi, I. (1993) 'Conservation in the Islamic world: current practice and critical lessons' in S. Barakat (ed.) *Architecture and Development in the Islamic World*, pre-publication, York.

Fisher, H. (1994) 'The image of a region: the need for a clear focus' in J.M. Fladmark (ed.) *Cultural Tourism*, London: Donhead.

Fitch, J.M. (1990) *Historic Preservation: Curatorial Management of the Built World*, Charlottesville: University Press of Virginia.

Fladmark, J.M. (ed.) (1993) *Heritage: Conservation, Interpretation and Enterprise*, London: Donhead.

—— (ed.) (1994) *Cultural Tourism*, London: Donhead.

Fleming, D. (1996) 'Making city histories' in G. Kavanagh (ed.) *Making Histories in Museums*, Leicester: Leicester University Press.

Floyd, M. (1984) *Policy-Making and Planning in Local Government*, Aldershot: Gower.

Foster, D. (1985) *Travel and Tourism Management*, London: Macmillan.

Fsadni, C. and Selwyn, T. (eds) (1997) *Sustainable Tourism in Mediterranean Islands and Small Cities*, Malta: Med-Campus.

Fyson, N. (1997) 'Second is best', *The Geographical Magazine* 69, 4: 40–1.

Gallego, J. (ed.) (1985) *Granada*, Granada: Editorial En Su Mano.

German Foundation for International Development (1987) *Report: Tourism and Development*, Berlin.

Gerosa, P.G. (1981) 'The contribution of trades and industry to integrated. conservation' in *4th European Symposium of Historic Towns*, Strasbourg: Council of Europe.

Ghirardo, D. (1996) *Architecture after Modernism*, New York: Thames & Hudson.

Goodwin, G. (1977) *Ottoman Turkey*, London: Scorpion Publications.

—— (1991) *Islamic Spain*, Harmondsworth: Penguin.

—— (1992) *A History of Ottoman Architecture*, London: Thames & Hudson.

Guardian (1971) 'The city of York', *Guardian*, 1 January: 12–13.

Guardian (1981) 'Classical welcome to the invaders of 1981', *Guardian*, 21 August: 25.

Günay, B. (1988) 'Ankara: case study', paper presented at SCUPAD 88, Salzburg.

Güney, N. *et al.* (1986) 'Antalya Kaleiçi', *Yapı* 66: 38–45.

Gutschow, N. (1980) 'Architectural and urban conservation in Nepal' in M. Meinecke (ed.) *Islamic Cairo: Architectural Conservation and Urban Development of the Historic Centre*, London: Deutsches Archäologisches Institut Abteilung Kairo.

Gzell, S. (1989) 'Tourism and small towns' in *Tourism in Historic Towns*, Strasbourg: Council of Europe.

Habitat (1984) *Upgrading of Inner-City Slums*, Nairobi: Habitat.

Hakim, B.S. (1986) *Arabic-Islamic Cities: Building and Planning Principles*, New York: Routledge & Kegan Paul.

Hall, A.C. (1997) 'Dealing with incremental change: an application of urban morphology to design control', *Journal of Urban Design* 2, 3: 221–39.

Hall, D. (1990) 'The changing face of tourism in Eastern Europe', *Town and Country Planning* 59, 12: 348–9.

Hall, M.C. (1997) 'The politics of heritage tourism' in P. Murphy (ed.) *Quality Management in Urban Tourism*, Chichester: Wiley.

Hall, P. (1992) *Urban and Regional Planning*, London: Routledge (third edition).

Hall, V. (1998) 'From the inside looking out', *In Focus* 27: 12–14.

Hannersley, R. and Westlake, T. (1994) 'Urban heritage in the Czech Republic' in G.J. Ashworth and P.J. Larkham (eds) *Building a New Heritage: Tourism, Culture and Identity in the New Europe*, London: Routledge.

Harrison, P. (ed.) (1990) *Civilising the City: Quality or Chaos in Historic Towns*, Edinburgh: Nic Allen Publishing.

Harrison, R. (1994a) 'Telling the story in museums' in J.M. Fladmark (ed.) *Cultural Tourism*, London: Donhead.

—— (ed.) (1994b) *Manual of Heritage Management*, Oxford: Butterworth-Heinemann.

Harth, V. (1975) 'Bamberg', *European Heritage* 3: 21–3.

Harvey, D. (1989) *The Urban Experience*, Oxford: Basil Blackwell.

—— (1997) 'Contested cities' in N. Jewson and S. MacGregor (eds) *Transforming Cities*, London: Routledge.

Harvey, J. (1975) *York*, London: Batsford.

Hassan, N.M. (1985) 'Social aspects of urban housing in Cairo', *Mimar*, 17: 59–61.

Hass-Klau, C. (1990) 'Traffic and transportation in cities' in P. Harrison (ed.) *Civilising the City: Quality or Chaos in Historic Towns*, Edinburgh: Nic Allen Publishing.

Heeley, J. (1981) 'Planning for tourism in Britain', *Town Planning Review* 52: 61–79.

Helu-Thaman, K. (1992) 'Beyond hula, hotels and handicrafts', *In Focus* 4: 8–9.

Herbert, K. (1998) 'Christmas in Margaritaville', *The Independent Weekend Review*, 19 December: 22.

Heritage Trust (1985) *Conservation and Tourism*, Second International Congress on Architectural Conservation and Town Planning, Basle.

Hoag, J.D. (1963) *Western Islamic Architecture*, London: Prentice-Hall International.

—— (1975) *Islamic Architecture*, Milan: Electra Edifice.

Holod, R. (ed.) (1978) *Conservation as Cultural Survival*, Istanbul: The Aga Khan Award for Architecture.

—— (ed.) (1980) *Toward an Architecture in the Spirit of Islam*, Istanbul: The Aga Khan Award for Architecture.

Hooper-Greenhill, E. (ed.) (1995) *Museum, Media, Message*, London: Routledge.

ICOMOS (1968) *Second Conference on the Conservation, Restoration and Revival of Areas and Groups of Buildings of Historic Interest*, Tunis.

ICOMOS (1971) *International Charter for the Restoration of Monuments and Sites*, Venice.

ICOMOS (1987) *Charter for the Conservation of Historic Towns and Urban Areas*.

ICOMOS-UK (1995) *Historic Cities and Sustainable Tourism*.

ICOMOS-UK (1998) *Sustaining the Cultural Heritage of Europe*.

Insall, D. (1999) 'Chester: a conservation plan 25 years on', talk given at Tourism and Heritage: A Practical Partnership, joint meeting between Tourism Society and ICOMOS-UK Members, London.

Jaakson, R. (1996) 'From Marx to market: deciding the urban form of post-Soviet Tallinn, Estonia', *Journal of Urban Design* 1, 3: 329–54.

Jacobs, J. (1962) *The Death and Life of Great American Cities*, London: Jonathan Cape.

Jagger, M. (1998) 'The planner's perspective: a view from the front' in J. Warren, J. Worthington and S. Taylor (eds) *Context: New Buildings in Historic Settings*, Oxford: Architectural Press.

Jansen-Verbeke, M. (1995) 'Involving people – Bruges', *Historic Cities and Sustainable Tourism*, ICOMOS-UK.

Jewson, N. and MacGregor, S. (eds) (1996) *Transforming Cities: Contested Governance and New Spatial Divisions*, London: Routledge.

Jokilehto, J. (1998) 'Organisations, charters and world movement – an overview' in J. Warren, J. Worthington and S. Taylor (eds) *Context: New Buildings in Historic Settings*, Oxford: Architectural Press.

—— (1999) *History of Architectural Conservation*, Oxford: Butterworth-Heinemann.

Josephides, N. (1992) 'Environmental concern – what is in it for the tourism industry?', *Tourism and the Environment: Challenges and Choices for the 90s* (conference papers).

Kavanagh, G. (1995) 'Museums in partnership' in E. Hooper-Greenhill (ed.) *Museum, Media, Message*, London: Routledge.

—— (ed.) (1996) *Making Histories in Museums*, Leicester: Leicester University Press.

Keleş, N. (1992) 'Geçmişten çağrı', *Ege Mimarlık* 92/1: 35–42.

Keown, R. (1990) 'Square one at Spitalfields', *Building Design* 1000: 1–2.

Khan, F.R. (1980) 'The Islamic environment: can the future lead from the past?' in R. Holod (ed.) *Toward an Architecture in the Spirit of Islam*, Philadelphia: The Aga Khan Award for Architecture.

Kirby, A. (1978) *The Inner City: Causes and Effects*, Newcastle upon Tyne: J. and P. Bealls.

Kışlalı, A.T. (1992) 'Turizm potansiyelinin yüzde 6'sı kullanılıyor', *Cumhuriyet*, 20 July.

Korça, P. (1993) 'Mass tourism: the social costs to destination community as perceived by its residents', paper delivered to International Conference on Sustainable Tourism in Islands and Small States, Malta.

Kostof, S. (1991) *The City Shaped*, London: Thames & Hudson.

—— (1992) *The City Assembled*, London: Thames & Hudson.

—— (1995) *A History of Architecture: Settings and Rituals*, Oxford: Oxford University Press (second edition).

Krippendorf, J. (1995) 'Towards new tourism policies' in S. Medlik (ed.) *Managing Tourism*, Oxford: Butterworth-Heinemann (second edition).

Kuban, D. (1978) 'Conservation of the historical environment for cultural survival' in R. Holod (ed.) *Conservation as Cultural Survival*, Istanbul: The Aga Khan Award for Architecture.

—— (1980) 'Toward an understanding of architectural symbolism' in R. Holod (ed.) *Toward an Architecture in the Spirit of Islam*, Philadelphia: The Aga Khan Award for Architecture.

—— (1983) 'Modern versus traditional: a false conflict?', *Mimar* 9: 54–8.

—— (1985) 'Direct and indirect uses of restoration for tourism' in *Conservation and Tourism: Second International Congress on Architectural Conservation and Town Planning*, Basle: Heritage Trust.

Küçükerman, Ö. (1985) *The Turkish House: In Search of Spatial Identity*, Istanbul: The Turkish Touring and Automobile Association.

Laant, R. Jr (1975) 'Responsibilities of local authorities and citizens' participation' in *Congress on the European Architectural Heritage*, Amsterdam: Council of Europe.

Larkham, P.J. (1990) 'Conservation and historical townscapes' in T.R. Slater (ed.) *The Built Form of Western Cities*, Leicester: Leicester University Press.

—— (1996) *Conservation and the City*, London: Routledge.

Laurance, R. (1979) 'Tourist crossroads', *Guardian*, 31 January: 18.

Laws, E. (1995) *Tourist Destination Management*, London: Routledge.

Lemaire, R. and Dumont, F. (1985) 'Heritage, economic revival and employment', *European Conference of Ministers Responsible for Architectural Heritage*, Strasbourg: Council of Europe.

Leu, W. (1998) 'Cultural heritage and tourism: a continuing partnership' in *Sustaining the Cultural Heritage of Europe*, ICOMOS-UK.

Lewcock, R. (1978) 'Three problems in conservation: Egypt, Oman, Yemen', in R. Holod (ed.) *Conservation as Cultural Survival*, Istanbul: The Aga Khan Award for Architecture.

Lichfield, N. (1988) *Economics in Urban Conservation*, Cambridge: Cambridge University Press.

Lowenthal, D. (1996) *Possessed by the Past: The Heritage Crusade and Spoils of History*, London: Free Press.

Lowenthal, D. and Binney, M. (eds) (1981) *Our Past Before Us, Why Do We Save It?*, London: Temple Smith.

MacCannell, D. (1976) *The Tourist: A New Theory of the Leisure Class*, London: Macmillan.

McCaskey, T.G. (1975) 'Colonial Williamsburg' in A.J. Burkart and S. Medlik (eds) *The Management of Tourism*, London: Heinemann.

MacDonald, S. (1995) 'Changing our minds: planning a responsive museum service' in E. Hooper-Greenhill (ed.) *Museum, Media, Message*, London: Routledge.

Machin, A. (1989) 'Tourism and historic towns: the cultural key', *Tourism in Historic Towns*, Strasbourg: Council of Europe.

McKean, C. (1993) 'The Scottishness of Scottish architecture' in J.M. Fladmark (ed.) *Heritage: Conservation, Interpretation and Enterprise*, London: Donhead.

McRobie, G. (1982) *Small Is Possible*, London: Abacus.

Maguire, P. (1982) 'Issues in conservation and protection' in R. Zetter (ed.) *Conservation of Buildings in Developing Countries*, Oxford: Oxford Polytechnic.

Malik, A. (1993) 'Muslim cities: recent history and possible future' in S. Barakat (ed.) *Architecture and Development in the Islamic World*, pre-publication, York, 1993.

Masser, I., Sviden, O. and Wegener, M. (1994) 'What new heritage for which new Europe' in G.J. Ashworth and P.J. Larkham (eds) *Building a New Heritage: Tourism, Culture and Identity in the New Europe*, London: Routledge.

May, R. Jr (1989) *The Urbanisation Revolution*, New York: Plenum Press.

Medlik, S. (ed.) (1995) *Managing Tourism*, Oxford: Butterworth-Heinemann (second edition).

Meffert, E. (1995) 'Will Zanzibar Stone Town survive?' in A. Sheriff (ed.) *The History and Conservation of Zanzibar Stone Town*, Athens: Ohio University Press.

Meinecke, M. (ed.) (1980) *Islamic Cairo: Architectural Conservation and Urban Development of the Historic Centre*, London: Deutsches Archäologisches Institut Abteilung Kairo.

Mercangöz, S. (1991) 'The conservation plan of Antalya and its aftermath' in International Symposium on Cultural Aspects of Urban Conservation in the Third World Countries, Istanbul (unpublished).

Middleton, M. (1982) 'Liabilities into assets: caring for the built environment' in *Whose Town Is It Anyway?*, Proceedings of the Conference held to review the European Campaign for Urban Renaissance in Britain, London: HMSO.

Middleton, V.T.C. (1994) 'Vision, strategy and corporate planning: an overview' in R. Harrison (ed.) *Manual of Heritage Management*, Oxford: Butterworth-Heinemann.

Middleton, V.T.C. with Hawkins, R. (1998) *Sustainable Tourism: A Marketing Perspective*, Oxford: Butterworth-Heinemann.

Millar, P. (1995) 'Heritage management for heritage tourism' in S. Medlik (ed.) *Managing Tourism*, Oxford: Butterworth-Heinemann (second edition).

Montgomery, J. (1998) 'Making a city: urbanity, vitality and urban design', *Journal of Urban Design* 3, 1: 93–116.

Moore, K. (1997) *Museums and the Popular Culture*, London: Cassell.

Morrell, J.B. (1981) *Studies in Conservation*, York: York Conservation Trust.

Mumtaz, K.K. (1978) 'The walled city of Lahore: directions for rehabilitation' in R. Holod (ed.) *Conservation as Cultural Survival*, Istanbul.

Murphy, P.E. (1985) *Tourism: A Community Approach*, London: Methuen.

—— (ed.) (1997) *Quality Management in Urban Tourism*, Chichester: Wiley.

Nasr, S.H. (1980) 'The contemporary Muslim and the architectural transformation of the Islamic urban environment' in R. Holod (ed.) *Toward an Architecture in the Spirit of Islam*, Philadelphia: The Aga Khan Award for Architecture.

The National Trust (1988) *The National Trust: Access and Conservation*.

The National Trust (1990) *The National Trust: An Introduction*.

Naylon, J. (1975) *Andalusia: Problem Regions of Europe*, Oxford: Oxford University Press.

Ndoro, W. and Pwiti, G. (1997) 'Marketing the past: the "Shona village" at Great Zimbabwe', *Conservation and Management of Archaeological Sites* 2: 2–8.

Negi, J. (1990) *Tourism Development and Resource Conservation*, New Delhi: Metropolitan.

Newby, P.T. (1994) 'Tourism: support or threat to heritage?' in G.J. Ashworth and P.J. Larkham (eds) *Building a New Heritage: Tourism, Culture and Identity in the New Europe*, London: Routledge.

Nuryanti, W. (1996) 'Heritage and postmodern tourism', *Annals of Tourism Research* 23, 2: 249–60.

Nuttgens, P. (1970) *York*, London: Studio Vista.

—— (1976) *York, The Continuing City*, London: Faber.

—— (1989) 'The impact of tourism on historic towns and their regions', *Tourism in Historic Towns*, Strasbourg: Council of Europe.

Oddermatt, P. (1996) 'A case of neglect? The politics of (re)presentation: a Sardinian case' in J. Boissevain (ed.) *Coping with Tourists: European Reactions to Mass Tourism*, Oxford: Berghahn Books.

OECD (1975) *Tourism Policy and International Tourism in OECD Member Countries*, Report, Paris: Organisation for Economic Co-operation and Development.

OECD (1986) *Tourism Policy and International Tourism in OECD Member Countries*, Report, Paris: Organisation for Economic Co-operation and Development.

Oliver, P. (1982) 'Cultural issues in conservation implementation' in R. Zetter (ed.) *Conservation of Buildings in Developing Countries*, Oxford: Oxford Polytechnic.

Orbaşlı, A. (1994) 'Historic towns: tourism, conservation and development with particular reference to Turkish towns', unpublished DPhil. thesis, Institute of Advanced Architectural Studies, University of York.

—— (1997) 'Historic towns and tourism in Turkey' in C. Fsadni and T. Selwyn (eds) *Sustainable Tourism in Mediterranean Islands and Small Cities*, Malta: Med-Campus.

—— (1998) 'Postcard from Tibet', *In Focus* 29 back cover.

Orbaşlı, A. and Worthington, J. (1995) *Architecture and Town Planning Education in the Netherlands: A European Comparison*, York: Institute of Advanced Architectural Studies.

Otan, Ü. (1991) 'Turizm satılığa çıktı', *Cumhuriyet*, 29 June: 11.

Özer, B. (1990) 'Türkiye'de restorasyon anlayışı ve uygulamaları üzerine', *Yapı* 105: 33–4.

Page, S. (1995) *Urban Tourism*, London: Routledge.

Paszucha, M. (1995) 'Managing places – Krakow', *Historic Cities and Sustainable Tourism*, ICOMOS-UK.

Patterson, K. (1992) 'Aloha for sale', *In Focus* 4: 4–5.

Perowne, S. (1962) 'Shades of Islam in Andalucia', *Times*, 11 August: 7.

Pettifer, J. (1990) 'Pride of Bath prejudiced by soaring shop rents', *Independent on Sunday*, 2 September: 4.

Pevsner, N. (1974) *Yorkshire: York and the East Riding*, Harmondsworth: Penguin.

Planning (1987) 'Community architecture still stealing the thunder', *Planning* 746: 89.

Prott, L.V. (1998) 'International standards for World Heritage' in *World Culture Report 1998: Culture Creativity and Markets*, Paris: Unesco Publishing.

Radecke, R. (1995) *Quedlinburg*, Cologne: DuMont Buchverlag (text by C. Rienäcker).

Raymond, A. (1984) *The Great Arab Cities in the 16th–18th Centuries: An Introduction*, London: New York University Press.

Repellin, D. (1990) 'Restoration in Old Lyon' in P. Harrison (ed.) *Civilising the City: Quality or Chaos in Historic Towns*, Edinburgh: Nic Allen Publishing.

Richards, G. (1996) 'Production and consumption of European architectural heritage', *Annals of Tourism Research* 23, 2: 261–83.

Rickson, I. (1973) 'Planning and tourism', *Royal Town Planning Institute Journal* 59: 269–70.

Rogers, P. (1982) 'Conservation and implementation' in R. Zetter (ed.) *Conservation of Buildings in Developing Countries*, Oxford: Oxford Polytechnic.

Ronchi, L. (1979) 'Rome from the inside: inhabitant's intermezzo' in D. Appleyard (ed.) *The Conservation of European Cities*, Cambridge, Massachusetts: MIT Press.

Rosenthal, R. (1991) 'Sustainable tourism – optimism v. pessimism', *In Focus* 1: 2–3.

RSS (The Royal Scientific Society) (1991) *Salt: A Plan for Action*, vols I, II, III, Amman: Salt Development Corporation.

Ruskin, J. (1849) *Seven Lamps of Architecture*, New York: Bryan Taylor.

Sammuels, I. (1990) 'Architectural practice and urban morphology' in T.R. Slater (ed.) *The Built Form of Western Cities*, Leicester: Leicester University Press.

Schauer, H.-H. (1990) *Quedlinburg, Das städtebauliche Denkmal und seine Fachwerkbauten*, Berlin: Verlag für Bauwesen.

Schembri, J. and Borg, M. (1997) 'Population changes in the walled cities of Malta' in C. Fsadni and T. Selwyn (eds) *Sustainable Tourism in Mediterranean Islands and Small Cities*, Malta: Med-Campus.

Serageldin, I. (1982) 'Housing the poor: the role of the public sector' in *Urban Housing: Designing in Islamic Cultures 2*, Cambridge, Massachusetts: MIT Press.

—— (ed.) (1997) *The Architecture of Empowerment: People Shelter and Livable Cities*, London: Academy Editions.

Seymour-Davies, H. (1972) 'White, red and gold in Andalusia', *Country Life* 152: 512–13.

Shackley, M. (1994) 'The land of Lo, Nepal/Tibet', *Tourism Management* 15, 1: 17–26.

—— (1996) 'Too much room at the inn?', *Annals of Tourism Research* 23, 2: 449–62.

Sheriff, A. (ed.) (1995) *The History and Conservation of Zanzibar Stone Town*, Athens: Ohio University Press.

Shivji, I.G. (1973) *Tourism and Socialist Development*, Dar es Salaam: Tanzania Publishing House.

Siembieda, W.J. and Lopez Moreno, E. (1998) 'Barrios and the Hispanic American city: cultural value and social representation', *Journal of Urban Design* 3, 1: 39–52.

Simpson, J. (1990) 'Whither conservation?' in P. Harrison (ed.) *Civilising the City: Quality or Chaos in Historic Towns*, Edinburgh: Nic Allen Publishing.

Sivri, M.A. (1988) 'Protection and development policies for traditional settlements in Greece: the case of Thasos', unpublished MA thesis, Institute of Advanced. Architectural Studies, University of York.

Slater, T.R. (ed.) (1990) *The Built Form of Western Cities*, essays for M.R.G. Conzen on the occasion of his eightieth birthday, Leicester: Leicester University Press.

Smith, V.L. (ed.) (1978) *Hosts and Guests*, Oxford: Blackwell.

Soane, J. (1994) 'The renaissance of cultural vernacularism in Germany' in G.J. Ashworth and P.J. Larkham (eds) *Building a New Heritage: Tourism, Culture and Identity in the New Europe*, London: Routledge.

Sordo, E. (1963) *Moorish Spain: Cordoba, Seville, Granada*, London: Elek Books.

Sparks, L. (1989) 'Future growth and characteristics of tourism in historic towns' in *Tourism in Historic Towns*, Strasbourg: Council of Europe.

Stadt Quedlinburg (1998) *Weltkulturerbe Quedlinburg: 7 Jahre Stadtsanierung*, 3–98.

Stancliffe, A. and Tyler, C. (1990) 'The other side of the camera', Supplement to *New Consumer*, Spring.

Stimpson, C. and Bhabha, H. (1998) 'Global creativity and the arts' in *World Culture Report 1998: Culture Creativity and Markets*, Paris: Unesco Publishing.

Stirling, Sir A. (1995) 'Keynote address' in *Historic Cities and Sustainable Tourism*, ICOMOS-UK.

Stuart, J.E. (1989) 'Future growth and characteristics of tourism' in *Tourism in Historic Towns*, Strasbourg: Council of Europe.

Talbot, M. (1986) *Reviving Buildings and Communities: A Manual of Renewal*, Newton Abbot: David and Charles.

Tandy, J. and Shostak, L. (1990) 'Balancing the "mega-attractions"', *Town and Country Planning* 59, 6: 173–5.

Tanghe, J., Vlaeminck, S. and Berghoef, J. (1984) *Living Cities: A Case for Urbanism and Guidelines for Re-urbanisation*, Oxford: Pergamon Press.

Tankut, G. (1975) 'Urban transformation in the eighteenth century Ottoman city', *METU Journal* 1, 2: 247–62.

Tekeli, I. (1978) 'Urban patterns in Anatolia: organisation and evolution' in R. Holod (ed.) *Conservation as Cultural Survival*, Istanbul: The Aga Khan Award for Architecture.

—— (1998) *Tarihyazım Üzerine Düşünmek*, Ankara: Dost Kitabevi Yayınları.

Teo, P. and Yeoh, B.S.A. (1997) 'Remaking local heritage for tourism', *Annals of Tourism Research* 24, 1: 192–213.

Thompson, I. and Georghiou, C. (1991) *Policy for Retention of Residential Uses in the City of York*, York City Council.

Thorncroft, A. (1998) 'Dubrovnik', *Financial Times: How to Spend It* (supplement), 31, December: 47–8.

Thrift, N. (1997) 'Cities without modernity, cities without magic', *Scottish Geographical Magazine* 113, 3: 138–49.

Times (1965) 'Costa del Sol after the building boom', *Times*, 20 February: 11.

Times (1976a) 'Holidays in Turkey' (Supplement), *Times*, 28 February: i–viii.

Times (1976b) 'Andalucia: a special report', *Times*, 25 June: 14–15.

Tout, T.F. (1948) *Medieval Town Planning*, Manchester: Manchester University Press.

Tramposch, W. J. (1994) 'Heritage recreated in the USA: Colonial Williamsburg and other sites' in J.M. Fladmark (ed.) *Cultural Tourism*, London: Donhead.

Turan, M. (1975) 'Vernacular architecture and environmental influences', *METU Journal* 1, 2: 227–46.

Turkish State Institute of Statistics (various years) *Statistical Yearbooks of Turkey*, Ankara.

Turner, L. and Ash, J. (1975) *The Golden Hordes*, London: Constable.

UNESCO (1972) *Convention concerning the Protection of the World Cultural and National Heritage*.

UNESCO (1980) *Protection and Cultural Animation of Monuments, Sites and Historic Towns in Europe*, Bonn: Bernecher Melsungen.

UNESCO (1998) *World Culture Report 1998: Culture Creativity and Markets*, Paris: Unesco Publishing.

van den Abeele, A. (1975) 'Four tourist towns: 1. Bruges, Belgium', *European Heritage* 4: 25–7.

van den Berg, G.J. (1971) 'Integration of monuments, ancient buildings and artistic sites into the economic and social life of the local community', *European Symposium of Towns of Historic Interest*, Split: Council of Europe.

van der Borg, J. (1994) 'Demand for city tourism in Europe: tour operators' catalogues', *Tourism Management* 15, 1: 66–9.

Wallace, M. (1995) 'Changing media, changing messages' in E. Hooper-Greenhill (ed.) *Museum, Media, Message*, London: Routledge.

Wallis, H.F. (1971) 'Conservation', *Local Government Chronicle*, 28 August: 1515–19.

Walls, A. (1995) 'The revitalisation of Zanzibar Stone Town' in A. Sheriff (ed.) *The History and Conservation of Zanzibar Stone Town*, Athens: Ohio University Press.

Warren, J. (1993) 'Ethics and aesthetics in conservation' in S. Barakat (ed.) *Architecture and Development in the Islamic World*, pre-publication, York.

—— (1998) 'The historic context: principles and philosophies' in J. Warren, J. Worthington and S. Taylor (eds) *Context: New Buildings in Historic Settings*, Oxford: Architectural Press.

Warren, J. and Worksett, R. (1983) 'Conservation and development in the Kadhimiyeh area in Baghdad', *Adaptive Reuse: Designing in Islamic Cultures 3*, Cambridge, Massachusetts: MIT Press.

Warren, J., Worthington, J. and Taylor, S. (eds) (1998) *Context: New Buildings in Historic Settings*, Oxford: Architectural Press.

Wates, N. and Knevitt, C. (1987) *Community Architecture: How People Are Creating Their Own Environment*, London: Penguin.

Wheeler, S. (1969) 'Preparing York for the eighties', *Architects' Journal* 161, 26, supplement: 1744–63.

Whitehand, J.W.R. (1981) *The Urban Landscape: Historical Development and Management*, papers by M.R.G. Conzen, Institute of British Geographers Special Publication 13, London: Academic Press.

—— (1990) 'Townscape and management: ideal and reality' in T.R. Slater (ed.) *The Built Form of Western Cities*, Leicester: Leicester University Press.

—— (1992) *The Making of the Urban Landscape*, Institute of British Geographers Special Publication 26, Oxford: Blackwell.

Williams, A.M. and Shaw, G. (eds) (1988) *Tourism and Economic Development: Western European Experiences*, London: Belhaven.

Wood, A. (1975) 'Responsibilities of local authorities and citizens' participation' in *Congress on the European Architectural Heritage*, Amsterdam, 21–25 October 1975.

Worksett, R. (1969) *The Character of Towns: An Approach to Conservation*, London: William Cloves.

—— (1978) 'Bath – museum or city' in G. Hones (ed.) *Bath: Museum or City*, Bath: Bath University Press.

—— (1989) 'Managing tourism: achieving a balance between commercial development, tourism requirements and historic preservation' in *Tourism in Historic Towns*, Strasbourg: Council of Europe.

The World Bank (1998) *Project Appraisal Document for Georgia Cultural Heritage Project*, Report No. 17275GE.

World Commission on Environment and Development (1987) *Our Common Future*

WTTERC (World Travel and Tourism Environment Centre) (1992) *World Travel and Environment Review*.

Yalim, G. (1978) 'The Antalya Citadel: a project for a leisure and commercial centre' in R. Holod (ed.) *Conservation as Cultural Survival*, Istanbul: The Aga Khan Award for Architecture.

York Chamber of Trade and Commerce (1984) *The Role of Tourism in the Future Prosperity of York*, extract from minutes of meeting held on Tourism on 20 November, York.

York City Council (1991) *City of York, Planning and Building Handbook*, York.

York City Council (1993) *York Town Scheme: Conserving the Historic City 1966–1993*, York.

York Conservation Trust (1981) *Studies in Conservation*, York: York Conservation Trust.

Young, G. (1973) *Tourism: Blessing or Blight?*, Harmondsworth: Penguin.

Youngson, A.J. (1990) 'Cities and civilisation' in P. Harrison (ed.) *Civilising the City: Quality or Chaos in Historic Towns*, Edinburgh: Nic Allen Publishing.

Zetter, R. (1982) *Conservation of Buildings in Developing Countries*, working paper no. 60, Oxford: Oxford Polytechnic.

Zivas, D. (1979) 'The future of the old sector of the city of Athens: Plaka' in D. Appleyard (ed.) *The Conservation of European Cities*, Cambridge, Massachusetts: MIT Press.

anon. (1935) *The Restoration of Colonial Williamsburg, Virginia*, F.W. Dodge Corporation, New York.

anon. (1992) *Managing Tourism in Historic Cities*, Krakow: International Cultural Centre.

http://www.worldbank.org/html/fpd/urban/cult_her/cult_her.htm (11.11.1998) (for 'Cultural Heritage')

Index